# Beyond Everest

# BeyondEverest

QUEST FOR THE SEVEN SUMMITS

By Patrick Morrow

Camden House

Canadian Cataloguing in Publication Data

Morrow, Patrick
   Beyond Everest

Includes index.
ISBN 0-920656-52-8 (bound)
ISBN 0-920656-46-3 (pbk.)

1. Mountaineering. I. Title.

GV200.M67   1986   796.5'22   C86-094427-1

Trade distribution by
Firefly Books
3520 Pharmacy Avenue, Unit 1-C
Scarborough, Ontario
Canada M1W 2T8

Distributed in Great Britain by
CORDEE
3a DeMontfort Street
Leicester LE1 7HD
ISBN  0  904405  53  2

Printed in Canada for
Camden House Publishing Ltd.
7 Queen Victoria Road
Camden East, Ontario
K0K 1J0

Cover: Climber Bernhard Ehmann makes his way up Mount McKinley's virgin Southwest Rib during a 1977 ascent of North America's highest peak. The climb was the first peak in author Patrick Morrow's seven-summits project, which took him around the world and to the highest mountain on each continent. Photograph by Patrick Morrow.

Designed by
Linda J. Menyes

Colour separations by
Herzig Somerville Limited
Toronto, Ontario

Printed and bound in Canada by
D.W. Friesen & Sons Ltd.
Altona, Manitoba

Printed on 80-lb. Jensen Gloss

Climbing partner Bernhard Ehmann watches the sun set over the Alaska Range from atop Alaska's Mount McKinley. It was our first high-altitude climb and, although I did not realize it at the time, the start of my seven-summits project.

# Acknowledgments

This project was a long and winding journey that would have been impossible to complete without the combined efforts of hundreds of people and organizations, some of whom are listed here.

With a special thanks to those who provided me with Morrow support throughout: Frank and Linda Morrow, Ed and Vera Auders, Aina and Hank Thomas, Russel and Bette Davis, Mike Breckon, Bill March, Lloyd Gallagher, George Kinnear, Jeremy and Wendy Schmidt, Linda Kuttis, Giles Kershaw, Rick Mason, Ric Airey, Peter Bruchausen, Don Edlund, Steve Drogin, Karen Paynter, Mauri Salo, Francie Cochran, Hugh and Cathy Macleay and family, Alejo Contreras, and The Merry Tweaksters: Martyn Williams and Maureen Garrity, Brian Finnie and Bart Lewis.

Thanks also to publisher James Lawrence for his endless personal encouragement and to editor Frank B. Edwards, who tirelessly guided the project through all of its phases and coaxed the manuscript along as though he himself had been with me on the climbs. David Barbour and Janis Kraulis assisted generously in the difficult task of selecting photographs. Baiba not only helped me get to these places, staying behind when financing was a problem, but also shared the mountainous task of writing this book.

More thanks to Barry Estabrook, Bart Robinson, Tracy C. Read, Linda Menyes, Patricia Denard, Joanne Bayly, Bob Jamieson, Tony Leighton, Tom Hopkins, Bruce Patterson, Jon Whyte, Brian Patton, Bev Hills and Stephen Bezruchka for pointing out the errors and inconsistencies in parts of the story—and adding some of their own.

The Everest chapter is based on Bart Robinson's "The Expedition Chronicle," which we co-wrote for *Equinox* magazine, January/February 1983. His edited versions of the Vinson and Carstensz chapters also appeared in *Equinox*. I borrowed heavily from Jeremy Schmidt, author of *Equinox* features on my Kilimanjaro and Elbrus climbs.

Corporations:

Bob Southey, Henry Myers and staff, Pentax of Canada; Steve Good, Custom-colour Labs; Randy Hooper, Colin Seddon, Dave Milligan, Coast Mountain Sports; Becky Parsons, North Face; Sally Ann Butler, Marmot Mountain Works; Ian McDonald, Sylvia Rempel and staff, Sunice Clothing; Dick McGowan, Leo LeBon, Dave Parker, Bruce Klepinger, Peter Cummings, Mountain Travel; John Bates, Johnson Diversified Canada Inc. and Eureka Tents; Shelley Turner, Optimus Stoves; Allen Slade, Karhu Ski Company; Andrea Dillon & Associates; Mike Mortimer, Calgary Hostel Shop; Al Thomas, Bob Williams and Graham Sandilans, Leisure Time Distributors; everyone at *Equinox* magazine; Jim Muir, Brian Smith and everyone at Programmed Communications; Bruce Patterson, the *Calgary Herald*; Mark Hume, *The Vancouver Sun*; John and Peggy Amatt, One Step Beyond; Brad Armstrong, Lawson, Lundell, Lawson and McIntosh; Michael Dunn, Expeditions by Michael Dunn; Cathy O'Sullivan, Jim Allen, Maureen Garrity, Martyn Williams, Ecosummer Canada Expeditions; Steve Fossett, Fossett Corporation; Milton Ward, George Mealey, Les Acton, Freeport Mining Co.; Consuelo Bonaldi, Mr. Perisoto, Scarpa Boot Company; Ekhardt Behrmann, Taiga Works; Tandy Corporation; Gilles Couet, Chlorophylle Clothing; Pierre Guevremont, First Light Associated Photographers.

Government Agencies:

Ambassador Adiwoso Abubakar, Husny Sunkar, Imam Soejandhono, Embassy of Indonesia, Ottawa; F. Guritno, Abdul Aziz, Indonesian Consulate, Vancouver; Dahlia Soemolang, Director of Social and Cultural Relations, Dept. of Foreign Affairs, Jakarta; Terry O'Connor, Gordon Morrison, Dept. of External Affairs, Ottawa; Jim and Heather Wall, Canadian Embassy, Jakarta; Don Javier Lopetegui, Juan Radic, Chilean Air Force; Monica Krassa, Servicio Nacional de Turismo, Chile; Helene Lafortune, Canadian Embassy, Buenos Aires.

# Contents

Pilot Giles Kershaw, plastic flamingo and Union Jack close at hand, makes his way up Antarctica's Vinson Massif. Having ferried two climbing teams to the mountain, he decided to take a firsthand look at the summit.

# High Adventure

## Coming of age in the mountains

Drawn to high, cold places ever since 1971, when I made a winter traverse of Mount Assiniboine in the Canadian Rockies, I have managed to combine photography with adventuring, *inset*—a numbing combination at minus 50 degrees F.

In October 1982, I became the second Canadian to reach the summit of Mount Everest. On my walk out from the mountain, my body and soul were completely drained, caught up in a psychic decompression period. I had spent the last 50 days in a zone where nothing lives and even the imagination is dulled. Ice, snow and cold had dominated my world, and the first whiff of vegetation—rock lichen—nearly made me swoon. Even the colourful wrappings of trailside garbage were a welcome sight to eyes that had been mercilessly bombarded by intense ultraviolet rays. Safely down the mountain, I was finally able to relax, and my mind was free to wander. There could have been no better landscape in which to turn my thoughts loose. Four years of preparation for this climb had left me with no immediate plans. Just what does a man do after he's been to the top of the world? I realized with a start that I had already reached the summits of three of the seven continents—McKinley in North America, Aconcagua in South America and Asia's Everest—and they were the toughest of the seven at that.

Suddenly, the answer seemed obvious. One hundred and thirty-one other climbers had been to the summit of Everest; of these, not one had gone on to climb the summits of all seven continents—no one had completed the grand slam of mountaineering. In climbers' terms, it hardly compared with such great feats as forging new routes up Annapurna or K2 or climbing all 14 of the world's 26,000-foot (8,000 m) peaks, but it was definitely a worthy adventure that would give me an excuse to travel to Africa, Europe, Australasia and, most exotic of all, Antarctica. It was only a matter of beginning.

Four years later, the adventure is complete. I find myself back home in Kimberley, British Columbia, contemplating my travels, writing about them and hoping that this book will convince a few readers that there are still chances worth taking and places left to explore.

My association with mountains began early. I was born in the town of Invermere, in the East Kootenay region of southeastern British Columbia, the first child of Frank and Irene Morrow, who lived at the site of the Giant Mascot Mine,

just 20 miles from the Bugaboos. My father worked as a maintenance carpenter in the lead/silver mine there until the following summer, when we moved a hundred miles south down the Rocky Mountain Trench to Kimberley, another mining town. British Columbia was experiencing a building boom, and we spent the next several years travelling around the province from construction job to construction job, stopping for a year on Vancouver Island in 1956 (where my sister Linda was born), before eventually returning permanently to the East Kootenay region.

Despite the industrial presence of Cominco's underground lead/zinc/silver mine and fertilizer plant, Kimberley offers its 7,000 residents some of the finest mountain scenery in the West. In this part of the Purcells, the peaks rise steeply to 9,000 feet (2,743 m). The Kootenays' glacier-carved valleys are quite distinct from those of the nearby Rockies, being more precipitous and having a tree line that rises a thousand feet higher, up to 8,000 feet (2,438 m). While a network of logging roads and old mining trails offers good access to the mountains, the coniferous forest is thick with dense chest-high growths of alders and willows, a significant obstacle to skiers and hikers already struggling with an elevation gain of 5,000 to 6,000 feet (1,524 m -1,828 m) from valley floor to mountaintop. Much of the range's remote heartland sees very little human activity, but for those who do manage to penetrate the natural defences, it is a wild and spectacular region, a rare treasure for those seeking reprieve from everyday urban pressures.

Like most kids growing up in the mountains of the world, I had been largely oblivious to the incredible beauty of my surroundings. In retrospect, it seems odd to have taken for granted what would become such an important part of my life, but after travelling through the Himalayas and the Andes, I realize it is a worldwide phenomenon.

During the 1950s and 1960s, ironically, climbing as a sport in this area was all but ignored, and there was only a handful of local enthusiasts. The granite spires of the Bugaboos, a hundred miles to the north, were bustling all summer long with out-of-province and out-of-

Pre-season warm-ups. Every spring, members of the Calgary Mountain Club congregate at Okotoks Rock, a 25-foot-high boulder south of Calgary, Alberta, for long evenings of climbing gymnastics, loud music and cold beer.

Previous page inset: Martyn Williams

country climbers. But in local recreational terms, the mountains were there to serve fishermen and hunters, if anyone at all, and climbing was a completely foreign concept. I suppose that after a hundred years of hard-fought exploration and settlement, the rugged passes and mountains here were naturally regarded as scenic barriers to civilization that, when mined and logged, could turn a profit but offered little else. Amazingly, this mentality persists.

## MAGIC SHADOWS

I went through a "mountain man" phase during the early 1960s, as did many of my friends. With my father, I hunted elk and deer and trapped beaver, marten and lynx on weekends through the Purcells and farther east into the Rockies. Our trapline was a hobby that gave us a chance to get away from the confines of a small town during the five-month-long winter season, and in summer and fall, we kept an eye open for likely fishing spots as we tramped around the alpine lakes. It was on these forays that I began to learn how to move freely and comfortably through this untrammelled world. To this day, I join my 71-year-old father on outings as he continues to explore the mountains.

Predictably, my boyhood dreams faded with my early teens, and I turned to other idiosyncratic pursuits. At 13, I joined the Kimberley Air Cadets and found an acceptable outlet for my gun mania through its competition rifle team. But by the time I turned 16, I had been won over by photography. One of the cadet instructors, John Daniel, introduced me to the mysteries of the darkroom, and every Tuesday night thereafter, I would watch white sheets of sensitized paper magically come to life with the images I had captured with a borrowed 4" x 5" Speed Graphic camera. My interest quickly became a passion, and I spent as much time developing film and printing pictures as I could, learning everything that John could teach and losing all track of time as we muddled around in the eerie half-light of the darkroom.

During the summer of 1969 and just a month before I entered my last year of high school, I spent a weekend at a

While much of my mountaineering has been cold-weather high-altitude slogging, I still enjoy rock climbing—especially on sun-warmed granite, such as this face climb in California's Joshua Tree National Monument. Here, a climber protects his lead by clipping his rope into a carabiner (a metal snap link), which in turn is clipped to an aluminum nut lodged in a crack, as he prepares to skirt around an overhang.

It was hard to ignore the call of the wild, growing up in the Purcell Range, which contains such scenic gems as Lake of the Hanging Glacier and, in the distance, the Bugaboos. Yet the more I explored the area, the more examples I found of poor mining and logging practices that were decimating the wilderness. Concerned, two friends and I produced a guidebook in the mid-1970s entitled *Exploring the Purcell Wilderness,* hoping that it might help to expand recreational use of the area and call attention to its unchecked exploitation.

friend's cottage 10 miles from Kimberley and thereby happened upon my first mountain climbers. We were lounging about at a picnic table when we heard the clear ringing sound of a piton hammer banging metal wedges into a nearby rock face. At that time, I did not recognize the noise, and we set out to investigate. On the cliffs, we spotted two climbers suspended in space 100 feet off the ground. We watched for hours, intrigued by their perilous situation and the painstaking way they pulled themselves up the rock, hanging nonchalantly from their piton-anchored slings whenever they needed a rest. It was a difficult pitch, and at one point, the man in the lead position lost his tenuous grip and fell, plummeting 25 feet before being jerked to a halt by the thin perlon line attached to his partner. It was an incredible moment, memorable because it dramatically confronted our innate teenage faith in immortality. We waited most of the afternoon, spellbound, until the two finally rappelled down to where we stood.

The white-haired elder of the two (who had prevented his partner's potentially fatal fall) introduced himself as Bob O'Brien. A 55-year-old geologist, he had been active in the hills all his life but had decided on impulse to take up climbing only five years before. With the commitment of a recent convert, he urged me to try an easier part of the face, scrambling 50 feet up before tying in and tossing me a line. I fastened it onto my borrowed harness and pulled myself up the vertical rock, somehow contracting Bob's enthusiasm as I felt a wave of adrenaline-induced excitement sweep over me.

## ESOTERIC SPORTS

Today, I look back at that meeting as a truly inspirational point in my life. Bob had opened my eyes not only to a fine new sport but, ultimately, to a fresh way of perceiving the world. What began innocently enough as my rebellion against adolescent boredom would sketch the blueprint for a fulfilling life style. Now in his seventies, Bob is still an adventurer, floating down rivers with little more than a wet suit and flippers, steering a truck-tire inner tube ahead of him that is rigged with netting to hold food and overnight

camping gear. "Even when you're in small rapids, your low body position makes it seem like a wild white-water experience," he says with a wink.

Although my parents were at first apprehensive about this rather esoteric and seemingly dangerous sport, it reassured them to know that it was all taking place under the guidance of someone who was a stickler for safety. Admittedly, neither my friends nor I could afford a proper climbing rope that would stretch the requisite 30 percent under load, so we did much of our early climbing on thick polypropylene water-ski rope. Fortunately, none of us had to test its tensile strength through falling.

As the stereotypical all-Canadian kid, I had spent thousands of hours sweating it out in a variety of repetitive games on hockey rinks and on the hardwood floor of the school gymnasium, but the exotic sport of mountaineering offered a whole new set of challenges. My school library carried two books on climbing: *The Cloud Walkers* by Paddy Sherman, one of the few books that describes climbs in Canada; and *Conquistadors of the Useless* by the great French climber Lionel Terray, who had, among other things, completed the first ascent of the Himalayan giant, Annapurna. Terray's spirited approach appealed to my anarchistic streak, while the message in *The Cloud Walkers* was clear: there were other ways by which I could enjoy and exploit the mountains in my own backyard. I started climbing with a vengeance, dragging whatever hapless friend I could find to accompany me or tagging along behind Bob whenever he would have me. A set of 25-foot-high (8 m) boulders on the outskirts of Kimberley provided a free outdoor gymnasium where we met two or three nights a week to hone our rock-jocking skills. Everything we needed to know about climbing, from safety procedures to rope-handling techniques and physical and mental training, we could practise here and apply directly to longer climbs in the nearby mountains.

In 1970, I moved to Calgary to study journalism at the Southern Alberta Institute of Technology and fell in with a knot of climbers from the Calgary Mountain Club (CMC). Straight out of Kimberley, where I had only recently discovered the

joys of cheap, fortified B.C. wine and rock 'n' roll (which I generously shared with my neighbours via the thin walls of our frame house), I was a willing victim of the climbing club's infectious and rowdy enthusiasm. The CMC's driving force was a wave of recent immigrants, mainly from Great Britain, who had fled the crowded mountains of Europe for the virgin summits of the Rockies. They were raucous and crazy, and I quickly realized that I had stumbled upon a new generation of climbers who were radically changing the tone of mountaineering in Canada.

## OUTLAW CLIMBERS

Taking advantage of Canada's lax immigration policies, they had headed to Calgary, many of them jobless after years of drifting from mountain range to mountain range in much the same manner as the ski bums of the 1960s. Most were in their late 20s when I arrived, and some had brought careers with them, while others stuck to menial employment that could be abandoned with few regrets whenever an upcoming expedition beckoned. Compared with the staid members of the Alpine Club of Canada and other established outdoor organizations that foster group outings in natural settings, theirs was a loose-knit group, held together by a love of adrenaline, dark ale and loud music, which more closely matched my youthful ideals.

There was an outlaw feeling to the club, and on weekends, members quietly pioneered bold new routes in blissful obscurity on local crags such as Yamnuska and Ghost River, regrouping midweek to swap stories and plan upcoming coups. Today, they are considered to be part of the foundation of contemporary climbing in Canada, and for all their past craziness and barroom antics, their names are well respected— Brian Greenwood, George Homer, Geoff Horn, Bugs McKeith, Chris Perry, Gerry Rogan, Jon Jones, New Zealander Archie Simpson and Swiss Urs Kallen—for they were instrumental in dragging Canadian climbing standards out of the Dark Ages and in influencing a generation of upstart young domestics.

Typical of his colleagues, Brian Greenwood worked in a Calgary bicycle shop,

Premier Cycle and Sport (one of the first to carry decent climbing equipment in the West), but was reputed to earn more at the pool table during lunch than in eight hours at the counter. While casual customers may have seen him only as a tousle-haired store clerk with a faraway look in his eyes, Brian, together with Calgarian Charlie Locke, established the first big route on the 4,000-foot (1,219 m) north face of Mount Temple near Lake Louise. Comparable to the notorious north face of the Eiger in the European Alps, this route has become a Canadian classic and was just one of many major rock and alpine climbs that Brian pioneered in the Rockies. Considered demanding even by today's standards, his routes were unthinkably difficult in those early days.

There was a handful of young, itinerant locals who fell under the émigré influence, including 1982 Everest summiteer Laurie Skreslet; Chic Scott, now a University of Calgary science instructor; Don Vockeroth, a B.C. ski-hill manager; Charlie Locke, owner of the Lake Louise ski resort; Murray Toft, a University of Calgary outdoor-pursuits instructor; Don Gardiner, a 1988 Olympics development manager; and Billy Davidson, a self-exiled recluse living happily out of a dugout canoe somewhere off the coast of British Columbia.

To be a club member in good standing, it was necessary to drop in on an informal Wednesday-night slide show every couple of weeks during the winter, supplemented by a weekly conference in the distinguished halls of local drinking establishments such as the Empress Hotel or the Cecil. We changed locations periodically, often at the insistence of a bar manager who would find various opportunities to suggest we search for new premises. The reasons for these requests varied from time to time but were usually related to the vain attempts by the younger members to match the beer consumption of the more seasoned Brits. Such heroics invariably led to damaged furniture, brawls and assorted foolish bets.

If the Alpine Club members were Phi Beta Kappa, with their handsome log clubhouse in Banff, we belonged to the campus "Animal House" and wore our colours proudly. While our counterparts brought to the mountains a social order and carefully planned guided outings, we maintained an informality that insisted on independent climbs and allowed only one kind of group activity— parties. Somehow, the loose network served our purposes well, and I regularly met top climbers who were always ready with offers of advice and invitations for weekend excursions. The only group climbs we sponsored occurred every spring, before the snow had melted from the nearby mountains. A couple of dozen members and whatever climbers were passing through town would drive out to the 25-foot-high (8 m) Okotoks Rock, located in a farmer's field south of Calgary, for an evening of rock gymnastics fuelled by music, beer and irreverent wit. Despite the boulder's relatively low profile, it was high enough to fracture bones, and the outings often ended with bruised egos and, occasionally, broken ankles and arms.

Inspired by the achievements of my fellow club members, I set out in the winter of 1971 with Skip King and Janis Kraulis (a Montreal-based photographer friend of Skip's whom I met on the eve of our departure) to make the second winter ascent of Mount Assiniboine. At 11,870 feet (3,617 m), it is called "The Matterhorn of the Rockies." The adventure took a sobering turn when we got caught by darkness just below the summit on our descent and had to dig a snow cave with our hands and ice axes to escape an oncoming storm. The temperature hovered at minus 26 degrees F (-32°C), but miraculously, I escaped with only superficial frostbite to my toes. Ignorance prevented me from abandoning the sport because, due to inexperience, I had no way of knowing just how close I had come to perishing.

At 19, I left school to join the photography staff of the *Calgary Herald* for a year. I married my high school sweetheart, Shirley Zaleschuk, and we moved to Banff for two years, where Shirley worked as a secretary to support us while I studied photography at the School of Fine Arts. During that time, I majored in Nordic ski touring and minored in winter waterfall ice climbing, with table tennis as an elective.

Over the next several winters, I joined my friends, Peter Zvengrowski, Tony

M artyn Williams, *above,* telemarks through a shower of wind-whipped ice crystals in the Swiss Alps. The lightweight telemark equipment we use adds an exhilarating and challenging perspective to our mountain-climbing expeditions. *Facing page,* Calgarian Jim Elzinga front-points his way up the chandelier waterfall ice of Banff's Weeping Wall. Waterfall climbs are pursued both for their challenge and as training for more extended expeditions.

Mould, Chris Perry and Steve Jennings on numerous technical and nontechnical ascents of peaks in the Rockies. Such was the start of my high-altitude apprenticeship in the thin, cold air at 11,000 feet (3,352 m), for the winter conditions in the Canadian Rockies were as severe as any I would encounter in the future. On weekend mornings, the floor of our small Banff apartment was cluttered with the bodies of CMC friends from Calgary who came out to join us on skiing and climbing trips. It was around this time that I became addicted to the thrill of skiing fast and out of control on skinny skis as I descended from a high pass in the mountains. The easy adrenal rush that this gave me surpassed that of slogging my way slowly up and down a peak, and it would, by the late 1970s, become my primary focus in the mountain experience.

## FINDING A JOB

Just before my graduation from the photography course in 1974, my mother died of cancer; it was a grievous loss. It was she who had bought me my first camera and had given me continuous encouragement throughout my early years as a photography student.

At about the same time, Shirley and I found that in growing up, we had grown apart. Our three-year marriage ended in 1975, and I moved back home to live with my father in Kimberley. It was a sobering period after several years of reckless fun, and I began to contemplate my future more seriously. I had seen some of the more talented photography students from Banff abandon their craft as soon as the going got tough, gravitating into more lucrative, if less fulfilling, occupations. As well, I had seen my climbing friends sacrifice months of their lives, grinding away at meaningless jobs in order to finance their next climbs. I was determined to live by my camera between climbs, forging a career from my two passions.

In those days, there was a group of climbers who, with puritanical zeal, refused to "sell themselves out" to the press. Ironically, as the bills for their global climbing habits began to eclipse their personal savings, they found themselves having to reach out for

sponsors through the popular press. Lacking basic business sense, promotional instincts and journalistic skills, they had nothing tangible to offer in return for donated services or finances, and they were forced into corporate panhandling that was often embarrassing both to themselves and to the climbing community as a whole.

With its century-old climbing tradition, Europe provided many more financial opportunities for its professional climbers, who could count on the same level of sponsorship as was afforded talented skiers, cyclists and racing-car teams. Corporate support and public interest tend to sustain one another, and many European mountain climbers and guides have realized comfortable earnings and gained folk-hero status among enthusiastic fans who glamorize the courage and spirit of such men as Reinhold Messner, Heinrich Harrer, Maurice Herzog and Gaston Rebuffat. The atmosphere began to change in Canada with Air Canada's sponsorship of our 1982 Everest expedition, but it is still all but impossible to survive as a professional mountaineer.

I'll remain eternally thankful to my father for housing me and my equipment during my leanest years. Thanks to him, I was able to spend most of my time on the road or in the hills, for he kept a roof over my head, acted as a repository for my mail (opening the occasional personal letter by mistake but discreetly resealing it with tape) and maintained a slightly hard-of-hearing answering service—"The name sounded something like 'Sonder Secklin,' but I'm not sure." He offered continuous support during the days when friends and neighbours good-naturedly asked when I was going to get a real job.

My first serious attempt at freelancing came in 1976, when my father lent me $1,000 to buy a bagful of Kodachrome and a plane ticket to the Austrian Alps so that I could photograph the first world hang-gliding competition. I had been following the sport of hang gliding for a couple of years but had discovered early on that hanging face down from a kite a thousand feet in the air terrified me. I decided it was safer to hide behind the lens of my camera and enjoy the sport vicariously. After a year of making count-

less submissions by mail, I made sales to five magazines and finally was able to repay my father. As a result of the satisfaction, the freedom and the exhilaration this kind of work provided—if not the money—adventure photography became the single motivating force in my life.

My intention in using photography to popularize such mountain sports as climbing and skiing is to demonstrate how people can maximize the potential of their leisure time—which our society squanders in vast quantities—and simultaneously learn something about themselves.

That year, I took my wares east to explore the precarious and competitive magazine marketplace. A 30-day Greyhound excursion ticket delivered me to the doors of editors in Toronto, Ottawa, New York and Washington. On this trip, I met Frank Edwards, who was working as an editor at the *Canadian Geographical Journal* in Ottawa. After I had shown him my portfolio and told him about my grand Greyhound adventure, he invited me to stay with him and his roommates on that and future trips. When he left, in early 1979, to take up an editing job with James Lawrence, the publisher of *Harrowsmith* magazine, he invited me to submit my photographs. Hence my continued association with that magazine and with Lawrence's subsequent publication, *Equinox*.

## ADVENTURE NETWORKS

During this critical period, I teamed up with landscape photographer and cinematographer Art Twomey, who had immigrated to Kimberley from Arizona in the late 1960s. I assisted him on a film he was making on winter in Yellowstone National Park at the invitation of Jeremy Schmidt, a former school teacher from Wisconsin who lived and worked as a winter keeper and later as a ranger at Old Faithful. As we skied through the frozen mist hanging in the geyser basin, photographing bison with masks of hoarfrost that had formed in the minus-30-degree-F (-34°C) air, we talked of warmer places and times. Art was a desert rat with a great flowing black beard that framed a perpetual smile. He had grown up exploring the subterra-

Baiba Morrow

L ong after the winter ski crowd has stored its equipment for the summer, I still manage to find enough snow in the Rockies to accommodate my telemark urges. The corn snow on the steep south face of Fisher Peak provides a fundamental skiing lesson in preparation for more serious endeavours.

Two Calgary Mountain Club members, *facing page*, belay one another while ascending a partially frozen waterfall in Johnston's Canyon, near Banff, Alberta. My favourite retreat from the rigours of cold-weather climbing is the magical subterranean world of the sandstone canyons, *above*, in the Arizona/Utah desert.

nean world of sandstone canyons in the high desert of Arizona and Utah. The three of us hatched a plan for a spring photographic expedition to the Rainbow Plateau in Arizona and, with various friends, spent almost three months in a serious attempt to document that amazing part of the world.

Summer storms spawn flash floods that churn across the flat pan of the desert on their way to the Colorado River, almost 5,000 feet below. The mineral-rich water has eaten its way through soft layers of sandstone over millennia, forming a complex and tortuous drainage system. Seen from a satellite, the canyons in that region resemble the countersunk veins of a leaf. We sometimes entered the labyrinthine maze for a week, taking with us enough food and climbing gear to carry out extensive exploration in the cavelike formations. Often, in the course of a two- or three-mile section, we would rappel several times, lowering ourselves with ropes into alcoves so deep that the narrow, red-coloured walls would converge like a dragon's jaw several hundred feet overhead, cutting out the sun for all but a few moments of the day. The rest of the time, the warm reflected light flowed in waves of changing colour, making it seem as though the rock itself was moving. The combination of climbing and caving and the chance to be the first humans to discover some of these secret places induced a lifelong fascination. To top it all off, the photographs we brought back, despite the arduous conditions under which they were taken, were delicate, otherworldly reflections of our psyches. It was to me such a sacred place that I returned to it in 1984 to exchange marriage vows with Baiba Auders. Several close friends, including Janis Kraulis, his wife Linda Kuttis, Jeremy Schmidt and Wendy Baylor, accompanied us and formed our bohemian wedding party.

That desert project established a compulsive ritual that lasted for the next several years. Each spring, I would migrate south in my decrepit old van, my

body acting as a carbon-monoxide filter for its leaky engine, to continue working on the desert jigsaw puzzle with Jeremy and Art as well as other friends. When the furnacelike heat of June drove us north, we eased ourselves back into a Canadian summer, hiking and climbing together in the interior ranges of British Columbia until the snow began to fly. With my climbing connections and these two longtime comrades, we began to build an adventure network that went beyond mountaineering, incorporating skiing, hiking, caving and rafting. During these starvation years, when my annual income seldom rose above $5,000, we came up with dozens of photojournalistic ideas and realized only those that could be accommodated by our shoestring budgets. The more sophisticated and lavish plans would have to wait a few years, until our credibility and contacts became equal to them.

My travels since that time have reached far beyond the high valleys of southeastern British Columbia. Yet I have applied the same inquisitive principles to finding my way on other mountains, taking some chances and learning both to deal with my fear and to use it to my advantage by harnessing and directing the energy it creates. Along the way, I have met dozens of people who have helped to broaden my way of thinking. Aldous Huxley, in *Along the Road—Notes and Essays of a Tourist*, observed that "for every traveller who has any taste of his own, the only useful guidebook will be the one which he himself has written." It is a philosophy that I have adopted more because of my own informal nature than by design. The magnitude of my wanderings has changed and the guidebooks have been useful, but in the spirit of discovery, I have always known when to set them aside and rely on my instincts.

I trust that *Beyond Everest* will serve a useful purpose to those who read it and that it will encourage them to explore the world and forge their own paths, rather than depend on the direction of others.

After three weeks on McKinley, climbing partner Bernhard Ehmann emerges from the top of the Messner Couloir into the still air of the summit plateau. Mount Foraker is seen in the background. Earlier in the climb, Bernhard, *inset*, warmed a warbler that had been blown seriously off course during its spring migration.

# McKinley

## Assault on an Alaskan giant

En route to McKinley, we conditioned our bodies with several numbing days in the confines of an ageing Volkswagen Beetle, complete with steel grate to deflect rocks on the Alaska Highway. Shortly after passing ice-covered Muncho Lake in the northern Rockies, we ditched the grate in favour of improved visibility.

Early in May 1977, Bernhard Ehmann and I crammed ourselves and our gear (including fishing rods and a net large enough for the brawniest king salmon) into his rusted-out Volkswagen Beetle and headed north for Mount McKinley, North America's highest peak. The snow-capped Rockies towered above the first sprigs of green in the valleys below, and as we pulled away from the larch-covered slopes of the Purcells surrounding Kimberley, I drank in the scenery, mindful that I might never see all this again. Bernhard and I had never climbed above 12,000 feet before, but we had been smitten by McKinley and were heading toward it with the same kind of fever that had lured gold-hungry "cheechakos" to the Klondike Gold Rush in 1898.

We had become involved in the expedition just a couple of months before when Bugs McKeith, "father of the Ice Age" in Canadian frozen-waterfall climbing, had asked me to join a Calgary Mountain Club (CMC) outing to Alaska. Typical of CMC activities, arrangements were loose. "Bring a friend," he said. "We have only one stipulation, that each group of two be fully responsible for its own food, equipment and transportation." In a single sweep, the one thing that could make organizing a large expedition such a pain was avoided. There was little need for communication and coordination among the various members, and we simply arranged to meet in Talkeetna on May 18.

Five days of driving lay ahead of us on 2,400 miles of gradually deteriorating road, which gave us plenty of time to reflect on the dreary descriptions of McKinley provided in 1906 by Dr. Frederick Cook to the Bulletin of the American Geographical Society. Claiming that his three-year expedition to the region included the first ascent of McKinley, he wrote:

"The area of this mountain is far inland, in the heart of a most difficult and trackless country, making the transportation of men and supplies a very arduous task. The thick underbrush, the endless marshes and the myriad vicious mosquitoes bring to the traveller the troubles of the tropics; the necessity of fording and swimming icy streams, the almost perpetual cold rains, the camps

23

in high altitudes on glaciers, in snows and violent storms, bring to the traveller all the discomforts of the Arctic explorer; the very difficult slopes, combined with higher-altitude effects, bring to the traveller the troubles of the worst Alpine climbs. The prospective conqueror of America's culminating peak will be amply rewarded, but he must be prepared to withstand the tortures of the torrids, the discomforts of the North Pole seeker, combined with the hardships of the Matterhorn ascent multiplied many times."

With such compellingly gloomy images of the troubles facing expeditions, it is little wonder that few climbers attempted McKinley. (Cook's accomplishments were tainted, though, when his summit photographs were proved to be taken at a point far below the top, which also made suspect his 1908 claim on the North Pole.)

As we drove along the limestone spine of the Rockies on one of the world's most scenic drives, the Banff-Jasper Highway, I caught glimpses of 11,000-foot peaks and valleys I had climbed and skied on over the past seven years. I hoped that all I had learned on their lofty, glacier-capped sedimentary layers had prepared me for the weeks ahead.

I had first come to know Bernhard a couple of years earlier while making the fourth ascent of the Purcell Range's second highest peak, Farnham Tower. He was a disciplined athlete who had recently become seriously involved in climbing and had trained year-round—a factor that gave him a marked advantage over his partners. Although this is now the norm for all serious climbers, it was considered radical in those days. He even changed his diet in the name of climbing, becoming a vegetarian. "I needed to knock off a few pounds so I'd have less to drag up those steep rock faces," he joked.

Bernhard carried the perfectionism of his training as a machinist into all phases of his life, which sometimes put us at odds with each other. My own lackadaisical, carefree attitude occasionally came into conflict with his more structured approach. However, this did not prevent us from teaming up and discovering some exciting new routes on the slippery lichen-covered cliffs near Kimberley and, later, on the firm granite

While waiting for better weather in Talkeetna, Alaska, so that we could fly in to Mount McKinley, teammate Ekhardt Grassman tried his luck at salmon fishing. A superb climber and an inveterate clown, Ekhardt had a doctorate in mathematics and a reputation for forcing his way up mountains. His climbing career ended two years later after a fatal fall on Mount Edith Cavell.

of the Bugaboos, the Valhallas and the eastern slope of the Coast Range in Washington State. The challenge of McKinley came just at the right time for both of us, and it served as an essential transitional step in our commitment to climbing. Bernhard went on to pursue a profession as a climbing and heli-ski guide for Canadian Mountain Holidays, a company based in Banff, Alberta; I became more deeply immersed in my career as an adventure photographer.

A stiff breeze scoured the fallow wheat fields near Dawson Creek in northern British Columbia as we came to the beginning of the Alaska Highway. This 1,520-mile all-weather gravel roadway had been gouged out of the landscape all the way to Fairbanks during eight frenzied months in 1942-43 by the U.S. Army Corps of Engineers, in response to the possibility of a Japanese invasion. Over the ensuing years, it has been improved with hundreds of miles of bituminous-covered surface and has helped put an end to the isolation of the North.

Mindful of the vulnerability of his windshield to flying rocks on the gravel-topped highway, Bernhard had ingeniously fabricated and mounted a large 50-pound steel grating on the front of the Beetle. In theory, it was intended to deflect whatever rocks transport trucks threw at us. But by the time we were halfway to our destination, the severe neck strain we had both suffered as a result of sitting in a full upright position in order to peer over the grating was enough to make us dismiss the danger. The grating was unceremoniously dumped.

Near Liard Hot Springs, 496 miles up the road, we crossed the Rocky Mountain Trench at its northern terminus. The same U-shaped valley runs past my home in Kimberley, 600 miles to the south, and was created by the terrible buckling action of the continental drift 50 million years ago when the Rockies were driven up against the interior ranges (the Purcells and Selkirks) from the bed of a great inland sea.

The scenery improved in the vicinity of Haines Junction in the western Yukon, where the road is squeezed up against the eastern slope of the Saint Elias Mountains by lovely Kluane Lake. Hidden from view by the lower front ranges is one of Canada's finest nature refuges.

Kluane National Park harbours most of Canada's tallest mountains and the world's largest icecap outside the polar regions, and I have returned many times to ski and hike in the area.

At the end of our fifth day, we jolted to a stop in Talkeetna, raising a cloud of dust. The rest of the team, being more solvent, had already arrived by jet, flying to Anchorage and then taking a connecting train. Roger Marshall was from Golden, British Columbia; Allan Derbyshire, from Bragg Creek, Alberta; and Jon Jones, Ekhardt Grassman, Dave Read and Bugs McKeith made up the Calgary contingent. I had climbed, or at least shared an ale, with all but Roger and Allan.

## PONDEROUS NEIGHBOURS

Talkeetna is a sedate little town in the taiga near the Arctic Circle and is distinguished from other Alaskan bush towns only by the fact that it is the launchpad for ski-plane expeditions into the Alaska Range. While McKinley is the prime target for climbers, other pristine peaks such as Hunter, Huntington and Foraker also offer excellent snow-and-ice climbs. The vertical rock-and-ice walls of Mount Dickey and the Moose's Tooth in the Ruth Gorge are available for the most adventurous spirits. As gateway to the range, Talkeetna fairly bustles during the two spring climbing months and in 1977 boasted a hotel, a gas station and two bars.

McKinley and its ponderous neighbour, Foraker, form the nucleus of the Alaska Range, a curved chain of mountains that stretches 580 miles across the lower third of the 49th U.S. state. Although most of the peaks are less than half McKinley's height, the range acts as a natural land barrier between the state's largest city, Anchorage, on the coastal lowlands and Alaska's interior to the north. West of Denali National Park, originally called McKinley National Park, the range forms a drainage divide for rivers flowing west to the Bering Sea or south to the Gulf of Alaska. The park, encompassing an area of 3,030 square miles, was created in 1917 largely through the efforts of naturalist John Muir, whose earlier attempts to publicize the importance of environmental preservation had resulted in the formation of Yosemite National Park in California.

At a latitude of 63 degrees north, Mount McKinley is the world's highest peak above 50 degrees north latitude, and its climate is as severe as that found on much loftier peaks in the lower latitudes of Asia. It has the greatest base-to-summit elevation of any mountain on Earth, and around its lower circumference, it is one of the world's most massive peaks. The mountain received its current name in 1896 for the 25th president of the United States, William McKinley. He was assassinated in 1901 and never saw the mountain that had been named for him. The native people called the mountain Denali, meaning "the high one," a name that has come back into vogue, particularly in the catalogues of equipment manufacturers. Being neither native nor Republican, we affectionately called it Big Mac.

The first ascent of McKinley's slightly lower north peak took place in 1910, when a bawdy group of three sourdoughs (prospectors who had spent at least one winter in the North) approached the peak by dogsled from Fairbanks. They had been financed on a romantic whim by Billy McPhee, the owner of Fairbanks' Pioneer Saloon and Hotel, and to mark their success, they dragged and carried a 14-foot spruce pole 36 miles and 18,500 vertical feet (5,638 m) from the taiga to the north summit. The main peak, 850 feet (259 m) higher, was first climbed by Hudson Stuck, the Yukon's archdeacon, who led a group of four in 1913 via the route used by the sourdoughs.

Our team began determining its own parameters over moose stew with cranberry sauce and home-baked blueberry pie in a cozy local eatery in Talkeetna. We had each come with varying degrees of experience, but most of us had not been above 14,000 feet before, so we shared a slight feeling of apprehension about how our bodies would perform in the thin, cold air of McKinley. All the climbers, except me, were in their early 30s and had had recreational climbing apprenticeships in the Alps. Bugs called me the "token Canadian," a label I was to wear on most of my climbs where I was the only indigenous member of a national team.

More than anyone in the group, it was Bugs who impressed me, not only with his irreverent and flippant attitude toward life but also as one of the world's most innovative and colourful climbers. He created a new route on the formidable north face of Switzerland's infamous Eiger in 1969 with a couple of friends from his native Scotland. He then spent the next 2½ years working as a dog handler for the British Antarctic Survey, after which he immigrated to Canada via climbs in the Peruvian Andes and Yosemite Valley, California.

Ekhardt Grassman had a Ph.D. in mathematics and was another strong member of the team. He had lost most of his toes to frostbite during various winter forays and had earned a reputation for pushiness while on big climbs. His nickname was "Dr. Death."

Tragically, both Bugs and Ekhardt would be killed two years later in separate climbing incidents in the Rockies. Ekhardt and his partner, spelunker-turned-climber Gary Pilkington, were found still roped together after falling off the north face of Mount Edith Cavell. Bugs plummeted through a summit cornice (the curling projections of wind-blown snow arcing out over the leeward side of a mountain ridge) down the east face of Mount Assiniboine.

In the course of my climbing career, I have lost several close friends. All of them, like me, had accepted the risk factor as being an integral part of the climbing experience. None of them had a death wish, but if given a choice, they would probably have opted to leave this life while engaged in the activity they loved best.

## EXPEDITION CLOD

In Talkeetna, we jokingly called ourselves CLODs, not simply because Webster's dictionary describes a clod as being a clumsy and uncouth rustic but because there happened to be several major CMC trips that spring which did not include us. We felt like leftovers—Calgary Leftovers On Denali. Expedition CLOD was, from the outset, a consortium characterized by wit, laughter, frustration, endearment and cockiness—the things that make an expedition tick.

The three days we spent in the Tee-

Using Nordic skis and plastic
sleds, we moved all of our gear
seven miles across the Kahiltna Glacier
to Base Camp. McKinley's main summit
is visible in the centre background.
Although park regulations stipulated that
climbing parties had to have at least four
members, our eight-man ''team'' split up
into pairs at the airstrip.

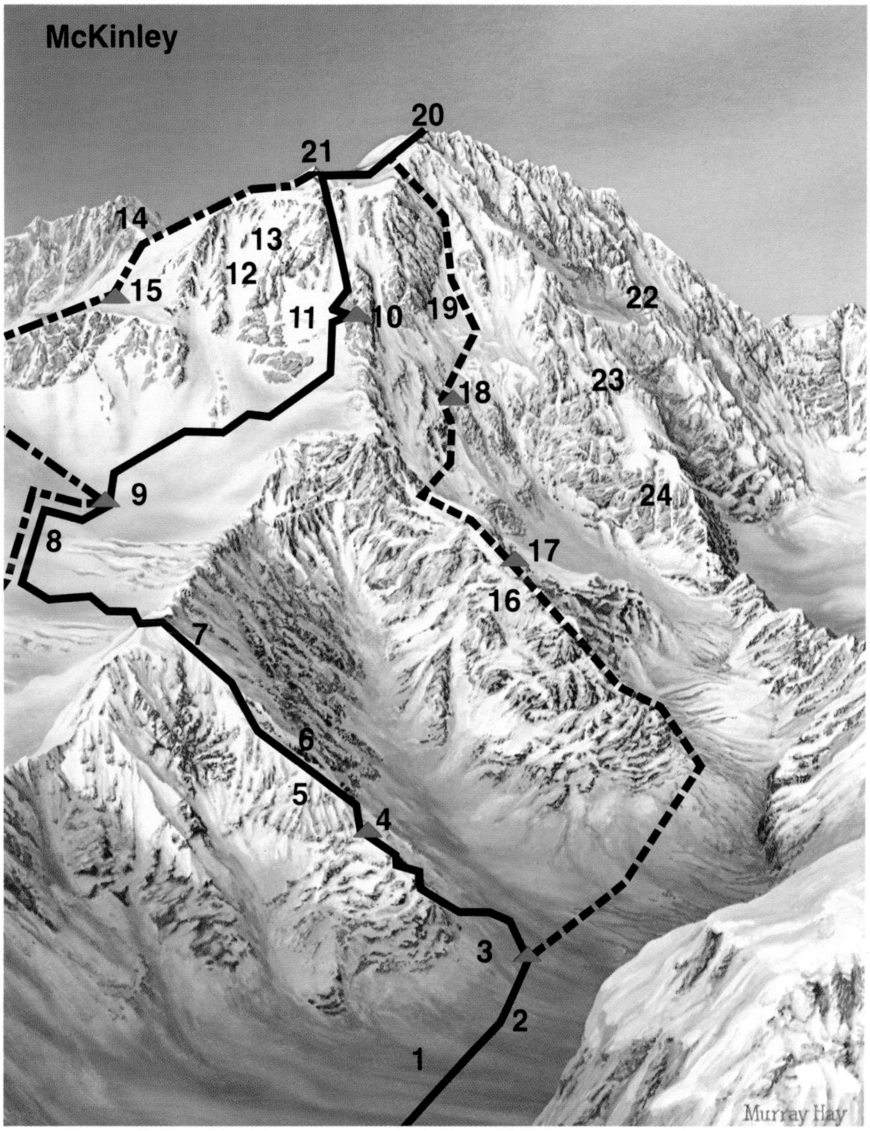

**McKinley**

Murray Hay

1. To CLOD Base Camp
2. East Fork of Kahiltna Glacier
3. Camp One (10,000 feet)
4. Camp Two (12,300 feet)
5. Southwest Rib
6. Double Cornices
7. Bivouac in Bergschrund (13,700 feet)
8. West Buttress Route (broken line)
9. West Buttress Route Acclimatization Camp (14,000 feet)
10. Our 17,000-foot Camp
11. Messner Couloir
12. West Face
13. Rib Bugs Took to Summit Plateau
14. Denali Pass (18,200 feet)
15. West Buttress Route Camp Three (17,000 feet)

16. West Rib
17. CLOD Camp Two (14,000 feet)
18. CLOD Camp Three (16,200 feet)
19. CLOD Camp Four Snow Cave (17,200 feet)
20. Summit (20,320 feet)
21. Summit Plateau
22. South Face
23. Cassin Ridge
24. Japanese Couloir

Our Route ▬▬▬▬

Calgary Mountain Club Route ▬ ▬ ▬

Main West Buttress Route ▬ ▪ ▬ ▪

pee Saloon waiting for flyable weather were not entirely wasted. Bugs picked up a guitar and led a seven-member Japanese team in a chorus of *Old MacDonald Had a Farm* and other favourites, which the Japanese soon learned by heart without ever understanding the words. It was something like an American grappling with the words to *O Canada* at the beginning of a hockey game. Outside in the driving rain, we jumped into an animated soccer game with the Russians, who had spent the previous two weeks acclimatizing at 17,000 feet (5,181 m) in the Soviet Caucasus Mountains. Unlike our team, they had to be careful not to let too much beer affect the physiological advantage of the increased capacity of their red blood cells to carry oxygen. Their superior prowess was not lost on the waterlogged ball, as they proceeded to win the game.

## STRETCHING THE RULES

The attraction of a peak of Himalayan scale that is easy and inexpensive to get to, with a minimum of bureaucratic hassle, has boosted traffic on McKinley. Between the time of the first ascent of the north peak in 1910 and the late 1960s, fewer than 250 people had climbed to the summit of one or the other of McKinley's two peaks. One of the climbers who would eventually join me on an expedition to Vinson Massif in Antarctica, Bill Hackett, had made the first ascent of the now popular West Buttress route in 1951 with other such noted climbers as Bradford Washburn and Barry Bishop. He also made the second ascent of that route seven years later. By contrast, on July 6, 1976, during America's bicentennial celebrations, 80 people followed his route to the summit. The percentage of accidents rose proportionately with the increased traffic, and 33 climbers were involved in rescue incidents on Mount McKinley and Foraker that year. They required 21 separate rescue operations (involving helicopters and light aircraft) and cost the U.S. government a total of about $82,000. During the first 64 years of climbing on this mountain, only three people had perished; in 1976 alone, four people died on McKinley and six on Foraker.

Statistics from that same year's record

Illustrations by Murray Hay

assault by some 600 climbers show the types of afflictions common to altitude climbs on any mountain: seven cases of high-altitude pulmonary edema (HAPE —the filling of the lungs with fluid), two cases of high-altitude cerebral edema (HACE—the swelling of the brain), five frostbite victims and a dozen instances of snow blindness.

Armed with these cheery facts, we crawled into Ken Holland's Super Cub on May 20, early enough in the morning that our watery-beer hangovers had not had a chance to kick in. Just as we slid through Gunsight Notch, a jagged cleft in a wall of rock leading out onto the Kahiltna Glacier, the first signs of motion sickness crept into the cockpit. Before it could develop into anything serious, the middle-aged bush pilot dropped us off at the snow airstrip at the park boundary, aptly named the Kahiltna International. Tipping the brim of his cap, he flashed us a cocky grin. "See you in about 25 days!" he called.

As we turned away from the departing plane, we were startled to see that the drop-off area was almost as crowded as the Teepee Saloon. We were surrounded by the familiar faces of a backlog of climbers who had also been waiting for good flying weather. In addition to several private teams, there was a mixed group of about 40 Americans and Germans milling about, each of whom had paid pioneer guide Ray Genet, who was preparing for his 21st ascent, and his assistants $1,200 to be shepherded up the popular West Buttress route. A few years before, Genet had been part of the fierce first winter ascent of McKinley when temperatures had plummeted to minus 148 degrees F (-100°C) with windchill. This garrulous bear of a man, with a flowing black beard and his head swathed in a pirate's kerchief, impressed me with his friendliness when he ambled over to find out what our plans were. Two years later, I was dismayed to learn that this powerful and experienced climber, along with his female teammate Hannelore Schmatz, had succumbed to sickness and deteriorating weather on their descent from the summit of Everest in 1979. Despite valiant efforts by Sungdare Sherpa to revive them, they perished before they could get down to the South Col.

Bernhard Ehmann, a flap of tape across his nose to prevent sunburn in the midday glare, climbs through a shadowy stretch of subzero temperatures on the second day of our first ascent of the Southwest Rib.

At Base Camp, we built several igloos to establish "CLOD" city and were later joined by two American Alpine Club hosts and their Russian guests, Sergei Etimov (left) and Valentin Ivanov (standing). We spent most of our nights on McKinley in snow caves or igloos, preferring them over cramped and cold tents.

The Denali Park regulations stipulate that teams of less than four are not allowed onto the mountain. For propriety's sake, we had posed as an eight-member crew at park headquarters in Talkeetna before flying into the park, but at the airstrip, we split up into our prearranged groups of two and began the daylong procession on skis up the seven miles of the Kahiltna Glacier in roped pairs. There, at the junction of the glacier's east fork, we established CLOD city. It was soon expanded by the Russians and their two American Alpine Club hosts, Riley Moss and Mike Helm, who constructed igloos in the suburbs to bring the total number of snow dwellings to six. Here, we got to know a couple of them a little better, including Valentin Ivanov, who was to become one of the 1982 Soviet Everest summiteers. (I would bump into him again in 1983 at the annual International Mountaineering Camp held by the Russians in the Caucasus Mountains.)

For our mountain food, Bernhard had been careful to choose a savoury high-calorie diet that included such culinary surprises as coleslaw sealed in foil and the most exotic gorp ingredients that the North Star Natural Food Store in Kimberley could muster—pumpkin seeds, dried papayas, coconut shavings, dried sugared pineapple and chocolate chips in combination with the usual mixture of nuts and raisins. When we prepared our dehydrated meals, we used a cooking method gleaned from a climbing magazine that saved us fuel and made tent life more efficient. After bringing water to a boil on our small single-burner stove, we added the dry ingredients and stuffed the pot into a nylon sack, which then went inside the sleeping bag. In this goose-down womb, the food was usually cooked within 20 minutes by its self-contained heat, and in the meantime, we were able to use the stove to melt a pot of snow for drinking water.

In the course of digging a pit for their igloo, Bugs and Jon uncovered a narrow 40-foot-deep crevasse. It was incorporated into the design of their entranceway and served as a convenient natural garbage disposal. We were to spend most of our 25 days on the mountain in the comfort and security of snow caves or igloos, preferring these to our cramped, frosty-walled tent. To those inside an igloo, all outside sounds are muffled, so a sizable storm can be virtually ignored—at least until wind-driven snow plugs the entranceway, cutting off the oxygen supply. Needless to say, we quickly realized the importance of keeping a shovel inside.

## LOFTY DIMENSION

Our original aim had been the classic West Rib route, a narrow ridge offering continuous, solid high-standard ice and snow climbing for its entire length. But once at the mountain, Bernhard and I were seduced by a steep and technically challenging alternative—a nearby virgin rib of 4,000 feet (1,219 m) of snow, rock and ice. A cone of steep pink granite and wandering ice ramps soared up the southwest face in a pristine sweep to a corniced, razor-sharp arête that, in turn, swept up into a final steep face to emerge on a small aerie only a short walk from Windy Corner at 14,000 feet (4,267 m) on the regularly travelled West Buttress route. It would add a day or two to the climb, but we were in no hurry and anxious to try something different. Inspired by its lofty dimension, we put our creative minds together and named it the Southwest Rib.

We decided to climb with a supply of only three days' food, leaving ourselves little or no emergency reserve, in order to keep our weight down for the strenuous technical climbing anticipated halfway up the steep rib. On reaching the West Buttress route, we planned to use it as an expressway down to Base Camp and return back up it with enough food to fuel the second stage of our ascent up the west face, a route that had been completed only once before. The rest of the CLODs were still intent on the West Rib, and we left them with wishes of good luck and a speedy reunion. "See ya later, Jimmy!" Allan quipped in his driest Yorkshire accent.

Soon after pitching our tiny tent at the base of our route, we were joined by the Americans, Mike and Riley, for tea. The Russian climbers had plans of their own, leaving their American hosts wantonly eyeing our route, which was in plain sight of CLOD city. Smacking their lips, they headed off into the twilight, planning to make camp somewhere among the rocks on the lower part of the rib.

Next morning, zooming up the stairway of their tracks that had frozen solid overnight, we whispered a greeting through the frost-laminated walls of their tent, which clung precariously to an icy notch hacked out of the slope. "We'll be up in a minute" was their sleepy reply. We hoped they would catch up before too long to help us with the lung-bursting task of trailbreaking on the ever-steepening slope. We had no idea it would be fully six days before we rejoined them.

Soon after, at 12,000 feet (3,657 m), we were setting personal altitude records with each step. Bernhard, in superb condition as always, surged ahead no matter how desperate the conditions, whereas I seemed to be left in his tracks, grappling with the weight of my pack and the mounting technical difficulties inherent in an increasingly rarefied atmosphere. The rope came into use at this point for more than just insurance against falling into crevasses. We relied on standard technical climbing precautions by placing ice-screw anchors for our belay points. One of us would feed the rope out through the eye of the anchor (belaying), while the other led to the end of its 150-foot length, protecting himself by setting ice-screw "runners" wherever possible for the rope to pass through to reduce the distance of a fall if he slipped. The "second" would then be put "on belay" by the first and climb upward, stopping to retrieve the ice-screw anchors. After an endless series of belayed leads in total whiteout, we reached the only natural tent platform on the rib at about the midpoint. It was an exposed site, and if our tent was destroyed in a windstorm, digging an emergency cave would have been impossible in snow that was only a couple of inches deep on top of a bed of solid ice.

## ON THE RIB

The next day, we awoke to a nondescript world. We could have been anywhere. Steering by sonar in almost total whiteout, we reached the most treacherous section of the entire climb by noon. At about two-thirds of its height, the rib narrowed to an arête with rotten cornices hanging over both sides of the ridge and

Having finished our ascent of the Southwest Rib, we made our way over to an acclimatization camp on the West Buttress route at 14,000 feet for a rest. Here we inherited a "trigloo" built by Alaskan guide Andy Butcher (left). It was so big that Bernhard Ehmann (centre) and I had room for overnight visitors like Jon Jones (right), who had just spent a chilly night on the mountain without a tent or sleeping bag.

perched above nearly 3,000-foot (914 m) drops. We wallowed through the loose sugar snow, adopting the clumsy but effective technique of straddling the rib and paddling along with ice axe in front. "It's kind of like kayaking upstream in frozen white water," I yelled back to Bernhard, "but forget about trying out your Eskimo roll here!" The occasional ice screw was augured into the leprous flank of the rib, giving more psychological comfort than actual safe purchase.

At around 5 p.m., the sun had once again flooded into the valleys as we rested under the ceiling of a large boulder to brew up a cup of tea. This same idyllic spot came close to being a disaster zone for Mike and Riley a couple of days later. They pitched their tent there during a snowstorm and were very nearly flushed off the mountain when a small avalanche shot through a hole in the back of the natural cave, collapsing their tent with them inside it. Such a scenario was far from our minds as we closed our eyes and concentrated on absorbing the sun's rays, luxuriating in a kind of reptilian lethargy.

Over on the West Rib, nearly a mile away, two specks appeared on the skyline. They were the Russians, well ahead of our counterpart CLODs, on the first day of an amazing three-day ascent of a route that can take up to three weeks. If they had been stranded in Talkeetna much longer in the wait for flyable weather, the residual effects of their acclimatization trip in the Caucasus would have worn off, but fate had been kind to them. Clinical tests have shown that the body retains its acclimatization properties, proportionate to time spent at altitude, up to a maximum of two weeks. Living at high altitudes for periods beyond that can cause severe mental and physical degenerative problems. Mental capacity is reduced by as much as 50 percent; individuals become physically weaker and have virtually no recuperative powers; psychological stresses are amplified, and lassitude saps the will to perform essential tasks such as melting snow for water.

The rather fickle weather appeared to be stabilizing, and although it was already early evening, we decided to press on. The persistent illumination of the "midnight sun" pushed us forward

over the 40-degree mixed snow-and-ice slopes. But the effects of ankle strain from the heavy packs and the 13,000-foot (3,962 m) elevation were beginning to tell when we faced two final pitches of 60-degree blue ice before reaching the broad slope of the upper glacier. Alpine faces always look steeper than they really are, and as we climbed it, it seemed the wall before us was perpendicular. We hung Bernhard's pack from the ice-screw belay, and he deftly front-pointed, digging the sharp front teeth of his crampons into the wall, the full length of his 150-foot rope. "Hey, this is fun . . . it's my first lead on ice!" he called excitedly and began to haul up our packs to his station, leaving me below to wonder begrudgingly about my role in his ice-climbing education.

My lead was short but tricky, for the steep ice wall terminated in a stack of fluffy hoarfrost crystals. Front-pointing to the top of the ice with virtually nothing for my hands to grasp, I sank my axe into the crusty surface of the upper glacier. Although I had climbed waterfall ice steeper than this in the Rockies, the combined effect of thousands of feet of gaping exposure and the ache in my oxygen-starved muscles forced me to rivet my attention on the task ahead. With the security of a rope from above, Bernhard followed, finishing with an ungraceful and fevered butterfly stroke to gain the last few feet. Reaching the stance I had chopped out in the ice, he happened to glance down at his harness to find the knot had somehow come undone during the excitement of the last couple of pitches. If he had slipped, he would have performed one of the world's highest and longest swan dives. We shivered at the thought and strengthened our resolve to stay on top of things from there on in.

It was now midnight. While we had been struggling with the world in front of our noses, the moon had been tracing its arc across the southern sky. A chilly wind blew colder; our tiny plastic thermometer had broken long ago, and it was just as well, since we found out later that it had been a steady minus 26 degrees F (-32°C) all night long. (Taking a lesson from this climb, I never again carried a thermometer in the mountains, figuring that if I knew just how cold it was,

Our Southwest Rib assault had been a lightweight affair, so before we could continue to the summit, we had to replenish our supplies. For two days, we hauled enough food from Base Camp to last 15 days, using the less strenuous and very busy West Buttress route up to the 14,000-foot camp.

The second phase of the climb was a rigorous ascent of the Messner Couloir, 6,000 feet of snow and ice. At the end of our first day on the route, at 17,000 feet, climbing partner Bernhard Ehmann looks down at the upper part of our Southwest Rib route as it emerges from the clouds to the left.

I wouldn't want to get out of my sleeping bag in the morning.) The ambience of the midnight sun was more than ample to light our way, so we kept easing ourselves across the steep glacier. In more than a few places, our probing axes found small crevasses over which we adroitly crawled.

At 4:30 a.m., we rolled out our ensolite pads in the mouth of a partially filled bergschrund (a crevasse at the head of a glacier) just as the sun kissed Mount Foraker. The pads shattered in the frigid air, but we had been climbing continuously for 20 hours, and sleep was all that mattered. A few hours later, when the heat became oppressive, we stripped to our long johns and finished the last couple of pitches to Windy Corner.

We spent that night at the 14,000-foot (4,267 m) acclimatization camp on the West Buttress, planning on a good night's rest before returning to Base Camp for supplies. But our sleep was fitful as we were kept awake until nearly midnight by the Styrofoam-squeaking noises of a large guided group walking around outside on the snow. After 2½ days of solitude on our own route, the traffic jam of people and tents seemed contradictory to our attempts to get away from it all. Next day, we headed down the gentle slope toward CLOD city to collect some food for the summit push. As it turned out, we could have continued upward by salvaging some of the many abandoned caches of provisions from the "Kahiltna Supermarket." The mountain was a storehouse of expensive freeze-dried foods, and unlike most teams that would rather be spared bringing their surplus supplies down, we eventually left the upper levels of the mountain with more than we had brought.

After seven hours of leaning downhill into stinging wind-driven ice crystals, we arrived at Base Camp to meet the "Squamish Hardcore" team (Steve Sutton, Hugh Burton, Gordie Smaille and Greg Shannon, all of Vancouver), who had just completed the formidable Cassin Ridge in a 15-day alpine push. They recounted how they had lost a tent and its contents low on the mountain when a rock avalanche had torn it off its platform. They were well into a bottle of vodka when the first of the Russians arrived from their five-day ascent of the same route. Proffering the bottle, Shannon said, "Hey, Ruskie . . . have some wwoddka!" But the Russian, as an elite representative of his country's climbing team, was on his best behaviour and politely declined. A few years later, in the Caucasus, I had no problem getting our Russian hosts to drink with us. In fact, the protocol had been reversed.

## ALASKAN TRIGLOO

We spent the next two days on Nordic skis slogging back up through 6,000 vertical feet (1,828 m) of fresh snow to the foot of the west face. Fifteen days' worth of food turned our little red sleds into submerged submarines. With the perplexing question "Why am I doing this?" burning a hole in the part of my brain that should know better, I ploughed upward through the knee-deep porridge snow and searing bacon-grease heat.

Climbers come to McKinley in May and June because of the bridge between the frigid chill of winter and the major avalanche season of midsummer. As the longer daylight hours insidiously weakened the snow bonds on McKinley and its neighbours, the constant roar of avalanches added unnecessary drama to our lives.

On the way up, we intercepted Riley and Mike, who were just coming off the rib climb. Since their Russian charges had already finished their climbs, the lads decided to save the summit of McKinley for another time and were going to return to the amenities of Talkeetna—specifically, the bar. They explained that they had hesitated during the unstable weather on the lower part of the rib and had been trapped by the same storm we had descended in. They had been tent-bound for a couple of days, but it had provided Riley with a chance to finish reading *Watership Down*. His main observation about the climb: "It was a pretty strange place to be reading about rabbits."

Back at the 14,000-foot (4,267 m) level, at the foot of the west face, we inherited a "trigloo," three sleeping igloos joined by a fourth that served as a kitchen/entranceway. The Alaskans who had built it were ski guides in the coastal range closer to Anchorage and had used sturdy aluminum grain shovels that

A post-climb group portrait of the "CLOD" team at the 14,000-foot camp. Left to right: Bernhard Ehmann, Jon Jones, Allan Derbyshire, Bugs McKeith, Ekhardt Grassman, Dave Read, Roger Marshall and me.

Halfway up the couloir, Bernhard Ehmann kicks steps in the snow during one of his leads. Hours later, his load was lightened when his pack dropped 4,000 feet, spilling its contents across the mountain face.

allowed them to toss up such a large snow structure in no time flat. Their other innovation was homemade packs, which were twice as big as anything I had seen before or since, and I wondered at the stamina it required to carry one at high altitude.

## PHASE TWO

Here, Bernhard and I rested in the sun for a couple of days, giving our bodies a chance to adapt to the thin air. We broke out of our sloth only to carry some gear for the Colorado Up 'n' Over expedition that was making a summit bid via the West Buttress route before descending the east side of the peak. Famed mountain runner Rick Trujillo was one of the climbers, and he admitted to being bored with the acclimatization process of high-altitude climbing. Back in the Colorado Rockies, where he worked as a geologist, he was used to running thousands of high-altitude vertical feet every week as part of his training regimen. Here, he was forced by conventional wisdom to limit the daily gain to 1,000 feet (304 m). Rock climber Jane Costantineau, bearing a ragged scar on her shoulder inflicted by a lightning strike while she had been climbing on the Diamond Face of Longs Peak in Colorado, agreed with Rick about the slow pace: "I'm used to blitzkrieging up a rock face in just a couple of hours and being back in the comfort of my own home the same day, full of the satisfaction of the climb."

From our trigloo, we spotted Jon, Ekhardt and Allan slowly descending from Denali Pass where they had been forced to bivouac. They looked thoroughly thrashed after spending a night in the open without sleeping bags or tents. They told us they and Bugs had completed a new route on the southwest face (which they named "Clodface"), branching off from the West Rib at about the 12,000-foot (3,657 m) level and angling over toward the difficult Cassin Ridge. After reaching the summit plateau, 300 feet (91 m) below the summit itself, Bugs had chosen to downclimb the southwest face to their snow cave at around 17,000 feet (5,181 m), where they had stowed their gear. The three of them, not quite feeling up to that strenuous feat, had decided to descend by the

normal West Buttress route and had ended up at the trigloo with us. They were now subjected to a second cheerless night wrapped in down jackets, dreaming, no doubt, of Bugs ensconced in their sleeping bags.

Meanwhile, Roger and Dave were high on the West Rib and were expected to finish it in another day or two. Their share of excitement had come when Dave sustained frostbite on his fingers and toes while resurrecting a collapsed tent in high winds late one night. Frostbite is a common malady on the mountain where wind gusts have been recorded at speeds exceeding 100 miles per hour (160 kph), while temperatures encountered between 7,000 and 20,000 feet (2,133 m/6,096 m) may vary as much as 130 degrees, from plus 80 degrees F to minus 50 (27°/-45°C).

For the second phase of our climb on the upper mountain, Bernhard and I chose to do the second ascent of the enticing 6,000-foot-long (1,828 m) Messner Couloir, on the right side of the west face. It had fallen to ace Italian climber Reinhold Messner the previous year in a mere 12-hour round trip from this acclimatization camp.

By late afternoon of our first day on the face (June 8, day 20 on the mountain), we had pitched our tent, a room with a spectacular view on a ledge at the top of a granite buttress just off the couloir at 17,000 feet (5,181 m). As we revelled in the warmth of the sun's rays far into the night, we caught glimpses of gilded ponds in the tundra and the vast soupline of peaks stretching away to the south toward the ocean. "I wouldn't trade places with anyone else right now," Bernhard whispered in an exalted voice. It was a fine place to be. We looked in the direction of the lower Kahiltna Glacier, from which an old friend, Joanna Coleman, had approached the mountain with another woman some years ago, in their own epic version of an Up 'n' Over expedition. They had lugged their supplies across 80 miles of moraine and glacier to the summit of the mountain, then descended by Karstens Ridge. On the descent, Joanna's partner fell through a cornice and had to drop her heavy pack, which tumbled 1,000 feet (304 m), in order to ascend the rope with Jumar clamps. Luckily, they were later

able to retrieve it and finished their expedition without further problems.

Despite nagging headaches, we dozed through the night and returned to the couloir on perfect crisp snow that rose up at a 35-degree angle. By noon, we were within 1,000 feet (304 m) of the summit plateau, sitting on the lee of a boulder enjoying a brew of oxtail soup. As we sat slurping the tasty concoction, Bernhard's pack, containing tent, sleeping bag and camera, displayed a rebellious mind of its own and began slithering off down the couloir. We stared, incredulous, as it gained momentum in leaps and bounds, spewing its contents across a quarter mile of mountain face.

We both groaned as it disappeared around the corner. We couldn't believe that our summit plans had been dashed, and the soup suddenly turned acrid in our mouths. "Wait a minute," said Bernhard, hopefully. "If we could make it to the summit tonight, we could descend the West Buttress route with the help of the midnight sun and find shelter in one of the igloos at 17,000 feet [5,181 m]." Already, life seemed brighter. The pack and its contents, which had fallen more than 4,000 feet (1,219 m), could wait to be retrieved from the trigloo camp in a few days. We could survive until then with the gear that was still left in my pack.

## HIGH-ALTITUDE ANGST

Up we trudged, in misty, unsettled conditions, pondering the intelligence of our decision. It was miserable going—one step, break through the crust of the deteriorating conditions, curse; another step, throbbing head, 10 to 15 breaths; another step . . . . Unburdened by a pack, Bernhard surged ahead on the wind-packed sections, the rope between us always taut. "Why don't you put some of that extra energy into nicking steps for me?" I yelled resentfully, my anger rising in a crescendo. I stabbed my way up to him, stiff-legged, two mongrels glowering at each other. Two extremely tired mongrels. Three weeks' worth of pent-up emotions from living in such close quarters had suddenly turned septic. Close friends were about to ruin their summit chances and mess up the scenery by planting ice axes in each other's chest.

Silently acknowledging the energy-sapping properties of a hollow debate, we backed away from the confrontation, fixing our glassy stares on the snow ahead as we resumed our task. When we emerged from the steep slope onto the summit plateau, the pure magic of the mountain took over. The constant metamorphosis of scenery, light and clouds had suddenly crystallized into a 360-degree panorama of mountaintops and cotton-candy cloud floor. Amazingly, the bitter wind died completely.

We floated up the final 300 feet (91 m) of the summit wedge through thick, lingering alpenglow and, at 11 p.m., topped out just as the sun was beginning to lose its grip on the edge of the world. A deep-freeze breeze oozed up from the dark south face like liquid nitrogen. Our faces and head gear were covered in hoarfrost in the still minus-30-degree-F (-34°C) air. The summit was a desktop-sized parking lot of bamboo wands and shredded flags, towering over an empty Japanese Asahi beer can. Everything was right in the world tonight.

## LAUGHING AT THE WORLD

On our way down, near Denali Pass, we came upon Roger and Dave in their tent, at 18,000 feet (5,486 m). The two had somehow descended from the top of the West Rib route and were now dangerously dehydrated because they had run out of matches with which to light their stove and thereby melt snow (matches don't ignite well at altitude). They fired up their first brew in three days with our lighter, while we hurried down to crash the pyjama party at 17,000 feet (5,181 m). It was at this point on his solo descent from the summit in winter seven years later that the great Japanese explorer and climber Naomi Uemura would last be seen.

As we snuggled up to our Up 'n' Over friends in their igloo, we received groggy congratulations as they tried to shake off the dopey effects of sleeping pills they had taken to combat the insomnia of high altitude. We didn't care to disturb them, only to share their body heat, and we gradually fell asleep, relieved to have made the summit and to have descended without being trapped by bad weather.

Next morning, a lone figure appeared on Denali Pass, and we all thought, "Oh, oh, someone's in trouble." It wasn't until the apparition was right upon us that we recognized Bugs. He had strolled over to the base of a couloir parallelling the Messner route on the west face at 10 the previous night and had polished it off in eight hours. After reaching the summit plateau at 6 a.m. for the second time in four days, he had snoozed in the early-morning sun and then continued down to join us just as we were emerging from the igloo. He had seen Roger and Dave making their summit bid that same day. We parted company once again, scrambling across the west face to retrieve Bernhard's pack before rejoining the others.

By noon of our 23rd day, we were finally all reunited, basking in the ultraviolet rays at the 14,000-foot (4,267 m) camp on the West Buttress, bringing each other up to date on what the "team" had done and generally laughing at the world. All of us had made the summit—Bugs had done it twice—and we had suffered no casualties.

Bernhard and I had used climbing skins on our Nordic skis to reach this camp a week before, and now we looked forward to an exciting run down the West Buttress route. On this and most other future altitude expeditions, I would bring Nordic ski equipment to serve both as a tool and as an adrenaline-pumping sport in itself. Unfortunately, the knee-deep powder that we had ploughed through on our way up had by now been blasted by the wind, and the bare patches of blue ice near Windy Corner required stints of down-climbing with crampons.

At 11,000 feet (3,352 m), the wind had merely compacted the snow and now the variegated surface provided us with a skiing challenge almost as great as the summit. If we had been using the technologically advanced metal-edged fibreglass telemark skis of today and proper leather telemark boots and bindings, we could have managed everything the mountain threw at us, including the ice. But we were on clunky wooden skis, with bindings that would often release our rigid double mountain boots when we reached maximum speed.

To top it off, our plastic toboggans, heavily laden with the booty salvaged from caches along the way, would zoom ahead of our ski tips, often riding right over top of them. The resultant pileups looked like a derailed passenger train, with bodies and luggage strewn everywhere. By the time we had reached CLOD city, rested a few hours and continued down the Kahiltna Glacier toward our plane pickup, we were skied- and climbed-out.

On our way down to the gentle lower glacier, we had passed lines of climbers in lockstep formation on their way up the West Buttress. Since the weather was good, we knew we would probably be picked up as soon as we arrived back at the airstrip. Indeed, shortly after our arrival, Ken Holland dropped in out of the sky with a couple of climbers and scooped us up. Within an hour, we were swilling beer at the Teepee Saloon. While the others hopped the train back to make their flights out of Anchorage, Bernhard and I strapped ourselves into his Volkswagen torture machine and set the controls for points south.

Bernhard Ehmann begins his final descent through the still, cold air as the summit and neighbouring Mount Foraker are bathed in a lingering midnight alpenglow.

# Aconcagua

## Tempting fate in Argentina

Aconcagua's frozen summit ridge, knife-edged and dangerous, seems a world away from its hot and dry lower reaches to climbers Roger Marshall (foreground) and Dave Read. *Inset*, Norman Croucher quenches his thirst in the parched Punta de Vacas Valley.

On our way south from McKinley, Bernhard and I made a side trip to the Queen Charlotte Islands, flying from Prince Rupert on the coast of British Columbia to Masset on Graham Island in a Grumman Goose amphibious aircraft. As in all future climbing expeditions, I tried to combine an assortment of activities to create a balance in what would otherwise be a rather one-sided experience. We had arranged to join some friends to hike the 60-mile-long white sandy beach of Naikoon Park, a dramatic change from the sterile world of ice and snow.

No sooner had I returned home from this extended trip and washed the dust of the road from my travel-weary body than I received a letter from Roger Marshall. He had learned through British climber Doug Scott that because a team had dropped off the waiting list for Everest, there was a permit available to climb the world's highest peak during the post-monsoon period of 1982. With a quick query to the Nepalese Ministry of Tourism on Canada's behalf, Roger had obtained permission for an Everest climb, even though he had no climbers. His letter to me was an invitation to join the team. "Let's keep it small," he wrote, "CLOD-style."

With only a few Everest permits issued each year by the Nepalese government, the mountain is currently booked into the late 1990s. Canada had previously received one of the coveted Everest permits for a 1975 attempt, an effort that foundered on financial and logistical rocks long before any Canadian climber ever touched Nepalese soil.

In my nine years of climbing, I had never had any Everest aspirations, but the opportunity to travel through the friendly Himalayan mountain kingdom of Nepal appealed to me. I accepted Roger's invitation with little hesitation. Living life a day at a time as I did, 1982 was four light-years away, and I couldn't stir up immediate enthusiasm for anything that far down the road, even the world's highest mountain. My interest in the climb itself would have to be kindled when (and if) we actually arrived at the foot of the mountain.

Roger favoured a small team of seven or eight climbers, which would make a lightweight foray costing less than $100,000. He proposed the same route that Sir Edmund Hillary and Sherpa Tenzing Norgay had taken through Nepal in 1953—the South Col. "It's a relatively nontechnical route," he reasoned. "It will give a small team the best chance for success. It is important that we make the summit. The ascent will give us not only some Himalayan experience but also some international credibility and will pave the way for future, maybe more ambitious climbs."

## PLANS FOR EVEREST

Roger's lightweight approach was not new. It had been attempted that same year by my Canadian adventuring partner and fellow photographer Art Twomey, with a New Zealand team of the type and size that Roger had envisaged, but with one exception: they had gone without Sherpas above Base Camp. The expedition had cost a mere $40,000 in total, and the eight team members had been able to come up with most of that out of their pockets. The team was a strong one that ferried all its own supplies, but when two climbers reached the Col at 26,000 feet (7,924 m), just 3,000 feet (914 m) from the summit, they were turned back by unusually icy conditions. Having travelled lightly and without porters, they felt the risk was too high should they have to rely on their small team for self-rescue. Their lightning-strike one-shot approach had been an exciting gamble that did not pay off, but with the national profile we hoped our expedition would assume, we could not afford this approach to climbing the mountain.

Shortly after planting the expedition seed, the thrill of sparking such a rush of excitement among the parochial climbing community of the Rockies was displaced by Roger's realization of the magnitude of the fund-raising and organizational campaign that would be necessary to mobilize the expedition. As any chance of its being CLOD-style vanished, he was quick to delegate the responsibility of leadership to George Kinnear, an instructor at the outdoor pursuits programme at the University of Calgary. His only stipulation, upon stepping down from the top post to assume a position as one of several directors of the climbers' committee, was that he be given the authorship of the "official" expedition book.

Under George's direction, the expedition quickly blossomed into a major event. "Because of the lack of experience most of the team members had had at altitude," he said, "I felt it was only natural that we would have more of a chance of success with a larger team." Applications from more than a hundred climbers were screened, and the concept of a series of training climbs was born—eight mini-expeditions, costing $160,000, designed to put every team member above 20,000 feet (6,096 m) at least once before the Everest attempt. The mountain selection depended on people's own preferences and on what their work schedule would allow. To his everlasting credit, George worked incredibly hard to provide a roster of highly motivated Canadian climbers with the unprecedented opportunity to make their mark in the international climbing arena.

Predictably, the sudden attention that was being paid to those of us lucky enough to be involved created a flurry of controversy among those in the climbing community who had been left off the team. The growing publicity also raised a few eyebrows among a suspicious public that could not see the justification for putting up so much money for a climbing expedition—even though our entire costs were hardly more than a season's salary for a single professional hockey or baseball star. For four years, we were to be reminded repeatedly of mountaineering's low-budget status.

Even our proposed route, through the treacherous Khumbu Icefall and up the South Col route, created problems. At the time of Roger's application, the much safer Tibetan side of Everest was inaccessible to climbers because of Chinese protocol. A team of our eventual size and strength would have been perfectly suited to any of several challenging routes on that side without being subjected to appreciable crevasse danger. But international politics forced us to make an attempt through the notoriously dangerous Khumbu Icefall, which, in its climbing history, had already claimed 11 lives.

While most of the team members were

Argentine *arrieros*, muleteers, from a local ranch ferried our loads the 30 miles from Punta de Vacas to Base Camp. They introduced us to a caffeine-packed tea called mate that is as powerful as it is bitter. Passed around socially, it is sipped through a stainless steel straw and is guaranteed to shatter the nerves and sleep of its initiates.

We were greeted on the arid lower slopes by a surreal world of dirty-snow stalagmites, created when snow deposited during the previous winter's avalanches decays under the direct rays of the scorching equatorial sun. Locally, they are known as *névé penitentes*, or snow supplicants.

resigned to the Khumbu's risks and to the relatively straightforward route, John Lauchlan, one of Canada's leading mountaineers, insisted on "a climber's climb": the South Spur, a new line branching off from the standard route above Camp Two that promised some technical rock-and-ice climbing above 25,000 feet (7,620 m). If we were going to do it at all, he reasoned, we might as well attempt a first ascent and make it worth our while. Unfortunately, just five months before the expedition left for Nepal, John was killed when an avalanche swept him off a solo ice climb in the Rockies.

Expedition business was reviewed at meetings in Golden, British Columbia, and in Calgary, Alberta, which accelerated from casual biannual beer bashes to a frenetic series of conferences day and night during the months prior to departure. To help offset the high overhead costs, each climber was required to put up $1,000. My own overland travels up and down the continent on self-assigned photography projects consumed all of my ready money, so I had to make my payments in installments.

As a freelance photographer, I had been successful enough by 1977 to become convinced that my career was on the right path, so I increased the scope of my wanderings and kept any Everest mania on the back burner. In November, I joined Jeremy Schmidt and Daryl Bespflug, a raft-trip operator from Edgewater, British Columbia, on an amphibious descent of the Rio Urique, a river that has carved a spectacular 5,000-foot-deep canyon through the Barranca del Cobre of Mexico's Sierra Madre mountains.

I spent the next spring exploring more canyons and rock faces in Arizona and Utah before heading north to the Yukon with Uldis Auders to work on a photography book of the territory. Uldis was busy putting off his medical internship, trying to get a good taste of life before starting his career, so on the way north, we took a 14-day 900-mile bicycle ride through British Columbia's Coast Mountains with our friend Ingrid Prouty before continuing to the Yukon.

We joined Janis Kraulis in Whitehorse and left almost immediately for the Saint Elias Mountains and Kluane National Park. Janis, who, like Uldis, was a Montrealer of Latvian descent, was working on a book about Canadian mountain ranges, and we used our projects as an excuse for a 10-day ramble.

## WIDE-EYED GRINGOS

The attrition rate of my camera gear had always been high, but one day in Kluane proved particularly costly. We had climbed 9,000-foot (2,743 m) Mount Hoge, photographing the rose-coloured dawn across the valley on the splintered surfaces of Donjek Glacier from the lazy comfort of our sleeping bags. But as we began our descent, Ingrid accidentally kicked my 20mm lens off a ledge. Assuring her that it was no great loss, I returned to our camp to find a grizzly bear demolishing Uldis's tent. Only after we had chased it away with timid shouts did we discover the remnants of my 500mm telephoto lens chewed beyond repair.

Upon the departure of Uldis and company, I joined my father on a drive through the central Yukon and then flew to Old Crow to spend two weeks photographing biologists collaring migrating members of the Porcupine caribou herd.

Sadly, that trip was my last chance to share Uldis's love of the outdoor world. Early in 1981, I was at work on another book project and had to turn down an invitation to join him and Ingrid in skiing the famous Haute Route of the Alps. A couple of weeks after his departure, I got the news that Uldis, another Montreal friend, Raymond Jotterand, and four Europeans had been killed in a major avalanche on the Grand Combin. Miraculously, Ingrid had been ill that day and had decided to stay behind while the rest of the group went off to attempt a ski ascent of the mountain.

It was a tremendous loss, for while I had been exposed to mountain fatalities in the past and had known several victims of mountaineering accidents, Uldis was the first close friend I had lost to the sport. Fortunately, 1981 was a busy year for me, and I had little time to brood. Choosing to remember the joys of our recent adventures rather than to mourn, I turned my mind to preparing for Everest.

To build up the team's profile and experience, we had chosen training climbs on such notable mountains as Nuptse,

Gangapurna and Dhaulagiri in the Himalayas; Logan in Canada; Peru's Huascaran; and Argentina's Aconcagua. In late January 1981, Gordon "Speedy" Smith, Roger Marshall, Dave Read and I set off for the latter, an Andean giant that we thought would best simulate the harsh conditions expected on Everest. At 22,831 feet (6,959 m), Aconcagua is the highest mountain in the western hemisphere and is relatively accessible. But rumours of its unforgiving and spiteful nature put us on guard. Within sight of its enticing snow-covered summit lay a well-stocked cemetery of 100 unmarked graves, testament to the fate of unprepared or unfortunate climbers. Aconcagua is climbed as often as is any mountain in South America; it has also killed as many climbers as has any mountain in the world. The trail to the summit and several *refugios* along the way encourage unacclimatized climbers to move too quickly.

We flew into Mendoza, a provincial capital that is 80 miles from the Chilean border, and relaxed for a couple of days. Thousands of miles from our Canadian winter, we basked in the warm sun, sipping ice-cold *cervezas* and soaking up the Latin American ambience. It was the height of the southern hemisphere's summer, and we were four wide-eyed gringos. Speedy, like Roger, was from Golden and, having once been to a Russian-hosted camp in the Soviet Pamirs, was the only one to have been on a major expedition abroad before.

The combination of the numbing effect of the beer that afternoon and our preoccupation with the prospect of meeting our destinies on the hostile slopes of the Americas' highest peak somewhat clouded our perception of the political realities of Argentina. The brilliant day soothed our jet-lagged souls, distracting us from the nuances of life under President Jorge Videla, but we soon found ourselves caught up in the ironies and contradictions of a South American police state. (My appreciation for the country has since risen with the election in 1983 of Raoul Alfonsin, whose civilian government has taken a courageous stand in the protection of previously violated human rights.)

There was a curious protocol forced upon those wanting to climb Aconca-

gua, one of the few peaks in South America for which permission to climb is needed. It was a screening process developed out of a practical need to limit the number of inexperienced climbers venturing onto the mountain's slopes, but to free spirits like us, it seemed a bit ludicrous in its application. In addition to supplying all manner of information in quadruplicate, we were obliged to bring from Canada a full medical report replete with an electrocardiogram (EKG) printout to be scrutinized by no fewer than two levels of the Mendoza police, as well as the fire department. Fortunately, the officials did not compare Roger's and my reports, for I had also done an EKG to help Roger, who had missed the appointment. As for Dave, he had been lucky to survive the examination: after several days of partying, he had nearly succumbed to the EKG bicycle machine on the day of the test when the attendant took his coffee break and left Dave pedalling for 10 minutes.

We had the good fortune of being taken under the wing of two Aconcagua-bound American guides leading a group for Mountain Travel (MT), an American wilderness-adventure company that has ranked Aconcagua in its most difficult category. MT founder and president Leo LeBon had magnanimously instructed his globe-trotting guide Bruce Klepinger, a Latin American specialist, and his assistant, Dr. Peter Cummings, to help us with our transportation and accommodation logistics at no cost to the Canadian Mount Everest Society, the official nonprofit administrative core of both the training climbs and the Everest climb. MT is one of many companies that have transformed mountaineering from a sport practised only by gentlemanly explorers into a viable middle-class option. The adventure-travel industry caters to those who don't have the time or the political connections to organize their own trekking, climbing or river-running expeditions but who do have the ready cash, the physical ability and the desire. By some estimates, more than 100,000 North Americans each year see the more remote regions of the world under the guidance of outfitters.

Bruce was more than just a guide in my eyes. I admired the courage it had taken for him to abandon a highly suc-

**U**nbearable heat turned to freezing cold by the time we reached Camp Two. Dave Read, Speedy Smith and Roger Marshall (left to right) share a joke during a morning snow shower that hit as we broke camp.

Clouds moving in from across the Andes marked the start of our summit day. This upper section of the Polish Glacier provided the only challenging climb on the route and had spelled disaster for several other teams. Just days prior to our ascent, two members of an Argentine party slid 1,200 feet down the glacier. One survived, and we came across the body of the second on our way past.

cessful career as a professor with a doctorate and qualifications in physiology, pharmacology and human development. "One day, I just woke up and realized that I was 30 years old and hadn't seen the world yet," he explained. He reversed the direction of his life and made the world his laboratory when he assumed a job as a guide that kept him out in the field for 350 days of the year.

## BAD MOVES

We left Mendoza on January 27 after consuming a delicate continental breakfast more befitting an artist in Buenos Aires' Boca Quarter than a mountaineer on his way to a rigorous climb. To get to the trailhead at Punta de Vacas, we fidgeted our way through several uptight military checkpoints. Since the mountain is strategically located near the Chilean border, we had to leave our passports at a military post until our return.

The round-trip 120-mile drive to Punta de Vacas cost a whopping $1,200, more than both the battered pickup trucks would have been worth on a used car lot in Canada. By the time we had arranged to pay for the three mules, two horses and drivers we needed in order to transport our gear 30 miles to the base of the mountain, Roger was seething. Among other things, he blamed our MT hosts for not finding us the best deals. Trying hard not to become angry with Roger's affected arrogance, Bruce was quick to point out that we were all at the mercy of the rate of inflation, that this was his sixth trip to Aconcagua and that MT was actually losing money on this one. Despite Roger's blatant ridicule of the guides, which often took place in front of their clients, our odd symbiotic relationship with the MT group miraculously survived the duration of the trip.

This high-handed attitude would later catch up with Roger on Everest. An impulsive man capable of enchanting charm one moment and derogatory vindictiveness the next, Roger liked to dominate his peers, with mixed results. I stayed quietly on the sidelines, biting my tongue, uncomfortable and somewhat angry. In an act that further eroded my respect, Roger and Speedy, thinking themselves clever or not thinking at all, had left our pressure cooker behind at

the hotel in the interest of travelling light and had substituted for it two bottles of our favourite wine, one of which promptly broke on the way to the mountain. Most of the high-fibre food, such as the long-grained rice and the spinach noodles that I had assembled for the team, required the pressure cooker to speed up the cooking time in the attenuated air of the higher altitudes. Consequently, by the time we got to Camp One, Dave's body began violently rejecting the partially cooked, partially ingested "health food," forcing us to break into our upper-mountain rations of less savoury but more easily prepared freeze-dried fare.

Aconcagua was first climbed in 1897. An Englishman by the name of Edward A. Fitzgerald took the partially built trans-Andean railroad to Punta del Inca, near our jumping-off point, in 1896. He had brought with him, in the best style of the times, three scientists, a cook, five porters and Mattias Zurbriggen, a renowned Swiss guide. There are two valleys by which the mountain can be approached, and Fitzgerald had selected the del Inca route, a frequent choice by present-day standards. Both it and the Punta de Vacas route are equidistant but take climbers to the base of the west or east side of the mountain, respectively. On January 14, 1897, Zurbriggen soloed to the summit via the now common West Ridge route to become the first person to stand atop Aconcagua. Fitzgerald never did make it, but a month later, two other team members did.

Millennia ago, forces within the Earth's crust pushed Aconcagua up through layers of volcanic silica-rich detritus, giving it a crumbly slag-heap appearance that has consistently failed to win the aspiring hearts of those attempting to find solid purchase on its flanks. Our sentiments were no different as we entered the dry and austere valley sizzling below it in the 100-degree-F (38°C) heat. "Oh well, at least we won't have a problem with bushwhacking on the approach," was Dave's observation. While I was upset about some of my teammates' behaviour, their senses of humour went a long way toward achieving their redemption in my eyes. When I wasn't scowling at their impertinence, I was chuckling uncontrollably at their antics.

**H**igh-altitude cerebral edema impairs the mind, with often fatal results. This Mountain Travel client, *above*, neglected to put protective cream on his face to shield it from the sun's strong ultraviolet rays and thereby added to his discomfort with a severe burn. Fortunately, we were able to get him off the mountain without his suffering a more serious injury. Dwarfed by the spectacular south face to their left, *facing page*, members of our party make their way along the edge of the Polish Glacier route. Only a few climbers, including Canadian Sharon Wood, a 1986 Everest summiteer, have scaled the difficult 10,000-foot south face—an impressive feat in light of Aconcagua's unforgiving nature.

**Aconcagua**

1. To Punta de Vacas Valley
2. Base Camp (13,500 feet)
3. Camp One (16,500 feet)
4. Camp Two (19,000 feet)
5. Camp Three (20,400 feet)
6. Polish Glacier
7. Scene of Argentine Accident
8. Helicopter Crash
9. False Summit (route continues behind ridge)
10. Main Summit (22,831 feet)
11. South Face
12. Argentine Wall

Route Hidden From View — — —

The boredom of the 30-mile three-day walk up the de Vacas Valley was frequently broken by our team comic's inspired travelling road show. At our first campsite, which we shared with half a dozen reluctant members of an Argentine cavalry border patrol, Dave wrestled a bone away from their German shepherd, then dropped to his knees with a crust of bread in his teeth. Smiles quickly replaced the worried looks on the soldiers' faces as the dog gently plucked the bread from his mouth, and Dave stood up to take a bow.

## ADOPTING A SLOW PACE

By the second dusty day, we were starting to sort out the various personalities of our teammates from MT. Easily the most garrulous, Norman Croucher from London, England, won our attention early. As a teenager, he had lost both legs below the knees in a tragic encounter with a train. But rather than admit defeat, he had taken up distance hiking and mountaineering to prove that life doesn't have to end with a handicap. He had had ice-axe pick attachments fabricated for his crutches but had lost one on a technical climb in the Alps. ''Imagine the surprise when other climbers discovered that crutch in the middle of the alpine face!'' he chuckled. His easy-going nature, which camouflaged an iron will, allowed him to be the butt of even his own jokes. ''Yeah, I've got it easy now. I don't have to worry about getting cold feet anymore.'' But his real claim to fame was and is his near-legendary capacity for ale, a fact to which I can heartily attest, having visited him at his neighbourhood pub in 1983. Still a climber, he is now the author of three books and makes his living by giving motivational lectures while travelling the world.

Our third day on the trail led us through a precipitous canyon with walls thrust upward for 1,000 feet (304 m) into the Andean sky. The Andes are the world's longest mountain system, extending 5,000 miles from Venezuela to Cape Horn, while their midsection (Peru) harbours the world's largest concentration of equatorial ice. As the trail steepened the last couple of thousand feet to Base Camp, at 13,500 feet (4,114 m), the effects of altitude began to manifest themselves, forcing us to shift into low gear. One of the MT clients who had been pushing himself hard all day in the hot sun collapsed soon after arrival. Bruce quickly fed him oxygen from the bottle in his immense pack, which helped bring some natural colour back into the pulmonary-edema victim's blue face. Peter then set up camp for him at a lower elevation and left him with explicit instructions not to attempt to go to altitude again. (Nevertheless, the client defiantly appeared at our Camp Three 10 days later, feeling better and harbouring summit aspirations, just as everyone was preparing to descend. His reception was anything but warm.)

As we had done on McKinley, we considered the options for ascending the mountain. There were three routes with a number of variations. We had ruled out the West Ridge because of the prospect of its being crowded, while the south face, with its incredible 10,000-foot (3,048 m) wall of steep mobile rock and ice, was more than we were prepared for at the time. (In December 1985, Canadian Sharon Wood, with partner Carlos Buhler, became the second woman to climb this formidable face. Sharon had embarked on her first altitude climb with the Calgary Mountain Club Women's expedition to Mount Logan in the late 1970s, a milestone for women's climbing in Canada. In May 1986, she won the hard-fought distinction of becoming the first North American woman to reach the summit of Mount Everest.) We looked, instead, at the Polish Glacier route on the east face, which offers some fine snow climbing on its upper slopes, providing a greater challenge than does the standard route. It had been pioneered by the Poles in 1934.

We allowed ourselves one day to rest in Base Camp among the rubble of the glacier moraine, 7,000 feet (2,134 m) below the Polish Glacier. For the next nine days, we would do multiple-load carries to Camp One, at 16,500 feet (5,029 m), moving on to Camp Two at 19,000 feet (5,791 m) and Camp Three at 20,400 feet (6,218 m).

The old rule of thumb—climb high, sleep low—seemed to be our most significant lesson. Our carries of 3,000 vertical feet (914 m) to stock an upper

Carefully making our way through sporadic whiteout conditions, with a 10,000-foot gaping chasm to one side, we make the final approach to the summit of Aconcagua.

camp, done twice in a three-day period (the third being a rest day), gave us a controlled height gain of 1,000 feet (304 m) a day. Any faster, and the body's capacity for producing oxygen-transporting red blood cells at the proper rate is jeopardized. The curse of improper acclimatization is a wringing headache, nausea and a fragile sense of reality, not unlike the effects of a hangover following a long night of drinking cheap wine.

The alternative to this "siege" style is to relay enough supplies to be able to sit at a camp above 14,000 feet (4,267 m) for about two weeks, exercising mildly every day. Then, with the body approaching optimum acclimatization, an "alpine" style ascent is begun, with just enough gear to climb continuously without having to relay loads from camp to camp. This is the method Reinhold Messner uses on his bold solo climbs on much higher mountains in the Himalayas.

Perhaps my most significant personal realization during the climb occurred when Bruce demonstrated the efficacy of adopting an exaggeratedly slow pace. I found that if I forced my body to slow down, rather than to plough ahead at the speed of which it seemed capable, I could maintain the pace, essentially without pain, for the entire day and arrive almost refreshed.

I had trained hard for this climb, skiing every day on the cross-country trails at Kimberley and carrying a heavy pack on Nordic ski ascents of the local mountains. I knew that on a mountain of this scale, it was important to make yourself more than strong enough for the task, in case you had to pull yourself out of an unexpectedly sticky situation. Once on the mountain, the game of self-preservation must be well balanced with your contribution to the team's goal, an incredibly delicate operation. How far *must* you push yourself and how far *can* you push yourself in a normal work day? How much energy will you have left after a week, two weeks, three weeks, in an atmosphere where nothing else lives? Saving your energy for summit day is not enough. Often, it is a couple of days or more before you can get back to the foot of the mountain, so your reserves must be bottomless. Every action must be deliberate with this end result in mind.

Six months after tackling Aconcagua, I headed to the Chinese Pamirs for another Everest training climb. After reaching the summit of Muztagh Ata (in distant background), we spent several weeks exploring the surrounding countryside. To celebrate our success, these Kirghiz villagers put on a rough-and-tumble game of *olagh tartish*, a sort of rugby on horseback. A freewheeling sport, the game occasionally got too close for comfort, and spectators had to flee to safety.

The dreariness of the route just above Base Camp was alleviated when we wandered into a fantasy world peopled by frozen spires that resembled kneeling supplicants. The direct overhead rays of the sun had carved down through the five-foot-deep debris of the past winter's avalanches, creating hundreds of free-standing pieces of a natural chess set, some of which we accidentally knocked over with our elbows as we walked past.

## DEATH ON THE GLACIER

A couple of hours after this bit of reverie, we came face-to-face with Aconcagua's unforgiving nature. Just as we were about to settle into our tents at Camp One, we were startled by three figures staggering down the scree slope toward us. They were the survivors of a three-day drama that had unfolded as we were slogging unwittingly on the lower mountain. Four days before, five Argentine climbers had left for the summit push, and as a result of circumstances unknown to us, one climber had slipped and pulled his partner, attached to him on the rope, 1,200 feet (365 m) down the abrasive, rock-studded glacier. A rock tore a gaping hole in his chest, while his 16-year-old partner was lucky enough to escape with only a smashed face and body and a deeply bruised psyche.

The four had huddled on a ledge hacked out of the ice at 21,000 feet (6,400 m), while a fifth raced for help. Three days later, a big military helicopter finally arrived. But their relief at seeing an end to their ordeal was short-lived. As it struggled up through the thin air, just beyond their reach, the chopper got caught in an upward blast of air and crashed into the mountain face. It exploded right in front of the incredulous climbers. The next day, a second machine arrived to remove the pilot's remains, delicately suspending itself over the wreckage until a cable hoisted free the charred body. Then the hapless Argentines understood what was happening. They would be left with their mortally wounded comrade. With their remaining strength, they wrapped him in warm clothing and left him tied to the slope in a delirious, semiconscious state. Dangerously weakened by their death vigil,

the three descended to Base Camp.

Four days after hearing their story, Roger and Speedy spotted the now lifeless body of the Argentine and dragged it down another 1,000 feet (304 m) in case the Argentines were planning a retrieval. When Norman Croucher returned to Aconcagua in 1982, he found two more bodies at the same site, sobering evidence of the ugly hand of fate.

My own routine on the mountain had developed a somewhat schizophrenic pattern: I would sleep with my teammates at night but spend the day load-carrying with the MT group. I preferred the company of the other team and managed to avert any blowups with my own companions by remaining aloof from them in this way. Their self-righteous, obnoxious behaviour had no place on a mountainside.

The next day, a frisky wind brought with it a flurry of snow and a rest day. Secure in our sleeping bags in a two-person tent, Speedy and I ignored our differences and allowed our minds to wander. Moved by the fact that we were on the highest peak in the Americas, we fantasized about the other continental high points. I was surprised by Speedy's claim that the highest mountain in Europe was Mount Elbrus; in the Soviet Caucasus, 2,710 feet (825 m) higher than Mont Blanc in the French Alps. Neither of us knew Antarctica's highest summit, but we had both read Austrian Heinrich Harrer's *I Come From the Stone Age*, chronicling his first ascent, with New Zealander Philip Temple, of Australasia's tallest peak, Carstensz Pyramid, in the remote Indonesian province of Irian Jaya. But for the time being, we had a big mountain towering over us, and any thoughts of expeditions to these other giants had to be stored in our imaginations. Such is the nature of the dreams that keep a mountaineer busy for the rest of his life.

On February 9, we forced ourselves out of our warm down-filled chrysalides at 2 a.m., prepared to make the summit bid. The clear star-speckled sky enveloped us with a numbing cold as Speedy and I stamped our chilled feet impatiently outside Roger and Dave's tent. They groggily pulled on their boots and crampons, as our twinkling headlamps helped cut the predawn blues. When we

were finally on our way, the sun began to cast its weak light on the granular snow of the glacier, a subtle but welcome warmth. By the time we reached the MT campsite 500 feet (150 m) higher, Peter Cummings stepped out to follow us with his two strongest clients roped to him. Speedy's eyes were already glazed over. Since he was feeling the drag of inertia, he swallowed humble pie and joined the slower-paced MT string led by Bruce.

Running at a consistent 35-to-45-degree angle, the slope finally offered some of the thrills of climbing that had been sorely lacking on the scree sections below. The unrelenting angle required continuous attention; the spectre of the Argentine's fatal fall the previous week was still fresh in our minds. For me, this was the most rewarding part of the climb. Rock-hard ice provided a bed just below a dusting of snow while crampons scratched for a hold on the iron belly of the sleeping monolith, and ankle strain made the breath come in gasps. The lessons gleaned from this particular expedition would come from within: learning how to endure long bouts of boredom while load-carrying, going through the motions of camp life and keeping the body going through storm and sun. The techniques of climbing had been stamped into my subconscious over the years. Now was the time to learn from high-altitude guru Bruce Klepinger how to adapt to the demanding rigours of life on a mountain. All I had learned on Mount McKinley was how to subdue pain. On Everest, I would be faced with the ultimate test.

## ONE STEP AT A TIME

Exhilaration swept over me as we pulled onto the knife-edged rib leading up to the summit ridge. The south side of the mountain was creating its own weather, puffing up globs of cumulus clouds thousands of feet thick and lobbing them our way. As quickly as we were engulfed in sporadic whiteout conditions, it was all vacuumed away to reveal the terminal plunge down the face.

At that point, Roger and Dave hit the "marathoner's wall," which, as in a Ralph Steadman illustration, resembles a human psyche being extruded through a vegetable shredder. In true British hard-man tradition, neither had bothered to train for this climb, and both appeared to be hurting a lot. Propped up against each other in the snow, they were ready for a break. When Peter and his rope of clients caught up with us, I joined them on the final two hours to the top. All four of us hit the wall soon after that, but rather than come to a complete stop, we turned our internal metronomes down to a slower rhythm . . . one step forward, two deep breaths . . . one step, two breaths . . . onward and upward, as though we were repeating a Buddhist mantra. The fog moved in and out. Our nearly stationary figures reminded me of sentries guarding one of the wilder frontiers of the world.

The sun gained in strength again, forcing the clouds to retreat. Our hunched human forms took on the shape of the aluminum crucifixes, bent over like wilted flowers by the jet stream, that marked the summit landscape. With his final few steps, the strongest client suddenly faltered. We attributed it to fatigue, but shortly thereafter, he began to stagger and slur his words. Cerebral edema. Wordlessly acknowledging the seriousness of the situation, Peter and I fixed 10-foot tethers on him and left the summit for the others to exalt in.

If he hadn't been so strong, descent along the glacial tightrope, with its fatal drops on either side, would have been impossible. As it was, Peter caught him twice from above as I helped steady him from below, constantly coaxing him to pay special attention to his feet. A couple of times, he pirouetted dramatically and then made brilliant recoveries, until at long last, we were on the broad lower slopes of the glacier. Dusk was close on our heels. By this time, both teams had made it back, with all but two people reaching the top. We collapsed into our goose-down bags and a dreamless sleep.

The next day, in the face of oncoming clouds, our team headed for Camp One. The MT group split into two, with Peter and two clients staying at Camp Three to make another summit attempt the following day. That night, it snowed. Within hours, the dry slopes above their camp had collected a layer of fresh snow, which released two consecutive ava-

Victims of border politics, the once nomadic Kirghiz have been restricted in their movements since China's borders with Russia and Afghanistan have been closed. Forced to live year-round in their 13,000-foot-high valley, they must store hay against the severe winters, when temperatures often plunge to minus 50 degrees F.

lanches, burying their tent with them inside. They blindly dug their way out and tried to escape downslope. After triggering a slab avalanche of compacted snow, they miraculously found a sheltered spot, repitched the tent and made it through until morning. We later found out that this same storm took the lives of three Koreans who had been caught unprepared on the normal route on the other side of the mountain.

## GOBBLING GUANACOS

On our final day of the climb, we dismantled Camp One and glanced up at the howling winds coming off the summit slopes. We realized how close we had actually come to being turned back or, worse, being launched into space by the weather. The blizzards that tear at the mountain are of legendary magnitude. The "white winds" can reach velocities of 160 miles per hour (257 kph), with temperatures plummeting to minus 45 degrees F (-42°C) in midsummer.

As we threaded our way through the treacherous, snow-covered talus boulders in whiteout conditions, Dave kept removing his dark glasses to watch for hidden holes. The intense ultraviolet rays penetrating the cloud layer consequently fried his corneas so that he spent a painfully sleepless night at Base Camp. He did not recover fully from his snow blindness for several days.

I stayed behind an extra day to watch out for the MT group, while my teammates headed back to the road in search of the soothing effects of multiple *cervezas*. I took this opportunity to clean my cameras after their rugged trip to the top. The year before leaving for Aconcagua, I had approached Pentax of Canada about using their MX single-lens reflex manual model on this series of climbs. Prior to this, I had used a miniature fixed-focal-length camera that lacked the capability of switching lenses. With its robust, lightweight features, the MX was perfect for the job and would withstand the abuse to which my cameras are usually subjected. Pentax's response was more generous than I had hoped—we worked out an arrangement whereby, in exchange for the use of my photographs in their advertising, I am supplied with camera equipment.

Early the next day, I left with the knowledge that everyone from the MT group was accounted for. My complacent walk down the brown and dusty valley was interrupted by the startling sound of what seemed, strangely enough, to be a turkey gobbling hysterically. Silence, then more gobbling. I was totally perplexed and waited for further signs of what form the noise would take. Suddenly, a graceful, sanguine guanaco appeared on the near horizon. There was no connection between the comic, guttural voice coming from its deftly curled lips and its dignified appearance.

Shortly after this, the trail dropped into a gorge on its steep descent back to the de Vacas Valley. It was at this very point, 10 days earlier, that Norman Croucher had nearly suffered his first major mountaineering accident. On his initial carry to Camp One, one of his prostheses had broken. Undaunted, he soloed a nearby 16,000-foot (4,876 m) peak on hands and knees in four days and descended on his backside in one. "First knee ascent," he later boasted. Hearing of Norman's predicament with the broken prosthesis, the sympathetic commandant of the army camp had brought mules up to our Base Camp and collected Norman to take back to their camp where they could keep him company. To secure his place in the universe, the good soldier had tied Norman to the saddle. At the most exposed spot on the trail, with the roar of the creek far below, the saddle slipped upside down under the mule's belly, leaving Norman hanging like a bat—a frightened bat. The soldiers, luckily, were quick to react and calmed the equally terrified animal as they spun Norman right side up. "Let me tell you," Norman recalled, "I've never been so scared in the mountains as at that very moment."

Back in Mendoza, both groups stretched out on the smooth, clean tiles by the hotel swimming pool, satiated in every way. Well, almost. Roger, Speedy, Dave and I had some time and money left, but they ached for a short vacation in the Caribbean and were anxious to leave Latin America. Bidding them farewell, I took a bus to Santiago and spent several days exploring the galleries and museums of the Chilean captial. After side trips to Patagonia and Rio de

The face of this teenage Kirghiz girl reflects her people's Indo-European ties. Her red scarf signifies her unmarried status.

Janeiro, Brazil, I headed back to Calgary in order to prepare for another pre-Everest training climb.

## DREAM SKI

Andrzej Zawada, the visionary leader of the 1979-80 Polish Everest winter and pre-monsoon expeditions, had given a lecture in Calgary in the autumn of 1980. At a party afterward, he convinced John Amatt, the expedition's business manager, that the gentle slopes of the Soviet Pamirs provided an ideal training ground for those wishing to chalk up altitude experience for Everest.

Acting on his advice, John led the first Canadian climbing expedition into China, just across the border from the Soviet Pamirs, in September 1981, with teammates Stephen Bezruchka, Lloyd Gallagher and me. We topped the Everest team's altitude record when we made a breathless ski descent from the summit of 24,757-foot (7,545 m) Muztagh Ata in the Chinese Pamirs. To add challenge and enjoyment to this big cream puff of a mountain, I had used lightweight Nordic ski equipment, cranking the world's highest telemark turn on the descent. I had felt great on the summit and knew that I could do well on Everest. Several days later, I joined Lloyd on a dream ski of 1,000-foot-high (304 m) sand dunes near our Base Camp in the Sarikol Valley. The fine sand particles had magically responded to the carving edges of our skis like spring corn snow; the difference was that, unlike snow, once lodged in your ears after a fall, the sand would not melt out.

Of our six weeks in the country, less than two were taken up with the climb. This reinforced the travel/self-discovery theme that had been started with my recent South American foray. On this expedition, however, I had felt a close bond with my teammates, unlike on Aconcagua. The rewards of a strong team spirit on the mountain spilled over to the rest of our trip. We all shared a childlike fascination with our surroundings and because of this, had a warm reception from our Chinese hosts. Our group was only the third party of Westerners to visit the remote Xinjiang Autonomous Region along the old Silk Caravan Route since Eric Shipton had been

a British consul in Kashgar 33 years before. This truly gave us one of the finest cultural immersions any of us had experienced.

Our sympathetic liaison officer, Song Zhi-yi—himself a climber and a representative of the Chinese Mountaineering Association (CMA)—allowed us to roam freely in the valley that borders on Pakistan, Afghanistan and Russia. The once nomadic Kirghiz welcomed us into their felt yurts and fed us yogurtlike dairy treats produced from their large herds of goats and yaks. Prior to the closing of the borders, the Kirghiz could escape the icy grip of winter (where temperatures in this 13,000-foot [3,962 m] valley drop as low as minus 58 degrees F [-50° C]) by travelling to the warmer climes of Afghanistan. The year after our visit, the Soviet invasion of Afghanistan displaced those Kirghiz who were living just across the border from here into refugee camps in Pakistan. Sadly, we know that the Kirghiz and the rest of the minority groups in this frontier region are subject to an assimilation programme which is not as blatant as the Soviet aggression but is just as effective. Hans from the heavily populated eastern part of the country are being systematically transplanted to the area and will eventually outnumber the native population.

These training climbs proved quite useful, both for giving us high-altitude experience and for publicity purposes, and the credit for their success goes to Everest expedition leader George Kinnear and to John Amatt.

John was a business-management course coordinator for the Banff Centre, and the team hired him in the fall of 1979 to deal with financial and promotional matters. His central objective was to obtain a major corporate sponsor who would assume 30 to 50 percent of the expenses while giving the expedition the credibility it needed to attract additional support. After a two-year search, John finally found a sponsor in Air Canada through advertising director Mike Breckon. Using 1 percent of its annual advertising budget, the national airline donated $280,000 and volunteered free air service for climbers and cargo on both the training climbs and the main event. It was the financial boost the expedition needed, and for the first time, I became

convinced we were really going to Nepal. Predictably, some critics complained of the expense, but in retrospect, our team's spending was surprisingly modest. At $26,464 (U.S.) per climber, it was quite conservative when compared with some others: $48,066 (in 1986 dollars) for each climber on the 1922 British team to the north ridge; $45,833 for each Spanish climber on the same route in 1985; and $87,463 for each member of the 1980 Japanese north face/north ridge attempt.

## NATIONAL EFFORT

Air Canada's gesture, however, had some strings attached. Any chance of this expedition's turning into a rambunctious Calgary Mountain Club outing disappeared, for the airline was promoting an image of "professionalism, integrity, candour, equality, adaptability and teamwork," and it demanded that the climb be given as high a profile as possible.

Accordingly, John set to work creating a communications and public relations network that would help make the Canadian climb one of the most publicized in the history of Everest mountaineering. With Air Canada's involvement, the whole thing snowballed, and the expedition soon took the shape of an organizational octopus that would do bureaucratic Ottawa proud. In addition to the Canadian Mount Everest Society, which was complete with a board of directors and tax-exempt status, there was CanEverEx, the promotional arm, responsible for all publicity, broadcast production, public appearances, advertising, licensing and funding; more than 100 cosponsors; and several dozen individual volunteers, each organizing, fund-raising and planning. When Teleglobe Canada agreed to provide a million-dollar satellite communications link to allow the first-ever live radio and television coverage of a Mount Everest climb, Air Canada and the sponsors were assured of national publicity, and we were committed to media coverage that would not go away, no matter what happened.

In the months preceding our departure, I was assigned my duties as expedition photographer. In addition to pho-

Thousand-foot-high sand dunes in the heart of the Pamirs inspired some memorable "dream skiing." The fine silica flecks were similar to the corn snow of late winter and gave us continuous slow-motion runs.

tographing our sponsors' products and documenting the team's progress, I was supposed to coordinate and encourage the other climbers to shoot their own material as much as possible. There was no compensation, but after the society and sponsors had used my photographs for one year, I would regain all rights. After years of having to pay my own film and travel expenses, it seemed a fair deal to me.

We devised a system of getting the exposed 35mm and video film back to Canada for distribution to the media while we were still on the mountain: after delivering it to Kathmandu with a Sherpa runner, it was to be sent by diplomatic pouch to Paris and then on to Toronto, where it would be processed and forwarded to Programmed Communications in Montreal. There, it would be stamped, identified and logged, photograph by photograph, into a computer, which would provide us with telexed printouts that would tell us how our cameras were working and how the photographs looked in general. All told, we would ship 18,000 expedition slides.

While I sat in on these organizational meetings, held at the University of Calgary, I realized just how difficult decision making had become in the Society's group structure. If it was tedious in this controlled environment, what would it be like on the mountain? Even though most of us by nature would have preferred a smaller, less cumbersome team, leader George Kinnear impressed me with his ability to meld the politics of the organization with the realities of the climb. With the right people in control, our strength could only multiply, and our corporate image, for all its complications, was going to ensure that we were provided with all the resources we would need to climb Everest. Our expedition had become a national effort, whether we liked it or not. We were representing Canada in the international climbing arena and therefore had a responsibility to put our best boot forward.

A scant five months before departure time, George Kinnear developed a retinal haemorrhage as a result of a training climb in Ecuador, and Bill March, an instructor at the University of Calgary, inherited what was soon to become a most unenviable position.

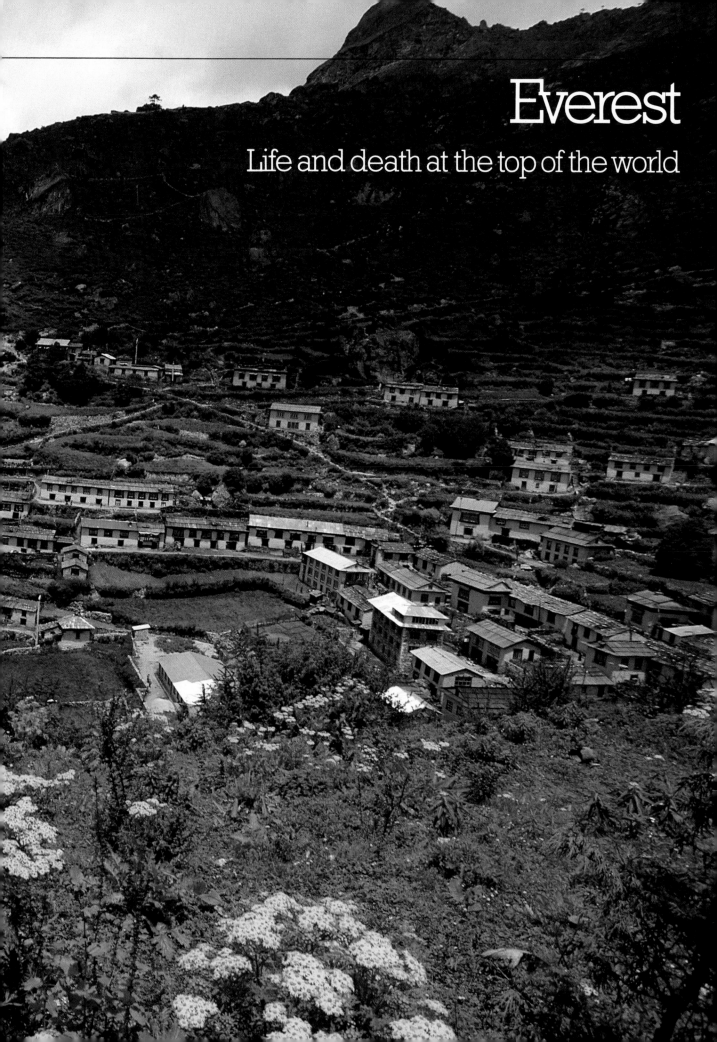

# Everest

## Life and death at the top of the world

I spent the spring of 1982 on a climbing spree that took me from the swirling sandstone slot canyons of Arizona through California and points north. Everest's jagged silhouette loomed ahead of me, and I needed to prepare myself for the mental and physical rigours of a high-altitude large-scale expedition. Three months of scrambling up rock faces with old friends proved to be the perfect solution.

While Everest and other high-altitude peaks require incredible endurance and survival instincts keen enough to cope with an array of dangers—cold, oxygen starvation, avalanches, anxiety—crag climbing is a pure and enjoyable form of mountaineering that demands speed and gymnastic agility. In many ways, it is a simpler, more individualistic pursuit, for the danger—gravity—is more immediately apparent; one relies upon finger holds and toe grips to survive rather than upon careful logistical planning. Rambling around in my dilapidated van, I could choose a rock face one morning and have it climbed by nightfall, while by contrast, the Everest expedition had taken five years to plan, and I had not yet seen the mountain.

As a final test before setting off for Nepal, I joined Vancouver friend Brian Finnie for a romp on South Howser Tower in the Bugaboos. Brian and I had made a 14-day ski tour the previous spring on the St. Elias Icecap around the 140-mile circumference of Canada's highest peak, Mount Logan. I knew I could count on his good nature to take the seriousness out of this climb. We were intent on the Beckey-Chouinard route, one of the all-time alpine classics in North America, with its 23 roped pitches of rock climbing up the continuously challenging crack system that splits the upper third of the pristine 11,000-foot (3,352 m) granite spire.

When we arrived in mid-June, our spirits were dampened by two weeks' rain before we could get onto the mountain. After leapfrogging with two other groups of climbers who had also been waiting for good weather, we politely slowed our pace to let them get ahead and out of our way. We were rewarded for our display of good manners when we ran out of daylight just two pitches short of the summit. Lashing ourselves

The bustling cobblestone streets of Kathmandu, *above*, provided a sharp contrast to the more serene pace of Namche Bazaar, the mountainside capital of the Sherpa district of Solu-Khumbu, *previous page*. Kathmandu clearly shows the influence of centuries of Hindu and Buddhist tradition, with a few concessions to the modern West, while Namche reflects the quiet spirit of the Sherpas who settled the area 400 years ago—migrating through Tibet from the Chinese province of Szechuan.

with nylon webbing onto a small ledge, we spent the cold, dark night pining for the warmth of the commercial hot springs in nearby Radium.

By morning, it had begun to rain. When the rain became snow, the high-friction granite face turned to slime. The mountaintop was lost in fog when we finally reached it, and we wandered through snow for some time looking for the start of a rappel series that would allow a straightforward descent. By the time we had waded through knee-deep snow in our thin rock boots on our way back to camp on Pigeon Col, our legs were just as numb as our brains. Yet oddly, I left the mountain almost satiated—convinced that it would not matter too much if I ever climbed another mountain.

## THE EVEREST SHERATON

Two weeks later, I was in Nepal, wandering through the monsoon-wet alleyways of Kathmandu, as fit as I'd ever been in my life, feet still numb and still not caring whether I ever climbed another mountain.

Kathmandu, the capital of the world's only Hindu monarchy, is a fascinating mediaeval city, a maze of narrow, cobblestone streets, any of which can lead to a colourful bazaar. Although our initial impressions were slightly distorted by the fact that our team was being hosted by the sumptuous Everest Sheraton Hotel, just on the outskirts of town, we were only a 20-minute bike ride from the central Thamel shop district.

We had studied the official Nepali tongue through voice tapes that team doctor Stephen Bezruchka had produced as a companion to his excellent A Guide to Trekking in Nepal, and as we wandered from shop to shop, we were able to interject a few words of Nepali into the requests we made in broken English, loudly and with an innate body language that is readily understood by merchants in all lands. The air was alive with the sweet scent of flowers left by early-morning worshippers at the numerous small Hindu and Buddhist shrines, while off in the distance, 50 miles to the north, the snowcapped Himalayas rose majestically. Kathmandu is a romantic, magical city with a mood befit-

ting the capital of an ancient mountain kingdom, and it is little wonder that 130,000 tourists visit each year.

Despite the onslaught of outsiders, Kathmandu, with its flexible, congenial Nepalese citizenry, has managed to retain a charm that would quickly have become poisoned in most other cultures. The broad-ranging tolerance made necessary by the mixture of religions and languages, and perhaps by the proximity of the mountains, seems to have allowed the people to transcend, if not ignore, the foreign influx. The city still rolls up its doormats at dusk, around 7 p.m. in summer, and life resumes at dawn. Aside from the presence of Western hotels on its outskirts, Kathmandu shows few signs of changing, although in 1982 there was one charming crack in its ancient facade, a tiny late-night disco called "The Up 'n' Down Bar," unpretentiously dedicated to unadulterated rock music.

Back at the Everest Sheraton, the Canadian press corps' Base Camp, the politics of our expedition were about to override the ambience of Nepal. Expedition founder and onetime leader Roger Marshall was on the verge of being dismissed. His position on the team had seemed in jeopardy from the start, as he partied his way from training climb to training climb, leaving a legacy of antipathy. Following our return from Aconcagua, then leader George Kinnear had received no fewer than three letters, one from Leo LeBon, the president of Mountain Travel, the others from his guides, complaining strongly about Roger. Worried about the possibility that Roger's behaviour might reflect negatively on our team and on the corporate sponsors upon whom we depended, George had consulted the team members to see how we felt about it. Admittedly, Roger had provided a minor embarrassment for our team's image, but he had, after all, obtained the permission we needed to climb Everest. I said this much to George and, along with several other team members, asked that he be given a chance to make amends. George relented and cautioned Roger to watch his step.

The warning had little effect, and at a climbers' meeting on the evening of July 25, immediately prior to the start of the

long walk to Base Camp, Bill March announced that he was sacking Roger. He cited a number of offences he believed contravened the climbers' contract that all members of the expedition had signed before leaving Canada—a contract specifying that no member would commit any act that might embarrass the expedition or jeopardize its position vis-à-vis its sponsors. Bill apologized for bringing the subject up at such a late date but felt he could not ignore a final alleged offence, which had come to light only a few days before the team departed Canada. Because Roger had already left for Nepal in advance of the main team, Bill had waited for the planned Kathmandu rendezvous to expel him, but Roger had decided to head to Base Camp alone, an action that did his case no good since it was yet another violation of the agreement. At the conclusion of Bill's presentation, all of the climbers present voted to support his decision. Robert "Rusty" Baillie, one of the most experienced climbers in the group, summed up the team consensus: "On any climbing expedition, there are times when you have to trust your partners with your life. If something comes up that causes you to doubt that trust, it's better to be wrong than sorry."

## MAVERICK CLIMBER

To ensure Roger's departure, Bill had his Nepalese visa revoked. Now forced to return to Canada, Roger became a convenient if skeptical media commentator on the expedition's progress, blaming his dismissal on his failure to fit the promotional mould into which Bill and John wanted to shape their climbers. Having climbed with him as much as had any of the team members, I felt that Roger had been given a couple of chances to redeem himself and had chosen to ignore the cues. Since Everest, he has embarked on a successful solo-climbing career that better suits his style, free as it is from the confines of teamwork, and he seems to relish his role as the maverick of the Canadian climbing community.

Ironically, Roger's expulsion had an unexpected result. "It was our first crisis, a testing," recounts Tim Auger, "and it really pulled us together. We started the walk in with a feeling of solidarity that hadn't been there before." We needed that solidarity, for we were 16 free spirits, with a couple of prima donnas thrown in for good measure, working together for the first time.

The "walk in" to the Everest region is a 150-mile hike and an integral part of any Everest expedition. The trail is a rugged one, cutting across the grain of the land, and rises from 4,000 feet (1,219 m) at Kathmandu to 17,600 feet (5,364 m) at the Everest Base Camp. Climbers arrive at the mountain in top physical condition and, if the trek has been a leisurely one, well acclimatized to the oxygen-thin air and to each other's eccentricities. The latter consideration was a particularly important one for our large team, and Bill hoped to use the hike both to accustom the climbers to his leadership and to bridge the gaps between the disparate elements in the team.

Recent experience in the Himalayas has demonstrated that the happiest expeditions are those constructed around a strong leader who handpicks a team of climbers with whom he can get along and who can get along with each other. Bill, as the third leader of a team that had evolved somewhat haphazardly, recognized the need for a bit of last-minute fine-tuning. He saw two groups in the team: the older British-born Canadian climbers and the younger Canadians, both groups coincidentally containing several members from the Calgary Mountain Club. There was no noticeable tension between the groups, but Bill still felt the need to bind the two into a more cohesive unit. "In retrospect, I needed more time than I had," he admitted later, "but I did feel I was making good progress toward that goal by the time we reached Base Camp."

On the morning of July 26, with spirits soaring, our team hopped off the bus that had taken us to Lamosangu, a small village that was a two-hour drive from Kathmandu. After ceremoniously slipping a large stone into Bill's pack, we shouldered our own modest loads and started up the trail, impressed by the heat of the day and by the length of the hill rising out of the village.

The distance separating Lamosangu and Base Camp is frequently covered in 12 days, but we decided to stretch it to

Canadian reporter Bruce Patterson greets a youngster with the traditional Nepali greeting: "*Namaste*," I salute the god within you. It rained every day during our approach to Base Camp, an inescapable result of our decision to do the trek at the end of the monsoon season.

20, making the acclimatization process as gradual as possible. Our destination was a small rocky plateau at the foot of Mount Everest, the lone peak that towers above all others. The raw unfriendliness of the camp was in direct contrast to the magical beauty of the countryside, and our trek was a first-class affair in the finest British tradition.

A typical day began with tea served to us in our tents, a practice initiated by the colonial British. Watching our string of 20 porters, complete with umbrellas rolled up on top of their 60-pound loads, it was easy to imagine being part of the entourage of the Survey of India when it passed through these same hills 130 years before.

The discovery of Everest's record height was made in 1852 during the Survey's compilation of data. At that time, the mountain was simply known as Peak XV. Thirteen years later, it was suggested to the Royal Geographical Society that the summit be named after Sir George Everest, who had been the surveyor general of India from 1823 to 1843. To the people of the Khumbu Himal, bordering the Kingdom of Nepal and Chinese Tibet, however, the mountain aptly remains, as it always has been, Chomolungma, Tibetan for Mother Goddess of the Wind.

Bending the sky at 29,028 feet (8,848 m), the mountain is a jutting, angular pyramid of black rock, white snow and riven blue ice. The scale is immense, and few photographs do it justice; it is the yardstick by which all other mountains are measured. The summit itself is the 2½-by-15-foot gable of the world, lying above two-thirds of the planet's atmosphere and catching the howling brunt of a jet-stream wind each winter. During these months, the winds are incessant, often reaching velocities of 130 to 140 miles per hour (209-225 kph), and temperatures dip to minus 50 degrees F (-45°C). Even at the best of times, it is an inhospitable peak. It is a mountain that makes climbers aware of their temporal places in the universe.

And yet ever since the British invented mountaineering during the Empire's finest days in the mid-1800s, men and women have dreamed of climbing the world's highest mountain. It is safe to say that those who do not climb mountains

Loaded down with our kitchenware on their backs, our lowland porters approach the village of Junbesi, still 10 days away from the snowy core of the Himalayas. Upon reaching the village of Namche Bazaar, the porters gave up their loads to yaks and Sherpas.

As sahib clients, we enjoyed huge breakfasts in spectacular settings, all part of the service provided by our Sherpas and porters. Our entourage of 50 was certainly different from the lightweight expedition we had envisaged in 1977, and occasionally, such scenes made me think back to the colonial days of the British Empire.

will never fully understand those who do, but George Mallory—who disappeared forever in a lowering cloud near Everest's summit in 1924—at least clarified the question when he wrote: "If you cannot understand there is something in men which responds to this mountain and goes out to meet it, that the struggle is life itself, upward and forever upward, then you cannot see why we go. What we get from this adventure is just sheer joy. And joy is, after all, the end of life."

Largely because of Mallory and his like-minded colleagues, Everest has become a testing ground for adventurous spirits. The testing continues today. The British sent their first team of mountaineers on a reconnaissance expedition in 1921. It is an indication of both the mountain's remoteness and the ferocity of its heights that it took 32 years and eight expeditions before Sir Edmund Hillary and Tenzing Norgay stumbled down off the mountain to announce their success. "We've knocked the bastard off," exulted Hillary in an adrenaline-fuelled comment somewhat at odds with his later sentiment that Everest knows no victors, that those who reach the summit do so only with the mountain's tolerance.

By 1985, Everest had been scaled by an estimated 201 people from 22 countries—the number is questionable owing to the secrecy cloaking the efforts of the Chinese—using six different routes. In the spring of 1985, a single Norwegian team led by British climber-summiteer Chris Bonnington put 17 climbers on the top, but the most outstanding assault belongs to Reinhold Messner who climbed alone from Tibet, without oxygen. Still, the mountain is not to be taken lightly. Of the more than 100 attempts, fewer than half have succeeded. For every two climbers to reach the summit, another has died in the attempt. And climbers continue to die at an alarming rate, even on the nontechnical routes: during the 1982 winter pre-monsoon and post-monsoon climbs, eight Sherpas and four other climbers died in pursuit of the Goddess's ultimate secret.

Because we wanted to begin our ascent of the mountain at the first possible moment after the rains that last from June to August, we had elected to make our approach during the tail end of the season. Mornings dawned clear and

bright, but by noon, the clouds began to build, and we would be enveloped in a steamy drizzle that often turned into an outright downpour by evening. The weather, brought on by moist air from the Bay of Bengal, represented a minor threat, for it often rained two inches a day, making the trail a treacherous stream within moments of the start of the shower. But, aware of the hazards, our expedition had sent the bulk of its supplies to Base Camp in April—using several hundred porters, yaks and a STOL (short-takeoff-and-landing) aircraft—well before the rains began. Unfortunately, the monsoon also provided a medium for the proliferation of small brown leeches, which eagerly attached themselves to our succulent bodies at every chance. As a primary line of defence against these insidious nuisances, each member of the team was issued a salt-shaker. The leeches proved to be nearly as great a diversion for us as Rusty's daily T'ai Chi workouts were for the children in the villages along the trail.

## SHERPA CO-OP

My spirits picked up considerably when we started to pull away from the dripping forests in the valleys and get into the open alpine region in the heart of Sherpa country, near the capital of the Solu-Khumbu district, Namche Bazaar. Our lowland porters would leave us here, our loads taken over in the rarefied atmosphere by better-acclimatized Sherpa porters and yaks.

The Sherpas are believed to have migrated to this region from their native Szechuan province in China in the early 1500s, when pressure from the Mongols forced them on their 1,300-mile march. According to Tibetan documents found at Solu, a group of 50 or more Sherpas (meaning people from the east) crossed over Nangpa La Pass in 1533 and came upon an area that was hidden, uninhabited and covered with virgin forests. The Sherpas have lived undisturbed there for 400 years.

Until the border was closed by Chairman Mao in 1950, the Sherpas, with their yak caravans, plied rugged trade routes from Tibet to northern India. Coincidentally, climbing, and later trekking, in this region became popular at just

about the time of the closure. The Sherpas, being astute and business-minded, capitalized on the situation by developing the lucrative service industry of catering to Western tourists. With a "tea and sleep house" never more than a day's walk from one to the next, Nepal has some of the world's most civilized mountainous areas for foot travel.

The Sherpa Cooperative has been set up to make certain that working conditions and wages are kept at a reasonable level. An average wage for manual labour, such as smashing rocks with a hammer to create gravel for road building, is about 25 cents a day, but the Sherpa Cooperative has ensured that the risks taken by a high-altitude porter are rewarded with up to $4 a day, with a bonus system the higher one travels on a mountain. In addition, the Sherpas are allowed to keep the high-tech clothing and equipment issued to them by each expedition, which in our case was valued at approximately $3,000. The "new" gear is often set aside and offered for sale at half price in their shops in Namche Bazaar and Kathmandu, while their old gear is used on each climb. During the main trekking and climbing seasons of spring and autumn, when the men are off working as high-altitude porters or trekking guides, their wives manage the shops.

Medical studies have shown that the Sherpas' bodies have developed a superior oxygen-carrying capacity, earning them their reputation for being tigers at altitude. Their slight build is deceptive at first glance. With less body weight to carry and less muscle bulk to consume valuable oxygen supplies, they are well suited to high-altitude work. As of 1984, 25 Sherpas had been to the summit of Everest. The United States, having put 24 climbers on the top, has come closest to the Sherpas' record.

Namche Bazaar sits in a shallow amphitheatre at 11,300 feet (3,444 m), at the convergence of two river systems. Its loftiness reminded me of the Inca ruin of Machu Picchu, as did the pungent, acrid smell of dried dung smouldering in the cooking fires. After many nights in a tent, it was an uncommon pleasure to sleep on the clean, polished wooden beds of the Sherpa hotels and to eat traditional meals of *tsampa* (roasted barley flour), whole red-hot chiles and potato pancakes served with sharp Roquefort-like yak cheese. In 1850, the introduction of potatoes from English gardens into the Nepalese diet had a profound effect on the life style of the Solu-Khumbu region. The extra nourishment changed the entire economic structure and even precipitated a modest population explosion. Having to forage less for food, people with time to spare became painters and sculptors who engaged in various forms of religious art such as Tanka painting. These are colourful mural-type depictions of Tibetan Buddhist deities, or stories about them, where the figures and objects in them are drawn to very exact proportions.

According to government edict, the Sherpa schools (established by Everest summiteer Sir Edmund Hillary) teach English and Nepali, and the Sherpa language, unfortunately, is taught only in their monasteries. Even though they are multilingual as a result of their association with visitors from many different nations and can converse in basic English, we tried our best to use our guidebook Nepali on them. This would usually elicit wild laughter and even warmer hospitality.

## CHURNING STICK

At this point in the walk in, the effects of the altitude were beginning to show, although they were alleviated by the increasingly spectacular scenery. Just up the trail, there had once been a pastoral alpine lake feeding the Dudh Kosi River. In fact, we had found postcards of it in Kathmandu. In September 1977, an avalanche fell from the upper slopes of the magnificent 22,350-foot (6,812 m) Ama Dablam into the lake, triggering a 30-foot wave that roared down the valley, washing away seven bridges and part of the trail we were walking on. Signs of a less dramatic but more perverse phenomenon illustrated the fact that the Himalayas are continuously falling to pieces. In response to increasing demands for firewood by tourists, the Sherpa people have systematically eliminated the forests that had previously kept erosive forces from washing the Himalayas into the Bay of Bengal. Even though it is illegal to cut

Unlike their Hindu counterparts to the south, who are embroiled in the Indian caste system, these Sherpa girls have a large degree of equality in their Buddhist society.

wood for fuel in Sagarmatha National Park, the Sherpas continue to strip the land of its foliage because it costs less than kerosene. (Sagarmatha is the Nepali name for Everest, meaning Churning Stick of the Ocean of Existence.) We saw two tree-seedling nurseries near Namche that showed a token tree-planting attempt which was only slightly less pathetic than our own reforestation programmes in British Columbia.

The expedition reached Base Camp on August 15, several days after Peter Spear, the Base Camp manager, and climber David McNab had arrived to start erecting a comfortable camp in a most uncomfortable location. The site, a rubble-strewn stretch of glacier at the foot of the Khumbu Icefall, has been used by expeditions for 30 years. Garbage from past climbs littered the ground, and it seemed that the camp was no more than a historic fecal deposit. The situation was little improved by the fact that, along with several others, I was suffering from a spiteful strain of dysentery. This, combined with the effects of altitude, laid me up for a whole week until I wondered if my body would ever be able to recover from the malaise at this altitude. Out of curiosity, when I had regained my health, I took my resting pulse rate at Base Camp. It was 119. I didn't even bother to measure it above that point.

We shared the site with a team of Catalans attempting Everest's highly technical West Ridge route. Together with the Sherpas from both teams, we observed a Buddhist ceremony and then proceeded to help the Catalans drain some of their magnificent stock of Base Camp cheer, which amounted to 500 cans of *cerveza*.

On August 17, while several members of the team conducted a training session with the Sherpas to standardize climbing techniques and rescue procedures, Bill March, Lloyd Gallagher and Alan Burgess scrambled up a short distance to reconnoitre a route through the icefall. The climbing, at last, had begun.

The overall strategy was to lay siege to the mountain in the classic fashion of past expeditions. The team would establish a series of camps up the mountain, stocking each with the supplies needed to push up to the next camp. This style

Prayer flags fluttering in the constant breeze at Namche Bazaar send their messages of blessings and requests for protection heavenward. While young Sherpas take advantage of the setting and climb for money, their elders have traditionally viewed the mountains as gods who shape their lives and their fortunes. Expeditions can, they believe, occasionally anger the gods, and misfortune is sure to follow.

Like his father, this young boy—the son of one of our porters—will probably grow up to work in the tourist industry as a high-altitude porter, a trekking guide or, perhaps, in a Kathmandu trekker supply shop.

of climbing is considered necessary whenever a mountain presents an obstacle, such as the Khumbu Icefall, that might require many days to surmount. Unlike almost any other popular mountain in the Himalayas, Everest sits right on the Tibet-Nepal border and so the only easy access from Nepal is through the Khumbu region. Because Tibet's borders were closed to foreigners at the time we were planning our expedition, we chose to approach the mountain through the treacherous icefall, a route that makes no mountaineering sense at all and would normally be avoided at all costs. Since the Khumbu Icefall was considered almost a separate climb in itself, we needed a large climbing and support team. In spite of our manpower, we soon found out how vulnerable we still were to the dangers of the ever-shifting mass of ice.

## MOVING ON AIR

The climb assumed a pyramidal structure—a wide base of supplies and climbers at the bottom that gradually tapered to a carefully selected cache of provisions and one or two climbers at the highest camp. The high camp might require a scant 10 loads to stock, while the one below needed 40 or 50, and so on down the mountain. Consequently, our Base Camp consisted of 700 loads of supplies, 15 Canadian climbers, 5 support personnel and 29 high-altitude Sherpas.

To facilitate movement on the mountain, polypropylene ropes were fixed between camps and anchored by ice screws or, in the case of deep snow, snow flukes and pickets. Also known as "dead men," snow flukes resemble snow-shovel blades and are pushed into deep snow, as are the T-shaped aluminum pickets, to offer resistance to any tug on the rope. Together, the ropes constitute a mountain lifeline to which climbers attach themselves as they shuttle supplies from camp to camp. If a climber slips or falls, the rope will secure him, thus eliminating the need for two or more climbers to rope themselves together and move as a unit. During the course of the expedition, we fixed more than five miles of rope on the mountain.

Everest's first challenge, the icefall,

was to be one of its most severe. From the bottom, it appeared impassable, a tumbled confusion of massive seracs (pillars of ice formed as a glacier moves down a steep incline of bedrock and splits apart) and gaping crevasses made all the more menacing by the continual reshuffling of glacial elements. Taken one step at a time, however, possibilities appeared and lines of approach opened up, and it became feasible, if nerve-racking, to move gently through the frozen, creaking maze.

The first 1,000 feet (304 m) went smoothly enough, but then we encountered a severely broken section that was dubbed The Traverse, and progress literally slowed to a crawl. There was nothing there but 30-foot-high (9 m) seracs above and 150-foot-deep (45 m) crevasses below, which forced us away from the centre of the icefall and into a position of vulnerability under the west shoulder of Everest. Our route lay across chunks of ice that had fallen from the seracs and become wedged in the crevasses, meaning we were moving more or less across air, rather than substance. As our Sherpa porters struggled upward under heavy loads, their breathing came in gasps for not only did they have to suck in enough air to breathe, but they also had to force a continuous stream of mantras through their clenched teeth as they exhaled. Their prayers ceased higher on the mountain, and it was hard to determine whether that was a sign the hazards had lessened or whether there was not enough oxygen to fuel them.

Fixing ropes through the traverse involved inching delicately down a rib of ice, leaping across a crevasse, tentatively working up the far side, crawling across a yard of serac crumbs to another gaping chasm and then starting all over again. To make subsequent progress easier, eight-foot aluminum-ladder sections were used to bridge the worst spots; several of the crevasses needed three sections.

Despite the severity of the task, our team, working in pairs, penetrated the icefall in three days and secured the route with ropes and ladders in five, a record time that surprised and delighted us. One climber would usually lead the route, another would fix ropes and ladders, and one or two would improve the

The hike into Base Camp, which took 20 days, allowed us to acclimatize to the increasingly oxygen-thin air and to revel in the pastoral scenes that unfolded around us. Our porters bought milk for our tea from this young boy who was driving his water buffalo past the terraced rice paddies of Namdu.

passage somewhere below. On August 22, Jim Elzinga, still limping from a fall suffered in Kathmandu, and Laurie Skreslet moved beyond the icefall to establish Camp One at 19,600 feet (5,974 m). The next several days were devoted to improving the route and carrying loads to Camp One. Almost without exception, we were all well acclimatized, strong and working hard. The team leaders had to threaten to tie David McNab down with a rope before he would take a day off. By the end of the month, the team had ferried more than 130 loads of food and supplies to Camp One and had selected a site for Camp Two at 21,000 feet (6,400m). "The way we were going," said Lloyd, "I thought we were going to be up the mountain by the end of September. That would have been a little embarrassing, since we were supposed to be gone until the end of October."

## BUBBLE OF IMMORTALITY

The passing days brought an easing of the initial apprehension about the icefall. The dangers were still obvious—so much so, in fact, that we began our day's work by headlamp at 3 o'clock in the dark, cold early morning when the glacier was least active and the chance of avalanche minimal—but as Rusty noted, "The team was building up a nice little bubble of immortality."

The bubble was not to last. On the morning of August 31, I set out from Base Camp with Rusty and two lightly loaded Sherpas to break a trail through snow that had fallen the previous evening. A larger complement of Sherpas, accompanied by Peter Spear, freelance cameraman Blair Griffiths and Bruce Patterson, our Southam reporter, was to follow. A short distance into the icefall, we found one of the crevasse-bridging ladders beginning to twist, but we were used to such phenomena by then and measured the icefall's motion by the torque on the ladders and the tension on the ropes. Rusty and one Sherpa decided to straighten it while I moved ahead with the other Sherpa. By the time we reached the traverse, the snow was boot-deep. More troublesome, however, was the strength of the wind: whatever snow had accumulated would be wind-deposited and thus prone to avalanching.

Moving out of the traverse, I thought of turning back and decided to do so if I came to a slope where my feet disturbed the surface of the snow enough to release its bond with the glacier and trigger a slide. I rested in the darkness, eating a chocolate bar and drinking water, trying to get a feel for the situation. It was still early, still cold. We had worked in fresh snow for the past two weeks, but nothing we had passed through so far had been avalanche-prone, and the disconcerting roar of big avalanches high up on Everest and its satellite peaks seemed to go on regardless of the time of day or the weather.

I decided to press on but radioed up to Camp One, where Bill, Alan, Tim, David McNab and three Sherpas—the first team to spend a night above Base Camp—were just awakening. As I talked on the radio to Bill about the possibility of his group's breaking trail down to meet us, Blair and six Sherpas caught up to me. After exchanging a few words, they moved upslope, but I only got 30 paces before being enveloped in a tremendous hissing of wind and snow. The snow was being driven so hard that it felt like grains of sand, and the rush of wind tore the breath out of me. It was very confusing, and I became totally disoriented. I couldn't see, I couldn't hear, and I couldn't breathe. I tried to shield my head with my arms and dived for the shelter of a serac I knew was in front of me, but I kept being dragged out from behind it. I was clipped into the fixed rope, and every time I got behind the serac, the rope, which was being torn off the mountain, would drag me back out. "Well," I thought, "this is it. It's finally caught up with me."

As suddenly as it hit, the avalanche passed, and I could see and breathe again. I first spotted Blair a bit below me on the edge of the avalanche path and slid down the rope to see if he was all right. Assured that he was, I worked back up to the Sherpas. They, too, were intact, although one had a badly bruised leg. Then, just minutes after signing off from the first call, I radioed back to Camp One to say that we had been hit by an avalanche but that everyone seemed all right. Next, I radioed down to Base Camp and, after a quick conference with Lloyd, decided that it would be best to evacuate the mountain immediately. A major avalanche is sometimes followed by another, and we wanted to leave the zone as quickly as possible.

## MOUNTAIN GRAVE

As we picked our way back across the 200-yard-wide (182 m) swath of debris, we found ourselves crawling over cakes of ice the size of refrigerators. The avalanche had been massive: it had picked up entire seracs and beaten them into smaller pieces as it roared down the mountain. We later estimated that it had begun almost 3,000 feet (914 m) above and, at its widest point, measured well over a mile. The snow that had swept over our team was one small tongue of a much larger slide.

On the far side of the avalanche path, the radio crackled again with the message from Base Camp that Rusty, Peter and three Sherpas had narrowly escaped serious injury on the downslope side of the avalanche. Rusty had been knocked down the mountain and buried up to his chest, and Peter, spinning on the fixed rope, had been completely buried except for one foot. Rusty and one of the Sherpas were able to dig him out. Three other Sherpas were missing. The snow had stopped just 150 feet (45 m) below us, and we couldn't believe that there were three men somewhere in there. Disregarding the threat of another avalanche, Blair and I began a frantic search, but the wet snow had settled like cement. It was impossible to probe the debris, and shovels bounced off the surface. Although we were soon joined by others from Camp One and later from Base Camp, it was well over an hour before we found the only body the slide was to yield—Pasang Sona. Stephen Bezruchka, our team physician, had come up from Base Camp and arrived in time to help recover the body. Pasang and the two others had been together and were buried just a couple of yards into the edge of the avalanche path. If they had been able to walk back down the fixed rope just a few more paces, they would have been missed by the slide as closely as Blair and I had been.

Stephen recalls the moment: "The

Destined to become the first
Canadian to reach Everest's
summit, Laurie Skreslet adds his own
prayer flag to those of the Sherpas at
Base Camp. The infamous Khumbu
Icefall stretches upward in the background, its reputation cause enough for
anyone to seek help from the gods.
Aware of the dangers ahead, the porters
built a small altar at the base of the
prayer-flag pole and burned juniper
each morning and afternoon.

Base Camp, its rocky, garbage-strewn moraine masked by nightfall, was less than appealing by daylight. With Catalan and New Zealand teams sharing the site, the population pushed 100—possibly qualifying as the world's highest (17,600 feet) inhabited village at the time. During my first week there, I suffered a nagging bout of dysentery that left me with less-than-pleasant memories of the place.

grim reality became clear when a hand was uncovered near the bottom end of the fixed rope. It took an eternity to clear the snow away from the body, and while Pasang was being uncovered, James Blench asked me if I had any idea what to do. I suggested I try CPR [cardiopulmonary resuscitation]. It seemed so hopeless, and there was so much frustration that I was at the point of tears; but I knew that if it were me, I'd want someone at least to try. We put him in a sleeping bag, and Rusty and I climbed in with the body to try to warm it. We worked on him for about 30 minutes, but Pasang never came back."

## PREMONITION OF DISASTER

The loss of the three men was an immense blow. The single recovered body, bound in a sleeping bag, was lowered to Base Camp and placed in a rock enclosure with a burning light to guide its spirit into the next life. With no place to go, we wandered around camp disconsolately, trying to sort out what had happened. "It was shattering," says Rusty. "It's one thing to sit in a bar in Calgary and say, 'Geez, you know 11 men have died in that icefall; we'll have to be careful in there,' and quite another to be carrying the body of a friend down through it. I don't think we truly understood the full implication of what we were up against until that moment."

In the afternoon, we gathered in the cook tent to analyze our situation. Although we were unable to isolate any particular reason for the accident (other than being on the mountain during the post-monsoon season when the Himalayas are heavily snow-laden), we did decide to travel in smaller groups; to spread out more; to use the radios to make scheduled early-morning weather reports; and not to make any subsequent climbs during snowfalls, no matter how mild it was. A year after the climb, I came across an eerie reminder of the occasion in a calendar photograph taken by Jonathan Blair, who himself was later killed in an avalanche on a Chinese peak. Jonathan had been at the site of our Camp One when he had photographed a massive, billowing release of snow along the identical path ours had taken. But the photograph had

been taken at midday, under a clear blue sky, indicating to me that this was a haphazard occurrence that could take place in any weather. It was simply bad luck that we had blundered into, and nothing short of a premonition could have averted the disaster.

More than just adding to the nuts-and-bolts aspect of climbing the mountain, the avalanche added a tremendous emotional burden to the climb. "It was about the worst possible accident," recalls Tim. "Not only had we lost three expedition members, but those members were Sherpas who were on the mountain solely because they could help us, the crazy Westerners, get to the top. It's true that most of them really do like to climb and that they are paid very well for it and that those who are successful become heroes among their own people, but that doesn't diminish the responsibility you feel for them on the mountain. And all this is in addition to the fact that they are such a warm, gentle people, so loyal in a way Westerners can barely comprehend that you just don't want them to be hurt." Those killed were Ang Tsultim, 20, who had worked with trekking groups before but was on his first climb; Dawa Dorje, 40, who had extensive climbing experience and had joined our training climb on Annapurna IV; and Pasang Sona, 40, also an experienced Himalayan climber.

Their deaths raised an old question that every climber must consider sooner or later: is any mountain worth the loss of a single human life? The team had decided back in Canada that the expedition would continue despite a serious accident, but it now seemed that the matter deserved reconsideration. Stephen, remembering the Japanese ski expedition of 1970 in which six Sherpas died, recalls: "I always resented that expedition for continuing. Now I was suddenly asking myself if three were so many fewer than six that we could continue ourselves." Rusty, a fine climber with a long history of dangerous, difficult ascents, surprised us at the meeting when he announced that he was considering quitting. Donald Serl, who could not reconcile recreation with death, said it was definitely over for him.

The following morning, a party of eight Sherpas carrying the body of Pasang

Sona headed down the trail to Lobuche, a high-summer yak pasture that has recently become inhabited year-round to serve trekkers. Bill, Stephen and John Amatt went with them—Bill and Stephen to look after details concerning the Sherpas' deaths, John to move farther down the valley to Namche Bazaar to radio out news of the accident. The powerful Base Camp radio had a faulty antenna, and it was thanks to Teleglobe Canada technician Dick Cushing, who arrived a couple of weeks later, that we were finally able to establish a radio link with Kathmandu. The men had been in Lobuche only a short time before the bereaved relatives began to assemble, Pasang Sona's widow and youngest daughter arriving first, their wailing audible for a great distance. Next came Ang Tsultim's father, a middle-aged man with a limp, leaning on a stick for support and silently weeping. Dawa Dorje's widow was slow to appear—she had one infant and was pregnant with another, and no one had wanted to break the news to her.

## SERENE SETTING

The next few hours were the hardest of the entire climb for Bill: "My official responsibilities were to meet with the families, express the expedition's condolences, explain the insurance policies we had on the Sherpas' lives and give them some money and what we had of the men's personal effects. Unofficially, I wanted to do all I could to comfort them, which meant sitting with them while they mourned—and they mourn long and hard, day and night. They are a very emotional people; they don't hold much back. Three of us—Gyalgen, the Sirdar, or head Sherpa, Kshatri Pati Shrestha, the liaison officer, and I—took turns in two-hour shifts. The mourning went on for two or three days, but it seemed like months. The sorrow was overwhelming."

On the morning of September 2, Pasang Sona's body was carried down from Lobuche for cremation on a ridge below the settlement. It was a serene setting: the world opened up below to the south, and the majestic peak of one of the most beautiful of the Himalayas, Ama Dablam (meaning Mother's Jewel Box) rose against the sky. A lama who

The Khumbu Icefall, *left*, repository for the snow and ice that Everest and Nuptse shed, was a constantly shifting no-man's land that ultimately claimed four expedition members' lives. It travelled downslope at a rate of up to three feet a day, forcing us to use 60 aluminum ladders to bridge the yawning crevasses, *above*. In all, a dozen ladders were lost to the shifting ice.

had arrived the day before to help guide Pasang Sona's soul into the afterlife chanted while the body was washed, ritually fed, then braced as rhododendron wood was piled around it. Once the fire was lit, the group of mourners moved to a spot where food had been prepared. Distraught, Stephen talked to the lama about the calamity. But the lama's words caught him off guard: "This is just one of those things. It just happens."

At 2:30 that afternoon, as Bill and Stephen were preparing to move back up to Base Camp, two Sherpa runners arrived with more of the deceased Sherpas' equipment and a note for Bill. The message from Peter was short and to the point: at 9:15 a.m., there had been a collapse in the icefall. Blair Griffiths had been killed by a falling serac at the upper end of the traverse. The climbers had decided to recover the body and carry it down to Lobuche for cremation.

## ANTIDOTE TO SORROW

Two days earlier, after Bill had left for Lobuche with the Sherpas, the team had regrouped, resolving to move back onto the mountain. Action, it was agreed, was the best antidote to sorrow, and besides, the weather had become perfect for climbing.

Despite the momentary optimism born of the continuation of the climb, Tim described his feeling of apprehension in his diary: "In the hours preceding the full moon of September 2, 1982, I was awakened from an uneasy sleep by ominous rumblings in the Khumbu Icefall. It was shortly after midnight, the night clear and still, cold but brilliant with reflected moonlight—and filled with the sound of thousands of tons of ice slowly stirring, groaning in its steep glacial bed, restlessly moving at up to a yard per day toward the valley below. The noise was distressing, for the icefall was our choice approach to the mountain's summit, 12,140 feet [3,700 m] above, and our team had been nervously threading its way through the maze of precariously balanced blocks and spires almost daily for two weeks."

On the morning of September 2, a party of five Canadians, of which I was one, and 10 Sherpas had moved up to occupy Camp One, carrying loads,

while Rusty (who had decided to stay on after all), Dave Read, Blair and two Sherpas went into the traverse to repair a two-section ladder that was badly twisted. Dave and Nima Tsering were working at the base of the ladder, Blair and Pasang Tenzing at the top, and Rusty was sorting out ropes just behind Blair. At 9:15, just over an hour after 15 of us had passed through this same spot, "the whole glacier started to shudder and shimmy." Caught in the midst of the movement, Dave remembers the next few minutes clearly: "I thought at first that it was an earthquake, but then I realized the entire glacier was moving around me. The piece I was standing on started to slide into the crevasse, and suddenly, there were these big blocks of ice all around my head, and I was passing them, and they were going over the top of me, and I thought, 'This is it, mate. Too bad.' " Above him, Rusty and Tenzing were scrambling from toppling block to toppling block.

Rusty later recalled that when the collapse began, his major concern was that he die with dignity. His one thought was, "I want to go calmly." Then, when the first wave of falling ice missed him, he began to work at avoiding the next onslaught.

Seconds later, as the ice stabilized, Dave found himself still alive, wedged in a domino assortment of snow and ice within the crevasse. Two large blocks of ice had fallen against each other above him, leaving a space for his upper torso and head. While trying to orient himself, he saw a wool tuque lying in the rubble, and reaching out with his one free hand to retrieve it, he was startled to find it attached to a head. Gently, he scooped snow away from the face and cradled it with his left hand, pulling the head back. Sputtering out a mouthful of snow, Tsering came back to life with a shout. Panicking, the Sherpa freed his arms and shoulders and began struggling against the snow, using Dave as a combination ladder and pull-up bar. Dave, with little means of resistance, was pushed deeper into the unconsolidated debris beneath him, until only his head, shoulders and left arm were clear of snow. The two men's struggles were interrupted when a face appeared in a small hole 20 feet above, where Rusty, hearing the noise, had dis-

M ost of the technical climbing on the South Col route occurs in the Khumbu Icefall; New Zealand team leader Peter Hillary, son of Sir Edmund, hauls himself over the top of the vertical wall of a big serac. During the avalanches that hit us, some of these huge pillars of ice were smashed to pieces and swept down the mountain.

covered the site of their entombment.

"My God! You're alive!" said Rusty.

"Right, mate. But I won't be for long if this Sherpa has his way."

Rusty lowered a rope and managed to pull Tsering out. With the aid of a snow stake, knife and ice axe, it took Dave another 15 minutes to cut the ropes binding his left leg and to clear the ice from both. Finally liberated, he asked Rusty how Blair was.

"Sorry, Dave," came the reply. "He's dead."

Emerging from the crevasse, Dave had found Blair a scant 15 feet away, pinned between two large cakes of ice and remembers, "He had a very calm look, as though he were going to talk, to say, 'Hey, you know I'm only joking.'" Dave walked over to the body, shook Blair's hand and said, "I'm sorry about that, Blair." With that, the three climbers turned away and began to struggle through what was left of the traverse. The remnants of the fixed rope they had been following now dangled 25 feet above them.

I was sitting at the entranceway to my tent at Camp One when the news reached us on our hand-held radio. Dwayne slumped over and began to weep. "It just isn't fair," he said. Jim reached over to console him, and I turned to Laurie who was staring in disbelief down on the top of the icefall that had so recently taken three other lives. I had never felt my own mortality more than at this moment, looking around at my friends and knowing that any one of us could have shared Blair's fate.

As the news reached Base Camp, the remaining climbers stumbled into the cook tent for yet another meeting. With the spectre of the Sherpa deaths still haunting it, the team was faced with another numbing loss, and the accumulated pressures were reaching a flash point. The decision was made that four men would move into the icefall the following morning and meet us descending from Camp One, and then the entire team would carry Blair's body down to Lobuche. This plan, however, met with stiff resistance from Bill, and in an afternoon radio conversation, Bill advised the climbers to leave the body on the mountain. From a practical point of view, he felt that it was a completely empty

Having finished making a carry to Camp One, Rusty Baillie rappels down the same massive serac that is shown on the facing page, on his way back to Base Camp, 2,000 vertical feet below. Our strategy on the mountain was a standard one for large expeditions. By making a series of carries from a well-supplied Base Camp, we gradually stocked each of the camps one by one. By climbing higher by day and returning to sleep at lower camps, we managed to acclimatize to the increasing altitudes slowly, but it meant endless trips through the nerve-racking icefall.

gesture: the icefall had twice proved itself deadly, and to traverse it for any reason other than absolute necessity was to jeopardize more lives needlessly. Also, as Bill had learned from his recent descent to Lobuche, transporting a body down the steep, rocky trail from Base Camp was physically exhausting and dangerous in itself. Another consideration was that Blair was a Catholic, and Bill was uncertain whether cremation was compatible with that religion. The body, Bill insisted, could be given a fitting burial on the glacier, in a long-accepted tradition among mountaineers.

Several of the climbers, however, insisted on following their plan, and to keep the peace, Bill asked for time to think it over. After scheduling another call and signing off, he and Stephen retired to a sod-walled hotel named "The Promised Land." Stephen pleaded the climbers' case for catharsis, and following much discussion, Bill relented. In his second call to Base Camp, he agreed to the plan, provided risks to the climbers were minimized. The Catalans assured him that cremation was in fact suitable for a Catholic, and inquiries in Lobuche confirmed that there was an adequate supply of wood.

The following afternoon, the team arrived in Lobuche. As Bill had predicted, the journey had been exhausting and dangerous. Laurie, having injured several ribs in a fall, was in considerable pain. The trip down was—not surprisingly—an emotional forum, for the doubts that had arisen in the aftermath of the avalanche now gathered like storm clouds. It was a time for each man to wrestle with personal demons, to contemplate his commitment, to try to separate the emotional from the practical.

Blair was cremated the next morning on the site that had been used for Pasang Sona. It was a cold morning, full of mist and blowing clouds, a day suitably sombre for the task at hand. The team had a small service before the lighting of the pyre, and each member stepped forward to pay tribute to the man, the mountain and the nexus between. Blair had been very well liked, respected for his enthusiasm and hard work, admired for his quiet self-assurance. On the trek to Everest, at the Tengboche Monastery, he had spent an afternoon gazing

After two weeks of steady upward progress, our luck ran out. Wind action on a fresh snowfall far above the icefall triggered an avalanche that swept past cameraman Blair Griffiths and me and dumped huge seracs all around Peter Spear, Rusty Baillie and four Sherpas. By the time we scrambled down to join them, the word was out by radio that three of the Sherpas were missing and a search had begun.

toward the mountains of Ama Dablam and Nuptse and the valley below and had written in his journal: "I don't want to die, but if the pale horse should decide to come along, there isn't a better cathedral to stay in." Knowing Blair's love of poetry, Tim wrote a verse for the ceremony:

> This is the way of all eternity;
> As we see him now, so shall we be.
> When the time comes to follow him
> To where the mountain wind blows,
> Go as he does, with a good heart.

The day of the cremation also proved to be a day of decisions. Aware that several team members were considering leaving, Bill took each man aside and asked for his thoughts. At the end of his own emotional tether, Bill needed to know what sort of a team he had left.

"I had to get it out in the open," he said, "and I was afraid of the worst. In those early stages, I thought that we were going to lose a lot more than we finally did and that I was going to have to cancel the expedition." The decision, he determined, had to come from the climbers themselves. "There was no way I could guarantee that if we did go on, there wouldn't be another accident, another avalanche, and I didn't want to be responsible for persuading someone to stay on the climb who might die as a result. I told each man that if he wanted to stay, that was fine; if he wanted to leave, that was fine; and if he asked for time to decide, I told him to take it. The one thing I did insist on was that those who wanted to leave should leave quickly. One way to handle the problem was to have everybody sit on his decision for a day or two, but I was worried that the negative feelings of a few would spread to the rest of the group. And I also felt their gut reaction would be closest to the way they really felt."

It was the greatest crisis of leadership Bill was to experience. His inheritance—a diverse team whose members he had not chosen himself, a route that had lost its strongest advocate with the death of John Lauchlan and a last-minute appointment as leader—was showing its soft underbelly. Bill had consciously constructed his role as a tough leader for a tough mountain, explaining later that "if you look at the concept of climbing Everest, at all that is involved, at all the

The avalanche killed Ang Tsultim, Dawa Dorje and Pasang Sona, locking them in ice and snow that was packed as hard as cement. It took us an hour to find Pasang, and we never recovered the others. Wrapping Pasang, a 40-year-old veteran of the mountain, in a sleeping bag, we lowered his body down to Base Camp.

Two days after the first accident and the day of Pasang's funeral, Blair Griffiths, a freelance cameraman for the Canadian Broadcasting Corporation, was crushed by a collapsing serac. The next day, we carried his body down the mountain to Lobuche for cremation—a physically and emotionally demanding journey that forced us to reassess our commitment to climbing a peak that had claimed dozens of victims over the years. We held a sombre but heartfelt service in the cold, blowing mist, each of us saying a few words in tribute to one of the team's most popular members. It was a deep loss for all of us, and one that soon split the team in half.

details and all the risks and at a team the size of ours, then there is only one way. The leadership has to be autocratic—*very* autocratic—to get the job done. The only way it can be different is if you have a small, cohesive group of climbers who all have equal ability and equal judgment and who are willing to take responsibility for their actions." By his own rules, it was an all-or-nothing game, and suddenly, with the climbers taking their own lead, he found himself facing the possibility of nothing.

Many members did not appreciate Bill's tendency to make lone decisions without consulting the whole team, and he came under fire from those who thought that he should have been a more flexible leader and that his strong personality was too brusque at times. But with a number of oversized egos to contend with, Bill was forced to adopt a more domineering style than his followers were used to.

Personally, I felt that his leadership was brilliant. Every day, there had been a dozen crises, both operational and emotional, that had to be sorted out in short order. Team members were constantly approaching him with endless problems, and he had to address them all, 24 hours a day. Given the diverse, often contentious personalities, if everybody had had an equal say on every issue, we would never have agreed on how to exit the hotel, let alone Kathmandu. After the accidents, Bill was under tremendous pressure, trying to keep the climb going, trying to deal with the problems of men who had never had to come to grips with a teammate's death before and trying to sort out his own feelings as well. If he sagged a bit at times, it was understandable, and I thought those who weren't willing to take the pressures into consideration were being unrealistic.

Bill himself, reconsidering his decisions immediately after Blair's death, later believed that he might have been correct in his first judgment: "I think if I'd been really insistent and told them to leave the body and get the hell off the mountain until I could get up there and sort the whole thing out, it might have turned out better than it did. But I let them do it, bring Blair down, and their emotions just took over, and that's one thing

a mountaineer can't afford—at least while he's on a climb.

"You've got to be able to separate your emotions from the practical aspects of the climb. A death on the mountain is simply an event, a logistical problem—just as getting up a tricky rock band is—but a lot of guys had difficulty handling that. There's no doubt that if I'd really laid it on the line, some of the guys would have quit anyway, but perhaps not so many. People have to understand that it was a hell of a difficult time, and it called for a hell of a difficult decision. You don't get off too easy when you're in a position of authority and people are dying."

## PACKING FOR HOME

The day after the cremation, the team hiked back to Base Camp, some members to continue the climb, some to pack for home. Members of the latter group included Tim Auger, Rusty Baillie, James Blench, Jim Elzinga, Dwayne Congdon, David McNab and Donald Serl. A day's walk down the trail, Dwayne reconsidered his decision and returned to the team with new commitment. Although each weighed his decision differently—concerned to varying degrees with health, a family at home, the morality of a climb that had cost four lives, personality differences with Bill or other team members and disagreement with Bill's leadership—all had judged the mountain too hazardous to justify further effort. Rusty perhaps best expressed their belief: "At the core of mountaineering is an ongoing process of evaluation. One tries to determine the location of the line between the skills one has and the risks one faces. The secret is to recognize the line and to know when to turn back. Too soon, and nothing is gained; too late, and you've been reckless and die. It's interesting that the press accounts of this period said we dropped the climb because of what happened. In fact, we turned back because of what we thought *might* happen. It's certainly not a matter of courage, because one doesn't become a climber, let alone a climber in a class to attempt Everest, without courage. It's a matter of listening to what the mountain has to say. In our case, the weather was poor, the avalanche hazard seemed very high, and

**W**ith half his team gone, Bill March (left) adopted a more democratic style of leadership, initiating discussions with teammates such as Al Burgess (centre) and Speedy Smith.

New Zealand team leader Peter Hillary grabs a quiet moment atop the ragged seracs at the tongue of the icefall, no doubt thinking of his team's attempt on neighbouring Mount Lhotse. Bad weather set in shortly after the remnants of our team decided to press on, and along with the New Zealanders, we were stuck at Base Camp for almost two weeks. Having had to select a more straightforward route up Everest, we were forced to get permission from the New Zealanders to share their route on the upper slopes.

the Sherpas were saying that the glacier was more active than they could remember its being in years. The risk factor was just too high." Twenty-nine years before, Sir Edmund Hillary's team had had to use only one ladder in the icefall. It was so active now and the crevasses so numerous that we were forced to use 60.

## MOST LIKELY TO SUCCEED

Among those who decided to stay, the degree of commitment varied considerably. Al Burgess, Dave Read and Speedy Smith were unswervingly committed to the mountain; Laurie and I asked for a few days to mull it over; Lloyd Gallagher, after deciding that the climb should be called off following Blair's death, quickly changed his mind back to an upward course. As business manager, John Amatt was concerned about the expedition's sponsors and thought it would be best if the entire expedition folded with some sort of grace, but he was willing to stay on in a support capacity if the decision was made to continue. Bill, as leader, was personally committed to the climb, but he floundered briefly in a dark sea of logistical problems related to the other climbers' departures before Lloyd assured him we could and would find a way up the mountain. Peter was happy to stay on as Base Camp manager, and Stephen agreed that he would remain as Base Camp physician, a blessing given that our other physician, David Jones, was having respiratory problems owing to the altitude and was compelled to leave the mountain. The Sherpas were willing to stay.

The mood at Base Camp the afternoon after Blair's cremation was eerie at best. People wanted to verbalize their feelings but found it next to impossible to do so. Bill was upset and refused to have much to do with those who were leaving, and it was only after a discussion with Peter that he spoke with them, acknowledging the role they had played in the expedition. It was a difficult time, and although the departing climbers left with the respect of those who stayed, there was little sense of personal resolution.

In considering our options, few of us had thought in other than personal terms, but we were soon to learn just how public an affair our expedition had become. The news media, prompted by publicists back home to report the full romance of scaling the Mother Goddess of the Wind, was ready for news; and the worse it got, the more attention we received.

The problem in the early days following the accidents was one of quantity and quality of reportage. With a faulty antenna for the Base Camp radio, we had to rely on a combination of Sherpa runners and small aircraft to move Blair's videotapes, the team's 35mm film and Bruce's news releases to Kathmandu, but when the weather was poor, news was days late getting out. This had been acceptable while the climb proceeded in an orderly fashion, but once the first scent of disaster wafted down the mountain, the media's demand for information quickly surpassed the meagre scraps available to them.

In a frenetic rush to capitalize on the beleaguered expedition, reporters who knew nothing about mountaineering were tapping out major stories with little concrete information. Any source, any rumour, any personality willing to speak became eminently quotable.

Expelled member Roger Marshall, resurfacing in a fermenting vat of sour grapes in Canada, became headline material as he editorialized on events occurring half a world away; an early-morning Canadian Broadcasting Corporation (CBC) radio newscast in Calgary quoted an unidentified climber's letter to a friend at home; and Tim, who had been reading a book in his sleeping bag at Base Camp at the time of the icefall collapse, returned to Canada to find he had been injured in it.

Out of boredom and a lack of understanding of the sport, the media in Kathmandu took polls on who was most likely to succeed in reaching the top of the mountain. From their experience in covering professional team sports back home, they focused their attention on the climbers whose tongues wagged the hardest and placed their bets on them. CBC reporter Russ Patrick, beaten back by the 16,000-foot (4,876 m) altitude at Lobuche in a valiant attempt to reach Base Camp (which is visited regularly by trekkers up to 70 years of age), wrote later in *Saturday Night* magazine about

his hellish trials and tribulations in covering the Canadian Everest experience, most of which actually took place in the broadloomed lobby of the Everest Sheraton in Kathmandu. With virtually no nightlife in a charmingly mediaeval city that rolls up its carpets at dusk, the party-loving press corps was tackling its own Everest.

The nature of the reportage that reached us while we were still on the mountain left us incredulous once we began to perceive what was happening. John was the first to realize the extent of the media confusion, and shortly after the departure of part of the team, he returned to Kathmandu in a helicopter with a CBC television crew to deliver news of Blair's death and to help prepare the way for the returning climbers. After 24 hours in town and a long radio discussion with Bill, John exchanged his role as climber for one as expedition spokesperson. By the end of the expedition, more than 20 people from the press, radio and television corps were in Kathmandu, and John found himself regularly putting in 18-hour days. Through a Herculean effort, he was able to put things in their proper perspective, and the resultant coverage of the mountaineering event was among the best ever to come out of a foreign land.

## THE BOWLING ALLEY

In the week following Blair's death, the monsoon returned to Everest, blanketing the mountain in deep snow and making it unequivocally too dangerous for climbing—in the course of four days, the expedition's pace had gone from full speed to stop. This down time gave me a chance to reflect on my own vested interest in this climb. Like the others, I had been through the icefall about 11 times, and I knew that if I could get over the psychological hurdle of venturing through the bowling alley once more, things would improve above. The reduced size of the team made me more comfortable, and I knew that while I might not be compatible with a couple of the other climbers, I could persevere as I had done on Aconcagua. At this point, I felt a need to even the score by putting our bad luck behind us.

The Sherpas, as restless and frustrated as the rest of us, began to speak of the Canadian Mount Everest Base Camp Expedition. The camp, however, was not without activity. Rallying around Bill, our reduced team, now the size that Sir Edmund Hillary's team had been 29 years earlier, reappraised its strength and its position on the mountain. We decided to abandon the originally intended South Spur route and try for the South Col, a somewhat less demanding line. This decision, however, had two complicating factors: one was that permission to climb the route would have to be obtained from the Nepalese government; the other was that permission to use a portion of the route that ascended the face of Mount Lhotse would have to be obtained from the New Zealand team led by Peter Hillary, which had arrived after we had established our route through the icefalls. (Peter was the sole New Zealander on the team, two of the others being from Britain and one from Australia.) The first permission was almost automatic, subject to the approval of the other team. But the "New Zealanders" had reservations. They were trying to climb neighbouring Lhotse lightweight and without Sherpa support, and they were afraid that sharing the route with us would jeopardize the integrity of their climb. This was preposterous, since they were totally dependent on our fixed rope through the icefall and had secured permission to use our route all the way to Camp Two. It irked me particularly when one of the team members passed us as we were working on an askew ladder and muttered smugly that he believed there was safety in speed and that we wouldn't catch him hanging about the icefall any longer than he had to.

Relations between the two teams were further complicated by the fact that Al Burgess's brother Adrian was climbing with the New Zealand team. Even fraternal love could not improve our bargaining position, and the result of an intricate game of high-altitude blackmail was that the New Zealanders became entitled to the use of Canadian food and gear as well as the right to stay ahead of us until September 30. After that, we were free to pass them and make our own way to the South Col and thence try for Everest's summit.

Despite this extremely odd symbiotic relationship, we got along well enough with the other team. Peter Hillary—the son of Sir Edmund—found his estimation of his father's 1953 achievement rising daily and vowed to congratulate "the old man" when he returned home. He had brought one of his father's original canvas wall tents and had erected it alongside his own space-age dome tent at Base Camp.

The negotiations over, Bill moved down the mountain again, both to tie up administrative loose ends in the wake of the accidents and to gain some quiet time to prepare for the new assault. He was gone six days, returning with a fresh supply of lama-blessed rice and good-luck necklaces made from old nylon avalanche cord. It was still snowing.

## GRUELLING TOLL

The weather broke on September 16, a month and a day after we had reached Base Camp—two months after leaving Canada—and we moved quickly to repair the route to Camp One and to make the last few carries necessary in order to continue up the rest of the mountain. Our spirits rose as we started climbing again, and a new expedition that we jokingly dubbed CRASS—Canadian Remnants' Attempt on the Summit of Sagarmatha—was born.

Speedy, squinting up at the mountain, announced, "This time, it's for real." By September 24, our team of 8, plus 12 Sherpas, had consolidated above the icefall at Camp One, and we were well on our way to the South Col. Deputy leader Lloyd Gallagher, returning from a much-needed rest at Lobuche, joined us at Camp One on September 22 and reported that the condition of the icefall was deteriorating—"it was creaking and talking to me the whole way up." After consultation with the team (the first time the team functioned as a democracy), Lloyd ordered the icefall closed to further traffic. It was a directive that enraged Laurie, who had the misfortune of being caught back at Base Camp trying to recover from his damaged ribs. Asking for just one chance to catch up, Laurie was given permission to join us but at his own risk. He arose early the next morning and made his way through the icefall to

At Camp Two, our Sherpa team displays a lightweight titanium oxygen tank they found, left by a Russian expedition that established a major route on the 8,000-foot southwest face of Everest (background) in 1982.

Camp One, carrying some of our personal mail as well as some scary news from the Catalan camp. One night, a major rockfall had severed 700 feet of fixed rope from the lower part of their route. Had it occurred during the day, it would have wiped out anyone who had been in its way.

Above Camp One, the route up Everest traces the bottom of the Western Cwm (pronounced "coom"), a stunningly immense and beautiful valley, without a doubt one of the world's greatest mountain settings. The sheer walls of Everest and Nuptse rise 4,000 feet (1,219 m) up from the bottom of the Cwm, which narrows in spots to half a mile. It feels as if one could reach out and touch both walls. But it is as hazardous as it is beautiful, for the avalanche danger from the walls above is extreme. We were keenly aware of the debris that had come down one face and run halfway across the valley.

The climbing above Camp One proceeded smoothly, quickly becoming a routine of establishing and stocking the camps necessary for a summit bid. Usually one team pushed out in front, fixing ropes higher up the mountain, while others worked behind, ferrying supplies from camp to camp. Climbers would work one day, then rest for one or two, trying to find the energy to go just one day higher, overcoming fear and a dangerous altitude-induced apathy.

While our renewed pace was relatively swift, it was also hard work, and the altitude was exacting a gruelling toll. There were times when I thought I had never felt so miserable.

On an expedition of several days' duration on a smaller mountain, a climber can expect to put everything he has into the ascent until he reaches the summit. On a mountain the size of Everest, however, you feel as though your personal investments have been misdirected and your energy reserves have been grossly overdrawn, and you know that on return to the trailhead, you stand to face spiritual bankruptcy.

Because of the altitude, everything required maximum exertion: even putting on my boots in the morning left me exhausted. Dave and I had taken up where Blair had left off with the video coverage on the mountain, so in addi-

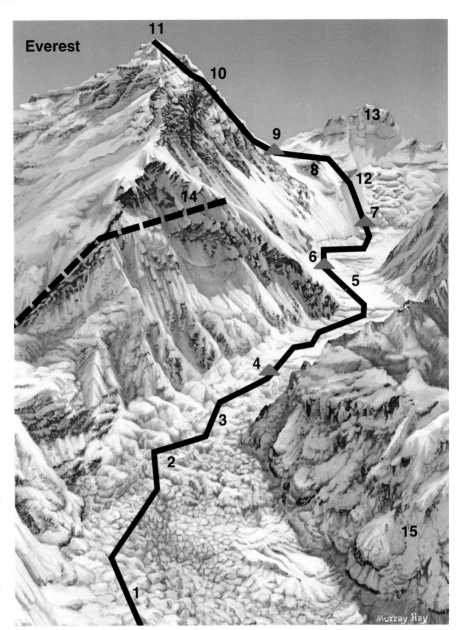

1. To Base Camp
2. Icefall Collapse
3. Avalanche Site
4. Camp One (19,600 feet)
5. Western Cwm
6. Camp Two (21,000 feet)
7. Camp Three (23,000 feet)
8. Geneva Spur
9. Camp Four—South Col (26,100 feet)
10. Summit Ridge
11. Summit (29,028 feet)
12. Lhotse Face
13. Lhotse
14. Fracture Line of Fatal Avalanche
15. Nuptse

Buffeted by winds from Everest's jet stream, Bill March and four Sherpas struggle to set up a box tent at Camp Three on a platform hacked out of the ice at 23,000 feet, halfway up the Lhotse face.

tion to documenting the expedition with my 35mm cameras, I had a 16-pound electronic monkey on my back that felt like 100 pounds. It detracted immensely from the enjoyment of climbing but was tacitly acknowledged to be a necessary part of honouring the agreement of our climbers' contract as video footage and photographs were critical to the sponsors. Most of the other climbers had made the mistake of using small, auto-exposure 35mm cameras for their own pictures. The intense cold and high reflectivity of the snow confused their meters and froze their electronic shutters, ruining most of their hard-won photographs. On the other hand, the manual shutter of my small Pentax-MX camera, kept within the warm folds of my jacket, continued to function even on the coldest days, and I had no reason to stop my photography. Perhaps the knowledge that dozens of photography editors would see the images before I would forced me to concentrate on portraying the physical dimension of the climb in a way that made the message as clear as possible. We were tired —I focused on the drama of the elements, the body language of my exhausted comrades, the remoteness of our playground.

The great reward of the Cwm was the sight of the summit, and that, still 8,000 feet (2,438 m) above us, was enough to keep me moving, day after day. The trick to the climb was to break it down into manageable portions. I couldn't let myself think of the climb as a whole; it was just too much to contemplate. The big push was always to make it just another five minutes, another hundred feet—and then another five minutes, another hundred feet. I did that for days.

Our team's good progress spurred us to greater efforts. The Sherpas, inspired by the examples of Sungdare and Pema Dorje, carried loads half again as large as the standard 30 pounds from Camp One to Camp Two. Relations with the New Zealanders warmed considerably, and climbers from the two teams often worked side by side to fix rope up the Lhotse face. The base of operations for the upper mountain soon shifted from Camp One to Camp Two, a site well up the Western Cwm featuring a Weather-port—a rugged, insulated 8-by-16-foot nylon hut providing a comfortable shelter against the elements.

The team's spirit, as well as its small size, spelled an end to Bill's leadership nightmare: each evening, the team sat together for an hour or so and decided what had to be done and who would do it. "It was fantastic," recalls Bill. "The commitment was really there. It was as though the mountain had brought about what was necessary. Instead of an unwieldy, diverse group, we were suddenly a compact, cohesive unit, and that was what we needed."

There is, in fact, some irony in Bill's statement, for there is considerable doubt that the expedition could have continued in any form had it not been for the efforts—and the split—of the larger team. With a supply dump at Camp One large enough for our reduced team size, we could now close the icefall and forget about the most dangerous part of the climb.

## HIGH-SPEED SPINDRIFT

Although most of the team members made one final carry through the icefall after establishing Camp Two, Bill took it upon himself to make three. "It was a really frightening thing to do," he says, "but I felt it was necessary both to show my commitment to the climb and to rebuild the Sherpas' confidence in us."

At the end of September, Bill and I moved up to complete the installation of Camp Three at 23,000 feet (7,010 m), near the bottom of the Geneva Spur, a prominent rock rib on the Lhotse face. Laurie had already set up one of the reinforced box tents that Woods, an outdoor equipment company, had specially made for our use on this steep slope. When we arrived with the two other tents, a pernicious wind buffeted us as we clung to the fixed ropes, hacking out a platform for the tent frames. In our hypoxic states and with high-speed spindrift particles nearly blinding us, it took more than an hour to erect each tent and secure it safely to the ice slope. Bill and I occupied one of them and Lhakpa Tshering and Pema Dorje the other. Bill melted some water with the hanging stove designed by Laurie, which burned a special mixture of butane and propane. We enjoyed a simple

At Camp Three, Bill March prepares a meal on a hanging stove designed by Laurie Skreslet. Laurie also helped design our climbing suits and our rugged ballistics nylon tents. These tents withstood nightly showers of airborne ice chunks, noisy collisions that contributed to our high-altitude sleeplessness.

foil-pouch meal of precooked stew that required minimal preparation and was still tasty enough to appease our finicky appetites. At Camp Two, our cook Pemba had fed us endless bowls of *tsampa*, which is easily digestible at altitude. I chuckled when I thought of the hot Szechuan foods I had wolfed down in restaurants at home and noticed the penchant the Sherpas had, with their Szechuan backgrounds, for swallowing chiles whole.

None of us slept a wink as the incessant wind raked the slopes above, shooting ice chunks down the slopes at us like artillery fire. When the chunks glanced off the tent walls of ballistics nylon, the sound was deafening, making us feel as if we were trapped inside a drum in a Shriners' parade. When we went up to fix rope the next morning, we found that several hundred feet of previously laid rope had been torn off by a spindrift avalanche during the night. While I stopped to replace it, Bill and the Sherpas continued to fix another 800 feet (244 m), halfway up the Geneva Spur. It was a major link of rope, and Bill pushed to his high point that day of 25,500 feet (7,772 m).

## YAK ROUTE

At this stage, the climbing had become as difficult as it was interesting, and we found ourselves negotiating pitch after pitch of steep ice and snow. A few days later, progress became even more difficult with the traverse across rock bands near the top of the Geneva Spur. The rock was so friable that it was doubtful any of the rope anchors would hold if a climber fell. Collectively, we agreed that whoever had named the South Col the "yak route" had never spent a day on the Geneva Spur picking a way across crumbling rock in 60-mile-per-hour (97 kph) wind gusts, shouldering a 30-pound pack. There was no protection should we slip, and our only prospect was a nonstop tumble down the Lhotse face à la Yuichiro Miura, the Japanese speed skier who miraculously survived his 3,000-foot high-speed slide when he fell trying to ski from the South Col. After three days, the team's superstar climber, Sungdare Sherpa, along with Lhakpa Tshering and Al Burgess,

fixed our final rope above the Geneva Spur and the most terrifying part of the climb was over.

Once on the Lhotse face, we used oxygen for the first time. Supplementary oxygen effectively reduces the altitude by 4,000 feet (1,219 m), and I found it helped measurably. Unfortunately, we soon discovered that one of the two types of systems we had bought from the 1981 American medical-research expedition on Everest was unreliable. The diluter-demand system, which theoretically supplied oxygen when a deep inhalation "demanded" it, seemed reluctant to supply oxygen under any circumstances. Even when it did work, however, the 40-pound weight of two oxygen bottles and the breathing apparatus came close to negating the physiological benefits, and there was little room for much else in a pack. Although bulkier and less efficient, the second type of breathing apparatus, which supplied oxygen continuously, worked. Fortunately, each climber needed oxygen for only 2 or 3 of the 50 days spent above Base Camp.

More and more, climbs at extreme altitude are being done without the use of this pulmonary crutch albeit with a dramatic (30 percent) increase in the loss of lives. Frostbite and the threat of irreversible brain damage are the main trade-offs for climbing light above 26,250 feet (8,000 m).

With the South Col tantalizingly close at hand, we suddenly found ourselves confronting a new obstacle. High winds, gusting to more than 100 miles per hour (160 kph), swept over the summit ridge sounding like snarling animals, and we retreated down to Camp Two for four long days, frustrated and totally exhausted. We realized that most of us had spent nearly three weeks above 18,000 feet (5,486 m), an altitude where our bodies had been clinically dying a slow, lingering death, despite a good diet and lots of rest. Lack of oxygen, the resultant sleepless nights, dehydration, sunburn, snow blindness and psychological stress were all taking their toll. With the jet stream howling on the slopes above, we considered returning to Base Camp for a few days' rest before attempting the summit push.

Lloyd, however, was insistent that we

stay on the mountain. "Everybody was so bloody wasted," he remembers, "that if they went down, most of them wouldn't make it back up. We were sitting on top of a full moon, and I knew that a full moon often brings a change in weather. It just had to happen." His intuition was confirmed, for even as we talked, the winds were dying on the ridge above.

## ALIEN BEINGS

The team, finding strength in what we dubbed "summit fever," moved quickly. Laurie, Lloyd and Dave were to go to the final camp, Camp Four, on the South Col at 26,100 feet (7,955 m), using oxygen to help them up the Lhotse face, and every able Sherpa would make a carry. The two strongest climbers, with Sungdare and Lhakpa Dorje, would stay at Camp Four overnight and then, weather permitting, would summit the following day, October 5.

On the morning of October 4, Laurie and the Sherpas left early, with Dave and Lloyd setting a slower pace somewhat behind them. Lloyd, unfortunately, had chosen one of the faulty diluter-demand systems and, once on the Lhotse face, discovered that it was not functioning. After spending an hour at Camp Three trying to fix the apparatus, he abandoned it, resolving to reach the South Col without oxygen, knowing that the Sherpas there had two extra bottles that he could use for the summit push. He felt strong but, without oxygen, was moving slowly, and Dave soon outdistanced him. It was late in the day when Lloyd approached the top of the Geneva Spur and, much to his dismay, found the two oxygen bottles lying in the snow. Obviously, a Sherpa had been unable to carry the 32 pounds any farther and had dumped them.

"That was it for me. I knew there was no spare oxygen above, and I was just too tired to pack it on up myself. I thought about it for a while, but there was just no way around it." He turned back the 300 vertical feet (91 m) from Camp Four, starting down by the light of the moon, keenly aware of the beauty of the view below. After 12 hours of arduous climbing, he had lost his chance for the summit, but his silent thoughts were broken

The south summit of Everest behind them, Bill March and Lhakpa Tshering work in the bitter cold to push the fixed line up the 5,000-foot Lhotse face. It was exhausting but necessary work if we were to haul loads to stock Camp Four at the South Col.

as his radio began to crackle, and he realized his failure to appear at the Col had put the team into a major panic. "It was terrible," says Lloyd. "I could hear them, but because of the rock bands, I couldn't contact them. The Sherpas from Camp Four were about to start down to look for me, and I knew if they came down any distance, there'd be no way they could go for the summit in the morning." Pushing himself hard, he worked down 600 feet (183 m) of rope to a location where he was able to make contact with the climbers at Camp Two who in turn radioed Camp Four. He was all right, he wheezed—not sounding so at all—and told them to call off the search, although Sungdare and Lhakpa Dorje had already been down as far as the Spur looking for him. It was the one moment of intense anxiety experienced by the team on the upper mountain.

At Camp Four, Laurie and Dave prepared for the next morning, sorting out equipment, making hot drinks from melted snow to rehydrate themselves from the day's exertions and to fill a vacuum flask for the following day. Routinely, they took off their boots and tucked them into sleeping bags, putting the insoles into their down sleeping booties so they would be warm and dry in the morning. Adjusting their oxygen regulators to the lowest setting, they donned their masks and made ready to sleep, or at least to lie quietly—alien beings on their own planet.

With only one oxygen mask working properly, Dave opted to wait at the Col, and the next morning at 4:15, he fed Laurie some tea and pushed him out the tent door, encouraging him with his own mantra, "Rock on!" With the temperature hovering at minus 30 degrees F (-34°C), Laurie, Sungdare and Lhakpa Dorje roped up and, by the thin light of their headlamps, began climbing the bare, green-blue ice curving up from the South Col. By 12:30, they were already back at the Col, having set a world record with their eight-hour round trip to the summit. They had put Canada on top of the world. "My major emotion, if I had one at all, was one of relief," Laurie said later. "I did hope, though, that Blair was up there with me."

Slumped over his evening meal with us that night back at Camp Two, Laurie

Psyched up for the top, Laurie Skreslet jumars up the fixed rope near Camp Three on his way to becoming the first Canadian to reach Everest's summit. His success buoyed our spirits and broke the psychological barrier that had threatened us continually after the two fatal accidents. Laurie had hurt his ribs in a fall while helping carry Blair Griffith's body down the mountain and had almost had to sit out the climb at Base Camp. But he managed to recover in time to travel through the Icefall solo, catching up with us as we began our push to the higher camps.

told me, "When I saw that sunrise over Tibet this morning, I thought of you and your Pentax." By this time, I had the only functioning camera and would have given anything to have documented the expedition's summit success and that sunrise.

## EASTER EGG HUNT

If the day had been a triumph for Laurie and our Canadian team, it was no less of a triumph for Sherpa Sungdare. At 25, Sungdare was a quiet, handsome man and the expedition's strongest Sherpa. His climbing career began in 1973, as a 16-year-old mail runner for a Japanese expedition. In 1975, he reached Camp Five on the British Everest Southwest Face expedition, and four years later, he summited for the first time with the German Swabian expedition—but not without paying a heavy price. He and the two climbers with him, American Ray Genet and Hannelore Schmatz, wife of expedition leader Gerhard Schmatz (who himself had summited two days previously), were forced to bivouac without oxygen at 28,000 feet (8,534 m) on the descent, too exhausted to continue. Genet died during the night, and in the morning, Sungdare moved down the mountain and came back with more oxygen. That, too, ran out, and Schmatz collapsed. Sungdare stayed with her until she died; the ordeal cost him four toes. Back on the mountain in 1981, he reached the summit a second time with the American medical-research expedition. Then, with our team, he became the first person to reach the top of Mount Everest three times. In 1985, he surpassed his own record and topped out for the fourth time, with a Norwegian expedition.

The following day, the remaining half of the team mounted a second attempt. Al, Speedy, Dwayne, Pema Dorje, Lhakpa Tshering and I left Camp Two for the 5,000-foot (1,524 m) vertical push with several other Sherpas who would carry gear for us as far as Camp Four. On our way up the face, remnants from the previous summit party's passage appeared here and there, left tied to the fixed line or on the steep slope at the point where the mountain turned a climber back. Our flag bearer, Speedy,

burned out just below the Geneva Spur, having drained his reserve of energy with weeks of dedicated hard work on the lower mountain. Dwayne, an obvious summit candidate himself, made a remarkable carry of two full oxygen bottles all the way to Camp Four without using any himself, selflessly leaving them for Al and me before he descended. (In May 1986, Dwayne finally stood on the top of the mountain when he and Sharon Wood summited from the Tibet side in the Canadian Everest Light expediton.)

When I arrived at Camp Four, I was surprised to find how strong I felt. Laurie's success had broken a psychological barrier for us, and I became more determined than ever to head for the summit the next day and catch a glimpse of that Tibetan sunrise. Al and I sorted through three decades' worth of brightly coloured oxygen cylinders that littered the broad saddle like flowers in an alpine meadow. Using a wrench that Al had carried up and our regulators, we tested those that had gas left in them and set aside two half-empty ones for me. Al would use a single one that was still nearly full and rely on using one of the Sherpa's two cylinders if his ran out. The Polish winter expedition of 1979-80, not having the resources of our team, had tooled a range of fittings for their breathing apparatus and had carried them to the Col, where they went on an Easter egg hunt just as we did. It was a clever gamble that saved them both money and precious energy.

I had shot video all the way up the Lhotse face, across the steep, horribly rotten rock of the Geneva Spur and to the camp on the Col. But, despite the fact that I had crammed the heavy batteries inside my pockets to keep them warm, the recorder itself was frozen solid. Although I had relished the thought of being able to film summit day, it was with some relief that I realized I would have to leave this extra weight behind. I had to slip the pick of my ice axe into the workings of the expensive camera to pry the videotape out.

Al and I spent the night in one tent, the Sherpas in the other. Whoever had used my side of the tent in the previous party had forgotten to take his crampons off, and the inflatable mattress was just a flat piece of fabric draped over the cold steel

**W**ithin a day of the summit, Al Burgess sorts through his oxygen equipment on the South Col. His choice of a diluter-demand breathing apparatus, a system that had been troublesome lower down the mountain, was to prove a fateful mistake.

of half-a-dozen oxygen cylinders that had been left on the floor of the tent as ballast to keep it from blowing away. With one of the salvaged bottles feeding me a trickle of oxygen, my back sought unsuccessfully to conform to the corrugated sleeping platform, and I dozed on and off until the gas ran out in the middle of the night.

## SUMMIT DEFEAT

At 5:20 on the morning of October 7, the four of us set out, following the blown-in tracks set by Laurie's team two days earlier. Starting at my usual slow but steady pace, I found myself unable to keep up with the other three and untied myself from the rope. Because we had started an hour later than Laurie's team, the Sherpas were anxious to make up for lost time. The mountain had been soloed before on this last stretch, so I was not concerned about being alone. Within half an hour, my body woke up, and I began to feel as strong as I had on summit days of lesser mountains, as if the mountain had finally decided to give me back some of the energy I had put into it.

On a short, steep pitch, I overtook the other three who had by this time slowed down. Resting on a rock ledge above, I looked back to see Al and the Sherpas huddled below, working on his oxygen set. It was a diluter-demand system that had predictably failed when needed most. I had opted for Laurie's less sophisticated set, knowing that it had taken him up the mountain and would likely work again. The three toiled for nearly an hour to get Al's set working again, but their efforts were to no avail. Al waved up to me and turned back to Camp Four, resigned to his second disappointing defeat on the mountain within one year, the first having been with an unsuccessful British expedition on the West Ridge. As a sahib, or Western, client, he could have requested one of the Sherpas' sets, but he refused that option, even though they would have many more opportunities than he to reach the top in the future.

It was an honourable act, but my memory of the scene has been soured as a result of Al's embittered account of the expedition in the team's official book.

The authorship had been conveniently designated to him as a result of an agreement negotiated between the Everest Society and Roger Marshall upon his departure from the team. Written with the assistance of a Calgary advertising copywriter, it was the story of the world's most gifted climber who deserved to make it to the top of Everest but didn't. In the book, he slammed the leadership and ignored the team effort that had gotten us all to our personal high points. He even intimated that he had expected me to abandon my own bid and give him my oxygen.

At precisely this stage during Reinhold Messner and Peter Habeler's oxygenless attempt on the mountain in 1978, Messner had mused: "It may be hard to understand, but up here, anyone who has aspirations to reach the top cannot help but feel some envy toward those who do. We try and keep such anxieties from our conversation, but if it should really come about that we no longer have any chance of success, then there would inevitably be a measure of criticism of the expedition leadership. We would need then to be able to blame this misfortune upon somebody or other."

The Sherpas moved up to me and tied in. I began to lead, gaining strength the higher I went, feeling like a hockey player on a wild-ass breakaway with an open net in front of me. The ice soon yielded to wind-crusted snow, and we found where Laurie had punched through the brittle veneer, floundering up to his knees. His tracks had blown in, and it was frustrating, heavy going. In the worst sections, even with oxygen, I had to stop and rest every five steps. Often, I'd turn around and ask how my partners were doing and would always get a steady thumbs-up signal. Again, I would push myself for the next five minutes, the next thirty steps, the next five steps . . . whatever I could handle. When we came to the slumped-over figure of Hannelore Schmatz frozen into the ice, all three of us crouched beside her and shared her silence, looking down at the eternal view she had onto the Rongbuk Valley. Her husband had offered a reward for the retrieval of her body, but I couldn't think of a finer resting place for a climber.

Shortly afterward, we passed the wind-scoured site of Camp Five at 27,880 feet (8,498 m), the launching site for most summit attempts of years gone by. Because we had spent so much time on the upper mountain, we had exhausted ourselves and our supplies to the point where we had to make a single push all the way from the Col. It reminded me of the excitement of our McKinley trip, where all the team members had given their best, not sure of their own potential. After nearly two months of drudgery, the joy of climbing was rushing back into my life.

Much of the summit ridge was corniced, and at times, we would be working so close to the edge that our ice axes would punch through the lip, leaving small holes with a clear view into space. The climbing was surprisingly demanding, and I remember thinking at one point that I was very glad all three of us knew what we were doing. A fall offered two alternatives: an 8,000-foot (2,438 m) tumble into either Nepal or Tibet.

## ONE STEP AT A TIME

The final hurdle was a 25-foot (8 m) vertical snow-and-rock pitch known as the Hillary Step. At sea level, it would be nothing; at 28,800 feet (8,778 m), it is a heartbreaker. As Laurie had described it, "Put on a snowmobile suit, big boots, heavy mitts, a face mask, steamed-up goggles, a tuque that slides down over your eyes and a 40-pound pack, then have someone knock the wind out of you and see if you can climb your own back fence." From the crampon marks, I could see where Laurie had fought his way up the right side of the step, one foot on loose, insubstantial snow and the other on steep, crumbly rock. Avoiding this, I swung up onto the left side of the rock and found to my delight that each move was rewarded with solid purchase for my scratching crampon points.

It was not until we reached the top of the step that I started to think of the actual summit, and when I did see it, I could not convince myself that in a few minutes, I would actually be standing there. Even in these last few moments, there were so many things that could go wrong—we were so extended—that it was just one step at a time, one step higher.

Laurie Skreslet had told us about the sunrise over Tibet, and I shared it with Lhakpa Tshering and Pema Dorje as we set out early on October 7 from the South Col. While not a particularly difficult pitch, it was steep, and I found it exhausting work slogging up through the snow. Not being able to keep up to the others' pace at first, I untied myself from their rope and let them go ahead, convinced that I could climb this last stretch solo if I had to.

At 11:30 a.m., arm-in-arm, we at last stepped onto the summit. All of a sudden, the hammering inside my skull stopped and was replaced by an overwhelming sense of well-being that swept over me, far stronger than any previous summit jubilation I had experienced. It was a fleeting moment for me, and having to concentrate so carefully on every movement as I did, I had to wait until I got down to reflect on the accomplishment. A month later, during an expedition slide show, when I first saw the photographs I had taken at the top, I was startled by a flood of emotions that I had not experienced at the time.

Except for Laurie's spent oxygen cylinder adorned with the happy faces Dave had inscribed on it, we found the summit wedge of pristine snow unblemished by climbers' memorabilia, the fierce jet stream having scoured it clean. Even the sturdy aluminum tripod left by the Chinese in 1975 was missing—buried or blown away. To the west, the Earth's curvature was emphasized by the diminishing size of mountains as they blended into the high plateau of Tibet; visibility was easily 100 miles in every direction. It was as though we were in a hot-air balloon, peering down on the tops of cumulus clouds two miles below. It was, quite simply, one of the most spectacular places I've been.

My photographer's ethic burned through my sluggish brain, and I painstakingly took one exposure after another. Pema Dorje took my picture with my oxygen mask and headgear peeled off. Within seconds, I was reaching for my mask. As we prepared to leave the summit, the Sherpas told me that they had forgotten to bring an offering for the gods: did I have anything we might leave? Keenly aware of my own position in the world at this juncture, I searched my pockets. As we started down, the last of my food, a Kit Kat chocolate bar, lay nestled in its bright wrapper in the summit snows.

Having met climbing's crowning challenge to stand atop the world and having prevailed against Chomolungma's defiant spirit, we descended slowly to the South Col. The final steep pitch below the south summit nearly proved to be our undoing.

The lenses of our snow goggles had been frost-covered most of the way to the top, and Pema Dorje had been propping his onto his forehead to see where he was going. Now, he was partially snow-blind and was not entirely sure of his footing. In one terrifying instant, the crumbly, treacherous snow surface gave way as he lowered his weight onto the next foothold. His crampons flailed uselessly in the air, and he shot off on a short tether of rope. Lhakpa Tshering and I were directly above him and could see it coming, and so we dug our axes in, in a self-arrest position. This happened twice, and both times, we were able to catch him before he could build up enough momentum to pull us down.

Somewhere below, approaching Camp Two in the gathering dark, I felt myself slip into a daze of elation and fatigue that would keep me sleepless for three days. Still, for the moment, I watched my feet, taking—as I had for six long weeks—one step at a time.

## ROUND-TRIP CLIMB

The push from Camp Two at 21,000 feet (6,400 m) to the summit of Everest had taken only two days round trip. And within 24 hours of our being on top, my Sherpa buddies and I were languishing in Base Camp, Pema Dorje in considerable pain due to the snow blindness he had contracted on summit day.

As we had descended through the Khumbu Icefall, we saw that whole sections of it had collapsed, springing ladders and ropes. It resembled the disastrous aftermath of a tornado. At the time, however, we had set our sights on Base Camp and were inured to marching through this icy minefield.

Stephen, Lloyd and Bruce came up to greet us at the foot of the icefall with a can of cold *cerveza*, compliments of the Catalans. After warm embraces, we stumbled back down the rocky moraine, tears of joy and sadness staining our shirts. I joined in a subdued celebration with my teammates, some still exhausted from three weeks up on the mountain and the others worn out with the insidious mixture of boredom and suspense of waiting at Base Camp. Peter had already started to dismantle camp and had sent a yak caravan into the valley with our extra gear and food. There was

**P**artway up the summit ridge, I turned to survey Lhotse (right) and Makalu, the world's fourth and sixth highest peaks, respectively. Below me, Al Burgess and the Sherpas were frantically trying to get his frozen oxygen system to function. They gave up after an hour, leaving Al, frustrated and disappointed, to return to Camp Two.

I t was not until we had climbed past the mountain's last hurdle, the rocky Hillary Step, midway along the ridge between the south and main summits, that I realized how close we actually were to the top. Only 25 feet high, it is a near-vertical snow-and-rock pitch that can be a heartbreaker for exhausted summit hopefuls.

little need to stick around any longer, so we sat down for our final Base Camp dinner. Having subsisted on a relatively bland diet on the upper mountain, I foolishly gorged myself on such exotica as canned trout in red wine sauce and olives washed down with beer. But my body was quick to reject this rich fare, and for the next couple of days, I stuck to a more rigorous regimen.

Bill and I left the next day for Namche Bazaar. We stopped off near Lobuche to help the others build a chorten (stone cairn) in memory of Blair Griffiths, Ang Tsultim, Dawa Dorje and Pasang Sona, set on a hillside studded with other simple memorials. The heft of every stone I picked up drove home to me the weight of our loss.

## BACK TO THE REAL WORLD

Our original plans had called for a live broadcast from the summit, but our specially rigged camera's batteries had died at Camp Two. (It was a year later that an American team with cameraman David Breashears managed to accomplish this same goal, transmitting frosty smiles into the living rooms of his compatriots from one of the least accessible points on Earth.) But early the next morning, I joined Laurie at an improvised studio set up near Kunde, just above Namche, and from the comfort of a balcony on the Japanese-built Everest View Hotel, we squinted into a camera lens to make contact with the outside world via newsman Ted Koppel, direct from Washington, D.C., for the ABC television programme *Nightline*. Having passed several friends on the trail the day before, including my friend Karen Paynter and my sister Linda, en route for a look at Everest, I was rapidly being reintroduced to the world I had left several months before.

Oddly enough, my mind was not tuned to getting back to normal but, rather, to directing my new-found energy and exhilaration. After two months of oxygen-thin air and weeks of high-tension exhaustion, I was gaining strength with every stride down the valley, and I wanted to focus it on something. The fantasy of a grand slam that had begun in that storm-bound tent on Aconcagua became an obsession.

I had already been to the top of North America's Mount McKinley (20,320 feet/6,194 m), South America's Mount Aconcagua (22,831 feet/6,959 m), and now, Asia's Mount Everest (29,028 feet/8,848 m). Those that beckoned were Europe's Mount Elbrus (18,481 feet/5,633 m) in Russia, Africa's Mount Kilimanjaro (19,340 feet/5,894 m) in Tanzania, Australasia's Carstensz Pyramid (16,023 feet/4,884 m) and Antarctica's remote Vinson Massif (16,067 feet/4,897 m).

The fact that I could become the first person in the world to accomplish the grand slam was in itself intriguing, although that alone was not reason enough to proceed. In mountaineering circles, there were more challenging peaks, but these seven particular summits were part of a cohesive theme that suited me well. It was a global project that offered much more than thousands of feet of snow and bitter cold, for in the shadows of those mountains were cultures and countrysides I had never seen before. Some claim that the Age of Discovery is long past and that space and the recesses of the mind are the last frontiers for true exploration. But I was convinced that there was a lot of territory left between the two. The mountains would simply be my passport to high adventure, and I would be able to finance most of my travels with photographs.

A few days later, back at the Rum Doodle restaurant in Kathmandu, I celebrated my thirtieth birthday with my teammates, Linda, Karen and other friends who had come to Nepal to seek the mountain experience on their own terms. It was a noisy celebration of life and marked an important beginning for me.

Our return to Canada was greeted with a flurry of public attention and was reported by news media that had forgotten the earlier controversy it had helped to create. Almost immediately after stepping off the plane in Calgary, we sat down in an audience with the press for a powerful audiovisual show hurriedly assembled by Montreal's Programmed Communications. It was an odd feeling to be seated in an auditorium, clothed in our bright red Air Canada outfits, only 10 days away from the mountain, watching photographs of ourselves, mixed with

Lhakpa Tshering, ice axe raised in victory, and Pema Dorje cling to the small snowy platform that is the highest point of the world, Tibet spread out behind them. It was a first Everest ascent for all three of us and Pema Dorje's first major climb.

the music of Nepal, in a setting that already seemed light-years away.

Without allowing any time for proper reentry into our culture, I would spend most of the next six weeks on the Ottawa, Toronto and Montreal banquet/publicity circuit, stealing as much time as possible to sift through the 4,000 photographs I had taken on the climb.

## THE NEXT LEG

They were heady days for all of us—lunch with Prime Minister Trudeau and dozens of speaking engagements—and it was gratifying to see that my photographs were in demand. The National Film Board put together a travelling exhibit of prints that was booked solid until 1986; the CBC used the footage I had shot up to the South Col and my stills from there to the summit in a one-hour television special; and *Equinox* magazine ran 28 pages of my work in their January/February 1983 issue. The extra effort I had made to get usable photographs had paid off.

As the expedition's official photographer, I had conscientiously taken pictures of a long list of sponsors' products in use on the mountain, but unfortunately, only a few took advantage of their association with our successful climb. While it did not bother me much at the time, I later realized that their failure to promote their involvement cost me future sponsors for my seven-summits bid. The conservative Canadian business community, having missed the boat on the Everest expedition, shied away a second time from an enterprise that smacked of adventure.

Between CanEverEx engagements, I stayed with friends near Camden East, the eastern Ontario home of *Equinox* magazine, where I worked together with writer Bart Robinson, tailoring the Canadian Everest story for the magazine. Publisher James Lawrence showed great enthusiasm for the seven-summits project and immediately pledged his support, with an offer beyond my wildest expectations. In return for a series of articles, he funded climbs in Europe and Africa and provided seed money for my Antarctic climb. His encouragement gave me the confidence to embark on the project that would con-

sume the next 3½ years of my life, and we all blindly chose to assume that the required $250,000 for an Antarctic expedition would come as easily.

Not until I had set the project in motion did I realize just how many others had set their sights on the same goal. Reinhold Messner, Gerhard Schmatz and Naomi Uemura were each in the running and looking for ways to reach the most elusive peak of all, Vinson Massif. Just that year, 1983, Americans Dick Bass, who owned coal interests in Alaska and the Snowbird ski resort in Utah, and his partner Frank Wells, president of Warner Brothers, had entered the grand-slam sweepstakes. Newcomers to the sport, the wealthy middle-aged businessmen stepped off their corporate ladders to try to climb all seven mountains in one year. Seen as black sheep by their corporate colleagues, Bass and Wells brought to the project the type of élan that had been lacking in the climbing world since the days of steam, when climbing was a rich man's sport and an expedition to the Himalayas could take a year or two. In this age of jets, the financially independent Bass and Wells were able to take an important time-saving shortcut because they did not have to search for sponsors. They surrounded themselves with the best climbing guides available, who led them in safety up the mountains and prepared their camps and meals.

Their interest in the seven summits threatened to turn the project into a race for the benefit of sponsors and the media, but I was determined to play down the competition angle. We were each climbing for our own reasons, and I did not think that one person's accomplishments should diminish anyone else's.

As the post-Everest madness subsided, I began to plan my 1983 itinerary. Karen and I had ended our relationship during the frantic days of November. During my weeks in eastern Canada, I began to form a strong friendship with Baiba Auders, an occupational therapist at the Ottawa Children's Hospital and the younger sister of my friend Uldis. Sensing that our destinies were about to mesh, I invited Baiba to join me and writer-adventurer Jeremy Schmidt of Flagstaff, Arizona, on assignment for *Equinox*, on the next leg of my seven-summits journey.

There were several tense moments on the way down the South Col. Pema Dorje was suffering from snow blindness and almost slipped into space twice. Fortunately, since we were roped together, Lhakpa Tshering and I were able to catch him both times, and we descended safely to Camp Two.

Pema Dorje

**P**ushing my snow goggles up for a few seconds, I posed for the requisite summit photographs with Lhakpa Tshering. Not as well equipped as I had supposed, we had brought no offering for the gods and finally left a chocolate bar on top of the snow. After several minutes, we headed back down, mindful that the mountain claims its victims going down as well as up.

Glacier-carved cirques in the Caucasus Mountains in the southwestern
Soviet Union are reminiscent of the Swiss
Alps. A month later, we got a taste of the
tropics as we descended through the
lush undergrowth of the southern slopes
of Kilimanjaro, Africa's highest mountain.

# Elbrus & Kilimanjaro
## Soviet summits and African plains

Getting away from it all, Soviet style. These tourists, with kerchiefs for sun shade, take their collective habits to the mountains with them. Fortunate to be granted a holiday at the Hotel Cheget, a Caucasus ski resort 64 miles from the Black Sea, these Eastern Bloc and Russian citizens were issued drab "mountain clothing" upon their arrival and then spent two weeks participating in a series of recreational activities that ranged from day trips on the lower slopes of Mount Elbrus to skiing and sing-alongs.

The 10-storey Russian Hotel Cheget was the most unlikely "Base Camp" I could ever have anticipated. Located in the Soviet Caucasus Mountains at the foot of a ski area in the Baksan Valley, a fast-developing resort area with three hotel complexes, the hotel's setting was every bit as impressive as anything I had seen in the western Alps, only on a grander scale. The mountains were several thousand feet higher than their French and Swiss counterparts and were just as charming, for they, too, were punctuated by green valleys and picturesque villages.

It was July, and the valley was crowded with vacationing Russians hoping to combine days of hiking and climbing with whatever nightlife the resort offered. Discos played loudly into the night at the hotels, while corner bistros featured unsophisticated light shows to the beat of vintage American rock music—Jimi Hendrix, Deep Purple and Janis Joplin live on in the Baksan Valley. Vendors hawked souvenirs, and roadside stands sold beer and shish kebabs, known as *shashlik*, while a small market offered fruits and vegetables as well as locally spun and knitted wool sweaters. Most people belonged to groups organized by trade unions or tourist agencies, as part of the "Mountain Tourism on Foot" programme, and it was not uncommon to see a file of 40 to 50 people happily trailing behind a leader along the numerous mountain paths, doing morning calisthenics in front of the hotel or standing in orderly formation while being led in song. These were odd concepts for our small, uncollectivized threesome from the West.

Accompanied by Baiba Auders and writer Jeremy Schmidt, I had come here to climb Europe's highest peak, 18,481-foot (5,633 m) Mount Elbrus. Through the services of California's Mountain Travel Company, we had booked into one of the International Mountaineering Camps that is offered annually by the U.S.S.R. Sports Committee in the Caucasus, the Pamir, the Tien Shan and the Altai mountains. The $920 (U.S.) package was perfectly suited to our modest budget. The cost of the 25-day Caucasus camp covered virtually all the expenses we would incur during our stay—meals, lodging, interpreter services, medical treatment, air and land transportation. We were also entitled to a sight-seeing tour of Moscow.

## BASE CAMP HOTEL

It was eight months after Everest. My feelings of "summit high" had been prolonged by joining some friends in February for a six-week tour of the Alps performing telemark ski demonstrations for the Karhu ski company. But my hedonistic days on the slopes had ended with a torn medial meniscus that resulted in a knee operation and a month-long recuperation in British Columbia. Now, with both my CanEverEx obligations and days of rest behind me, I was anxious to plunge into the seven-summits project.

After a one-day stopover in the Russian capital, we were rushed to the Moscow airport at 6 a.m., only to wait two hours for our jet to arrive from another destination, one of the typical hurry-up-and-wait syndromes encountered in any country with a surplus of bureaucracy.

We used the delay as a chance to meet some of our fellow climbers while sitting in the airport restaurant sipping coffee. There were 11 Westerners—two Britons, three Americans, four Catalans and two Canadians—amid 72 hardcore climbers from the Eastern Bloc who had come with big plans and relentless spirits.

We finally set out for the mountains, and after a two-hour flight on a rattling Aeroflot jet, we landed in the southern provincial town of Mineral'nyje Vody (meaning mineral water). After further confusion and waiting, we embarked on a four-hour ride southward along the Baksan River into the heart of the Caucasus. Our three buses, crammed with people, gear and backpacks, were operated by demonic drivers who relied on high-speed tactics to pass the slower, more conservative vehicles on the narrow, twisting roads. A busload of foreigners seems to arouse the racing instincts of every bus driver worldwide, and their madcap antics ensured we could not pay undue attention to the increasingly dramatic alpine scenery.

Upon arriving at our Base Camp hotel, we were assigned to our rooms and invited to a meeting where the rules and protocol of the camp were explained. There, we met our designated "coach," who would help us decide how to spend the rest of our stay.

Our plan was to climb Mount Elbrus, an extinct double-coned volcano, and then to spend as much time as possible in the neighbouring mountain region of the Georgian Soviet Socialist Republic, called Svanetia. Elbrus, with its upper 7,000 feet (2,133 m) coated with permanent snow and glaciers, presented no special technical problems to us, so we hoped to polish it off in a few days and then concentrate on exploring the exotic locale.

The next day, we rode a tramway and a chair lift that service the area to almost 12,000 feet (3,657 m), then slapped synthetic climbing skins on the base of our telemark skis and plodded past the summer training ground of the Georgian ski team. There were perhaps a hundred skiers, most of them on various Polish-made facsimiles of brand-name alpine skis. We tried to ski their gates, but the direct rays of the midday sun had turned the snow into cartilage-tearing mush. Having just recovered from my second knee operation in three years, I realized with some trepidation that I couldn't afford another injury, and we abandoned our attempts. We continued almost two more miles to Priut Hut, at 13,780 feet (4,200 m).

Sprawled outside the great aluminum-walled sausage-shaped structure were a few of its 60 Russian guests, hikers stripped down to their bathing suits intent on making the most of the fleeting sunlight and their summer holidays. They had come uniformly dressed in khaki-green pants and jackets supplied to them by their tour guides and had carried day packs with essentials such as bikinis, cigarettes and playing cards. They would stay the night at the hut and would be ousted the following day by another platoon of fun seekers.

Our naive misconception that a peak only 64 miles from the tepid Black Sea would be balmy itself, especially in July, proved wrong. Additionally, the fact that the 43-degree latitude corresponds with northern California, with prevailing southerly winds coming in from Turkey and the Mediterranean, was misleading. We quickly discovered that the innocuous-looking Elbrus, nestled in the im-

The classic twin summits of Mount Ushba (15,453 feet), resembling two Matterhorns that have been welded together, beckon climbers to rise above the clouds. Deceived by the area's proximity to the Black Sea, we were surprised at the ferocious summer storms that hit this region.

pressive 600-mile-long chain of mountains that divides Europe from Asia Minor, can be a seething cauldron of ferocious storms with a vindictive temperament. Even in the midst of summer, temperatures at the shelter often fell below freezing, and the wind never abated. The clouds, heavy with moisture, did their best to replenish the permanent snow cover in the range, and we quickly came to appreciate our fellow guests' frantic attempts at tanning.

We waited for three days to make our climb, twice starting out in the middle of the night under deceptively clear skies only to grope our way back in hasty retreat through whiteout conditions. Tennyson's lines "Cold upon the dead volcano / Sleeps the gleam of dying day" came to mind but were dismissed when we realized that the only thing which gleamed on this mountain were the lightning rods on the hut.

On one of our epic retreats from the malicious weather, we stopped by a camp of friendly Ukrainians who had pitched their tents in a notch just above the hut. Using their collective vocabulary of about 20 English words, they insisted we share a hearty homemade soup, which was served with hand-carved wooden spoons that were as ornately painted as traditional Ukrainian Easter eggs. They soon had us roaring with laughter at their good-natured antics. We huddled together under a plastic tarp as the hailstones began to pelt down, while the leader of the group, a doctor with a size 15 tricouni-nailed climbing boot, mocked our leather telemark boots, which he considered as old-fashioned as his own. As I got up to leave, the skis that I was now carrying upright on the sides of my pack caught a surge of electricity from the air as it arced from the metal edge of the ski, and I felt a stab of pain in the top of my shoulder. Despite the lightning risk, the Ukrainians refused to move to the hut from their camp on the exposed ridge, and for the rest of the night, we worried about their welfare.

After several days in the hut, we dubbed it Typhoid Tower, for the "outhouse" on the main floor had rendered the whole bottom area uninhabitable. Its outside replacement, requiring an exit into the howling winds, offered only a

Thoroughly enjoying their whirlwind vacation, these Latvian tourists spent one night at Priut Hut (background), which we later dubbed Typhoid Tower in recognition of its less-than-adequate plumbing. Baiba Auders' Latvian heritage and command of the language made us instant friends of this couple, and we spent part of a day on the slopes with them. Bad weather kept us at the hut for days as we waited for a chance to get up to the summit.

minor improvement. With frequent glances outdoors for signs of meteorological stability, we read, wrote and played endless games with my set of dice, which were already elaborately veined with lines of stress from overuse at the Everest Base Camp.

Seeing no window in the weather, we admitted only temporary defeat and withdrew to the Hotel Cheget. Within four hours, we were curled up in front of a massive rock fireplace in the lobby with another new friend, camp administrative assistant Mischa Rostov. Not only did he speak English well, but he also understood the nuances of the Western world. He had been trained as an engineer but was in the process of registering at a Moscow university to study his first love, literature. It seemed that he had already read more in English than the three of us put together, and he showed an insatiable interest in our perceptions of how close to reality the writers had been in depicting Western life.

Mischa, sensitive to our unspoken needs, steered us to an espresso café in the wings of the hotel. Although Georgian black tea appeared at every meal, coffee was always conspicuously absent. We sipped the precious liquid with the full appreciation it deserved, as conversation carried us into the evening. Later, we moved downstairs to the basement pub and stayed until its closing hour of 11 p.m., convinced that the East-West political stalemate could have easily been resolved if left to us.

When Mischa introduced us to the camp organizers, I instantly recognized Valentin Ivanov. I had met him six years before on Mount McKinley and learned that he had been one of 11 summiteers on the Russian climb of Everest in the 1982 pre-monsoon season, prior to our own post-monsoon climb. He arranged for a slide show of their impressive new route on the southwest face. It hardly looked like the same mountain I had been on, and they had strengthened their claim on the extremely technical route by putting a couple of climbers on the summit without the auxiliary use of oxygen.

The Soviet Union has a well-defined and interesting history of climbing, much of it in the Caucasus. As early as 1829, the eastern peak of Elbrus was said to have been climbed by the Kabard mountaineer Killar Khashirov, while the slightly higher west summit was reached in 1874 by English climbers Frederick Gardiner, Crawford F. Grove and Horace Walker in the company of Matterhorn guide Peter Knubel. Later, the 1920s saw the golden age of alpine exploration and achievement, beginning with the founding of associations that oversaw climbing endeavours. Unfortunately, shortly thereafter, two fatal accidents befell solo climbers, and strict regimentation of the sport was enforced that permitted only group climbing. In the summer of 1935, more than 2,000 people are said to have climbed Elbrus, and by the summer of 1937, alpine training centres existed in the Adil-Su and Baksan valleys near Elbrus.

Soviets interested in mountain climbing must participate in an alpine training programme, regarded by the authorities as an important system of physical strengthening. The title "Alpinist of the U.S.S.R." was authorized by the Central Executive Committee and introduced in 1937. Through central control, climbing became a mass affair, while the risk of accidents was minimized. Before a climb, each group submits its plans for approval and then reports to control posts maintained by the Mountain Rescue Service. Over 600,000 Soviet citizens have completed some alpine training, and over 1,000 alpinists have earned the title "Master of Sport."

In the month following our visit to the Caucasus, the All-Union Alpine Speed-Climbing Championships, first held in 1965, were to take place on a peak near Elbrus. The concept of speed climbing up granite faces was first developed in the Caucasus in 1945 by climbing-camp director Ivan Antonovitch, who saw that speed was essential in areas where the weather changes as quickly as it does on Elbrus. Competition and prizes also evoke great enthusiasm in the spectators, and there is no danger to the climber, who is safely secured by a steel cable in case of a fall. The paradox, of course, is that in North America, the mountains are usually regarded as a haven of refuge from the pressures of our workaday society. However, in a world that constantly strives for new avenues of competition and organized

challenge, it would be sad to see climbing go the way of cross-country skiing, which began as a form of recreation and transportation but is now part of the mainstream pursuit of gold at events such as the Olympics and World Cup Championships.

Viktor Markelov, who had been assigned to coach us, was one of the Soviet Union's current speed-climbing champions and was often confounded by the spectacle of us stretched out in an aromatic field of alpine flowers, staring complacently into space when we could have been speed climbing through life. Stronger than his aggressive competitiveness, however, was an underlying quick wit and energetic gusto that remained a source of pleasure for us.

## SVANETIA TREK

Despite the regimentation and emphasis on order, the atmosphere around the camp was agreeably lighthearted. Mealtimes in the cafeteria, especially, proved to be occasions for merriment, as all those who were not out climbing convened in the huge hall with its floor-to-ceiling windows. Tales of adventure were shared as we devoured meals of smoked sturgeon, cabbage soup, fresh vegetables, heavy rye bread, potatoes, rice and meat—three times a day!

As we dined in the evening, a band from Leningrad provided background music. The heavy-metal sounds were out of the 1970s, but while I found it exciting and an effective aid to digestion, Baiba, with her background in classical piano, winced occasionally between mouthfuls. Dinner was invariably followed by dancing with the Russian tourists who had filtered up the stairs. Mischa confirmed the popularity of rock 'n' roll in his nation's capital. Bootleg albums from the West make their way into an underground market and take their place beside domestic rock produced by bands in Czechoslovakia, Hungary and Poland.

While there was no shortage of fascinating guests at the camp, we were growing increasingly frustrated with our run of bad luck with the weather. Accordingly, Viktor Markelov and Svetlana Kravetz, our interpreter, suggested that we make our trek into Svanetia while

waiting for better conditions. We needed little convincing and immediately began preparing our packs. By the time we were ready to leave, our group had expanded to 12 to include not only Baiba, Jeremy and me, but the two other Americans and the Catalans.

The key to the success of our trip was indisputably Lado Gurchiani, a native of Mazeri, the first town we would reach in Svanetia. His knowledge of the local customs and the language, which is different from both Russian and Georgian, would ensure our acceptance by Svanetian society, but little did we realize the extent of his popularity and the sphere of his influence. He seemed to be related to almost everyone we met along the way, and this meant that we were welcome in any household. One of the top climbers in the U.S.S.R., Lado was also a Master of Sport and is now living in Tbilisi, the capital of Georgia.

Measuring roughly 70 by 30 miles, Svanetia is politically a part of the Georgian Soviet Socialist Republic. Culturally, though, it is still a world of its own, protected by formidable mountains that have resisted an endless chronology of invaders throughout history. The Caspian Sea, Iran and Asia lie to the east. To the west is the Black Sea, which provides access to the Mediterranean and Europe.

Svanetia has always been a melting pot of ethnic diversity. Ancient Arabs called the Caucasus "the mountains of a thousand languages," while in the first century, Pliny wrote, "We Romans conducted our affairs there with the aid of 130 interpreters." To the Greeks, the Caucasus were the end of the world, a region of mystery and romance.

The Romans came here under Augustus and were followed by Persians, Arabs, Tartars, Turks and Slavs. All left their mark, but none dominated for long. The tempests of war thundered past, as this vast mountain borderland between Europe and Asia became the refuge of successive waves of immigrants. Some cultures found a place of their own high in the mountains; others were absorbed by hill tribes and became lost to the world. The natural defences of these mountains resisted even the efforts of Genghis Khan and the Crusaders.

Russian aggression against the peo-

Jeremy Schmidt blasts down the gentle lower slopes of Elbrus, near Priut Hut, on perfect corn snow. Gazing across at the scores of challenging ridges and faces that were available to climbers, we realized why so many Russian climbers choose the Caucasus for training. Rising up to 3,000 feet higher than their Alpine counterparts, the Caucasus are one of the most beautiful ranges that I have visited, and it was somewhat frustrating to be kept off their peaks by bad weather.

Giving up on an Elbrus attempt for the time being, we headed into the Betsho Valley in the company of two Americans, including Pat Baker (above) and four Catalan climbers. Below the high Betsho Pass, the valley opened up into lush subalpine meadow, alive with the sound of cowbells and bleating sheep.

ples of the Caucasus began early in the 18th century during the reign of Peter the Great and continued with various degrees of ruthlessness over the next 200 years. Resistance to invasion has long been a characteristic of these defiant mountain people who even in the earliest centuries were described as "free citizens," but the military strength of the Soviet Union proved too powerful, and the Red Army invaded in 1921.

A new era unfolded in Svanetia in 1937 when the first road—and consequently the concept of the automobile —penetrated this mountain-locked region through the canyon of the Ingur River. For centuries, the only way in or out had been on foot, over high passes that were covered with snow for most of the year. It was in this extreme isolation that a bizarre and violent society evolved, based on the premise that no official authority was greater than the individual and that crime could be controlled through reciprocal suppression of criminals. In other words, murderers would keep each other in check as the unwritten law became "an eye for an eye, a tooth for a tooth." Each family was protected by a fortress—a stone defence tower rising 50 to 80 feet—connected to the house by a walkway that could be destroyed or closed off in case of attack. By all accounts, the fortresses were in constant use. Today, these towers—as many as 70 in a single village—are the architectural landmarks of the country, oddly reminiscent of the Italian mountain villages of Tuscany.

During the 18th and 19th centuries, there was no authority, either internal or external, to interfere with the business of domestic warfare, and by the time this lawlessness reached its zenith in the early 19th century, virtually every man in Svanetia had killed someone or had at least tried to. Between 1917 and 1921, during a brief period of independence regained from the Russians, there were about 600 murders by vendetta.

When British traveller Douglas Freshfield passed through the area in the 1880s, he wrote: "They were as lawless as the Cyclops of the *Odyssey*. They knew no restraint to their passions. No man could call either his wife or his house his own except insofar as he could defend them by force. The right of mur-

A Svanetian vendor in the small produce market in the village of Mestia takes a break from selling vegetables grown on the Caucasus' high valley farmsteads. Locked in on all sides by the mountains, Svanetia is a world apart from Soviet Georgia, to which it was annexed in 1921. Outside influences did not make any real advances until a road into the area was completed in 1937, and even now, the area remains relatively unchanged from past centuries.

der was the foundation of society. . . . When roused to passion, the Svan will occasionally use his dagger in open fight—I have more than once seen daggers drawn—but he prefers the safety of a neighbouring thicket, whence he can take a deliberate aim, with the help of his forked gun rest, and shoot his enemy unobserved." It was hard to believe that such mindless acts of terror had in the not-too-distant past reigned in this idyllic mountain setting.

## EPIC CROSSING

We set off late in the afternoon (Elbrus defiantly clear in a blue sky), moving up the Ozengi Valley to Betsho Pass, roughly six miles away and 5,000 feet (1,524 m) above our starting point by the Baksan River. We climbed steeply through a dense pine forest into perfumed meadows blazing with the rainbow-coloured blossoms of lupines, azaleas, marguerites, gentians and campanulas. Far above, the glaciers of Donguz-orun glistened in the setting sun.

As the valley opened up into lush subalpine meadow, the distant sound of cowbells and bleating sheep could be heard over the roar of the river torrent, choked by milky glacial runoff. Perched on grassy knolls were the tents and stone huts of shepherds.

From a camp beside an immense lateral moraine, Viktor pointed out the pass we would be crossing in the morning. Betsho Pass had been the scene of a bloody standoff where his father had been part of the Russian alpine troops (assisted by Georgian allies) who repulsed the German drive toward the oil fields of the Middle East. Lado added that during World War II, 2,000 residents of the Baksan Valley, many of them women and children, had made an epic winter crossing of the pass to escape from the Nazis. Despite the demands of war, the German invaders had taken the time to make an ascent of Elbrus.

The view on the other side of the pass was even more spectacular. Although we were standing at an altitude of 10,500 feet (3,200 m), there still remained an expansive world of rock, snow and ice high above us. We dropped down past a great hanging glacier whose calving ice chunks tore

**V**illage elders in Mestia, wearing their traditional felt caps, share stories of old feuds and hard-fought battles after a day of scything hay. The Russian presence has put an end to generations-old vendettas that accounted for 600 murders between 1917 and 1921.

great holes in the silence of the valleys below, the echoes hardly having time to die before more reverberations started up in this huge mountain amphitheatre.

It quickly became clear to us that Lado really was our ticket to instant acceptance by the Svans. Farther down the valley, as we approached the first shepherd's hut, we were greeted by a maniac shooting his rifle into the air. Fearing for our lives, we cringed in the lee of the hut until Lado arrived, all smiles. The reason for the noisy reception quickly became apparent. These people were his relatives, and he waded into the midst of men and women who had come out to embrace him and kissed each of them on both cheeks. We were ushered inside the dark, log-walled structure and offered freshly made *mazone*, a yogurtlike drink. A cauldron of curdled milk sat murmuring on the hot wood stove while conical bamboo moulds that are used to form and dry cheese curds hung from the rafters.

After an hour, Lado was released from his blissful custody, and we continued down the valley. Soon after entering the dense forest, the mountains closed in, towering above the wildly turbulent river. Mount Mazeri and the twin peaks of Ushba, at 15,453 (4,710 m), one of the world's classic climbs, soared above us, their lofty tops obscured by cloud. The huge waterfalls that crashed down the steep gullies bore further testimony to the abundant annual precipitation.

After walking 11 hours, we came out on a broad plain where two rivers meet. At the far side were the distinctive stone buildings and towers of Mazeri, Lado's hometown. We were content to postpone further exploration until the next day and retreated to our tents, dead tired. But around midnight, we were roused from a stuporous sleep by an enthusiastic Viktor who, together with Lado, had gone foraging on our behalf. They had brought back several bottles of local wine and a wicker basket filled with warm *hachapuri*, a flat bread with spicy cheese melted into it, along with green onions to dip in a specially herbed salt. Having spent hours trying to find someone to make it for us (and no doubt doing their share of visiting in the process), they were beaming with the success of their mission. Lado wanted our first Svanetian evening to be good, so we tucked this rich fare into our bellies before falling back to sleep.

First thing in the morning, a bleary-eyed Lado commandeered an ambulance, the only vehicle in the village, to drive us the 12 miles into Mestia, the administrative centre of Svanetia with a population of around 5,000. Seventeen of us, including the driver and his companions, and all of our bulky packs were jammed into a vehicle meant to accommodate a few patients at most. The road twisted through a steep-walled valley, with dizzying views down to a seething river that would have shot fear through the veins of even the most daring river rat. We caught glimpses of villages and tower clusters perched on alluvial fans that supported neat pastures and fields of barley and wheat. The calm emanating from this restful pastoral setting made us long to spend more than our allotted time here.

## COMRADES IN CLIMBING

Once in Mestia, we were housed in a newly completed tourist facility high on the far side of the valley, overlooking the town. From every point, towers were visible as constant reminders that the isolation had ended only recently. Svanetia, with a population of approximately 50,000 (by Lado's estimate), is economically a poor region, despite the presence of roads and electricity. Its population lives primarily by subsistence agriculture, the dearth of arable land preventing the large-scale collective agriculture practised elsewhere in the Soviet Union. Stalin's attempts at forcing collectivization on this part of his native Georgia in the 1930s were met with a spirited, if futile, gesture of resistance from the Svans, and the only blatant evidence of Soviet presence in the valley today is a billboard and a statue of Lenin in the square.

It took us 45 minutes to walk down to the town from our hotel. We were ushered into a restaurant whose design replicated the living quarters of a traditional Svan household. The interior was a huge windowless room. A square fire pit made of stone occupied the centre of the wooden floor, the smoke rising to the high pointed roof without benefit of a

In earlier Svanetian times, a man's home definitely had to be his castle as murderous feuds would keep families ensconced in the safety of their 50-foot towers for months or even years on end.

chimney and escaping through the eaves. A wooden rack hung over it, laced with chains to support kettles and meat for smoking. The furniture was equally rustic, with heavy wooden benches on either side of a grease-stained table. Traditionally, three sides of the walls would be lined with stalls for cattle, which helped keep that murky space warm in winter. In the floor near one wall was a trapdoor that in the old days led to an underground vault which served as a dungeon, not for enemies but for unruly children. That is where we would be locked up if the party got out of hand, we joked as we settled around the table.

The head of the local sports association acted as our host and welcomed us to his town. With Svetlana as interpreter, he began the first of an endless series of toasts that were an inherent part of Svan social protocol. At first, we enthusiastically downed the tasty wine, but as we began to realize that the night would be a long one, survival became a matter of temperance. But it was already too late. Carried away by Svan hospitality, we lauded the full range of life, from the spirit of mountaineering to those who had died in the mountains to peace, love, courage, good friends and the motherland (whichever one we chose) and to all of us around the table, one by one. We each had a turn at toasting. The power failed, candles were lit, and more amber-coloured wine was poured. Philosophical ruminations were embellished with the good peasant fare of fresh tomatoes, cucumbers, brown bread and grilled pork ribs smothered with onions, all of which were consumed heartily as we toasted.

As our cohesive little group finally straggled up the hill in inky darkness at the end of the evening, a small white car careened around the corner, headlights blinding us. It was Lado. He had found a Lada somewhere, and without checking his driving credentials, several of us climbed in and somehow woke up later in our beds.

The following day, a bus took us deeper into history as we entered the more remote villages some 15 miles away. When we arrived in the postcard setting of Chavdbiani, the people were busy with rural chores—hauling loads

A feeling of tranquillity has settled over the valley in the past several decades, and now the towers of Mestia remain as picturesque reminders of a not-so-distant past. Today, the village of 5,000 serves as the administrative centre for Svanetia and its population of 50,000.

down narrow lanes on the traditional sledges, sweeping the cobblestone streets after the passage of their livestock, and baking bread. Many of the women, as in the rest of the valley, were dressed in black. We were told that as part of Svan custom, every married woman must don black attire when a relative dies. Unfortunately, because the families are so large and interrelated, a woman sometimes ends up wearing black for the rest of her life.

We came upon the owner of a house who invited us up into the adjoining tower, which he claimed had been built in the 12th century. Several rooms, built one on top of the other, were connected by foot ladders from within. In the eerie darkness, we groped our way up two storeys and out onto a shake roof 70 feet above the ground. We could see the men in the fields, sweating in their nonfunctional brimless felt hats, gathering freshly scythed hay with their wooden rakes.

All too soon, we were on a bus headed for the trail that would lead us up Nacra Pass back to the Hotel Cheget. But road construction blocked the way, and we had to shoulder our packs nine miles short of the intended destination.

After walking awhile, we made camp 50 feet from the river. At 4 a.m., the sky dam that had been towering menacingly over us the previous day broke, and hail, followed by torrential rain, slammed into the walls of our tent. The sudden dramatic rise in the water began to disturb us. We could hear huge granite boulders grinding and gnashing against the riverbed. Lightning illuminated the inside of the tent, but it was not bright enough to tell whether we were going to be flooded. To avoid a disaster, we moved our tent farther away from the riverbank in case there was a flash flood. We found out later that this same storm had nearly wiped out several climbing teams on alpine routes and that a gravel bank above one of the hotels in the Baksan Valley had collapsed, completely filling the first floor with a slurry of mud and rocks.

Our first and only obstacle the next day was a major creek crossing, with only half a footbridge left intact by the raging floodwaters. Our group huddled on a cluster of boulders amid the frothing

After a violent storm had swollen this river and washed out half of the bridge, a group of shepherds crowded around to help us cross. At first, they threw Lado Gurchiani, our guide, a rope, but their goodwill turned to anger when we nearly lost their bridge in the torrent.

current at the end of the bridge, somewhat at a loss as to what to do. Finally, with supreme effort, we upended and dropped the crippled footbridge; it barely reached the far bank. The Svan shepherds who at first greeted us with smiles from the other side now attacked Lado with unexpected hostility. We fully expected that the legendary daggers would appear to add emphasis to the gestures. Since we were now well above the timberline, our antics on the wooden bridge had caused the shepherds to fear for its complete destruction, thereby cutting off their retreat to their homes. Our hopes for a cup of hot tea were abandoned as we hurried on toward the pass, leaving Lado to smooth things over in our stead.

## TYPHOID TOWER

This pass, as with Betsho, was adorned with plaques that commemorated those who had perished in the mountains, both as climbers and as heroes of war. Just before we began the descent to our hotel, the clouds lifted momentarily on the side from which we had come, revealing a breathtaking spectrum of peaks and glaciers that had been hidden from our view all day. With our heads full of this refreshing visual gift, we checked into our rooms, our feet leaden with the hours of walking, and considered our situation. We had three days left before the camp ended. Now, in the eleventh hour, we had no alternative but to go for it.

In the basement root cellar of the hotel the next morning, we once again loaded up with food provided by the sports committee. With provisions of bread, vegetables, rice, cheese and cans of fish filling our packs, we hopped on a bus destined for the base of the chair lift. We missed the last chair just as it shut down, so we slogged for an additional 45 minutes as heavy, wet snowflakes melted on the backs of our necks. The Americans, Pat Baker and Charles Roth, had also joined us for the ascent.

Next day, we found ourselves once again sprawled in the Typhoid Tower, in need of rest and trying to dry out our gear following the hike from Svanetia. In the afternoon, Baiba and I ventured out and skied up 2,000 feet (600 m) to a

prominent outcrop called Postukhov Rocks, feeling giddy in the dazzling sunshine. We swooped back down the perfect corn-snow surface, carving long telemark turns and yelping with glee. Back at the hut, we found Jeremy trying to tell a young aeronautical student that his attempt to carry a homemade hang glider to the summit and fly it down was even more esoteric than our "telemalarky." The pilot had been trying unsuccessfully to find some alpinists to assist him in lugging the heavy contraption, but given our tight schedule, we were unable to help. The next day was to be our only shot at the summit.

D day. We rolled out at the usual 1 a.m. to allow enough time for the long ascent. With Pat, Charles and a Hungarian, Zoltan, the six of us stalked the summit in a moonlit fantasy world. The moon and stars were so bright, our shadows became three-dimensional on the snow in front of us. The strong, steady wind caused some concern, but the brilliant sky promised warmth when the sun appeared. Just as we reached Postukhov Rocks, however, the curse of Elbrus descended upon us. A wind cloud formed on the peak, and within minutes, the sky coagulated into a cesspool of cloud. Backs against the wind in conference, we concluded, "To hell with it, it ain't worth risking our necks to continue."

Breaking away from our group, Zoltan dug out his compass, set it on coordinates given him by his friends and threw us a frost-encrusted smile. For half an hour, we deliberated after we watched him disappear into the wind tunnel. Finally, with our body core temperatures plummeting, we decided to continue upward for only another half-hour in case the weather improved. It didn't, of course, but we continued; our goal was too tantalizingly close to give up so easily, and our bus left for the airport on the morrow. The day before, we had gathered a satchel of willow wands from the valley bottom, and by planting one every 60 paces to mark our route, we could ensure a safe descent and not get lost in the dangerous glacier field to the southwest.

Buffeted by the storm, we finally came to a decisive point where we had to choose which of Elbrus's twin summits to climb. Knowing that there was only a 39-foot

(12 m) difference in elevation between the east and west peaks, we opted for the former. The slightly higher west summit, complete with its statue of Lenin, meant a two-hour slog across an exposed saddle that would have been impossible in the whiteout conditions. In quiet unanimity, we turned right for the final approach up the east peak, cursing our luck.

The gale-force winds bore down relentlessly on us from the south, hissing and biting into our faces. My left eye clouded over from the stinging snow crystals coming in from the side, and I was unable to focus properly for the next two days. This wind hyperchilled Pat Baker's feet, which had to be treated in a Moscow hospital two days later, as did the black-blistered fingers on one of Charles' hands. They were to cause quite a stir in Moscow medical circles, as doctors couldn't understand the origin of their afflictions when the city was suffering from sunburn and heatstroke.

## SEA OF CLOUDS

On ever-steepening slopes, we finally decided to abandon our skis in favour of crampons. To attempt a descent on these rock-hard wind-blown slopes, even in good visibility, would require supreme effort. Hunched against the wind, we continued to make good progress, feeling strong from the previous weeks of hiking and climbing. Windborne particles of ice stuck to the lenses of our glacier glasses, forcing us to risk snow blindness by peering over the rims. Miraculously, the slope eased, and Zoltan appeared out of the maelstrom. The top was a mere 20 minutes away, he told us, but the wind was even stronger up there. We pushed on, and he decided to turn around and join us.

As we approached the top, the clouds thinned momentarily, and we were thrown into a blindingly radiant world, the sun highlighting the hoarfrost that had formed on our clothing and faces. The peaks were totally obliterated in a sea of clouds, and our hopes of seeing the mountains near Mount Ararat, the alleged final resting place of Noah's Ark just over 185 miles to the south, were dashed by the furious wind. I took Baiba's hand, and we staggered like

Whiteout conditions on Elbrus threatened to keep us off the upper slopes on our fourth and final try, but we managed to persevere and made it up the east peak of the twin summits, carrying willow wands to mark our route so that we could find our way back down. Jeremy Schmidt (foreground), Pat Baker, Charles Roth and Baiba force their way through the storm; for most of the ascent, it seemed unlikely that we were going to make it to the top. On the way down, we spent several tense moments wandering about in the driving snow looking for our tracks and our wands.

**Elbrus**

1. To Ski Lifts
2. Priut Hut
3. Postukhov Rocks
4. West (main) Summit (18,481 feet)
5. East Summit
6. West Face

Route Hidden From View ▬ ▬ ▬

drunks the last few steps. Lying on our backs in the lee of the summit, we were bandied about by the roaring forces for about 15 minutes, not relishing the experience. Launching ourselves directly into the wind for the descent, we found it impossible to see anything. Stumbling, balking, walking backward, we couldn't find the start of our tracks. Minor desperation set in when one of my crampons fell off and I had to bare a hand to the unforgiving elements to refasten it. Survival instincts kicked in, and by contouring along the slope, we finally found the first of the wands.

The wind and whiteout conditions continued, but they had become part of the experience by now. We were back down at the hut before noon, having made the round trip in less than 10 hours. Determined to make it down to the Hotel Cheget for lunch at 2 o'clock, we assembled all our gear with haste and continued down. Although we had been gone only two days, the green valley's refreshing summer fragrance brought our senses back to life. We were welcomed with congratulatory handshakes and apologetic smiles, for not many people had had such rotten luck in trying as many times as we had to climb the peak. I vowed to return later to climb the west peak, a promise I kept during a 1986 visit to the U.S.S.R.

That evening, everyone was treated to a royal banquet replete with champagne and wine and hearty conversation, and later, we danced for our last time to the music of the hottest band out of Leningrad. Viktor and Lado broke house rules and came to our rooms with gifts of ultralight Soviet-made titanium ice screws (a by-product of armament technology and the only quality climbing equipment available domestically). We, in turn, presented them with gifts of climbing gear, and Lado and I exchanged hats—my baseball cap for his traditional Svan hat. Now that they had done their duty by shepherding their Western charges around in the mountains, they could get on with a month of serious climbing in the upcoming speed championships.

Viktor sent us a card later that autumn saying that he had won the alpine climbing competition and that he had enjoyed the time he had spent with us. "Hallo Pat and Baiba. Best congratulations from your Soviet friends! We wish you to win some Everests yet, not only in mountains but in your life too. Since really your friend, Viktor.''

## KILIMANJARO

Having put Baiba on a plane for Canada, Jeremy and I continued on to Tanzania, only to find ourselves stuck at the Kilimanjaro Airport with an immovable load of gear.

Three months before, I had sent a letter to a friend of a friend, Jim Thorsell—a longtime resident of Banff who was working as an instructor at the College of African Wildlife Management in Mweka on the southern flank of Mount Kilimanjaro—warning him of our arrival. But I had not received a reply and had no idea how to contact him from the airport. Wendy Baylor, a friend of Jeremy's (and now his wife), had flown in from Arizona to meet us and had spent the previous week in nearby Moshi trying, without luck, to reach him. Now, the three of us sat staring in exasperation at our pile of luggage.

Optimistically, Jeremy jumped up and headed outside, assuring us that he would ask around in the parking lot until he found someone with a vehicle large enough to accommodate us. Minutes later, he strode back into the waiting room wearing an award-winning smile, saying, ''I've found a way of getting this stack of gear out of here!'' Hopeful, we alternately dragged and carried our packs full of insulated clothing out into the withering rays of the equatorial sun and tossed them, along with our skis, onto the roof rack of a mud-splattered Land Cruiser.

When the owner came back to the parking lot, he surveyed the loaded vehicle and asked where we were headed. ''Into Moshi, I guess,'' I suggested. ''But we actually wanted to get up to Mweka to look someone up.''

''Oh,'' remarked our spectacled chauffeur, raising his eyebrows with interest. ''Who are you looking for?''

''A guy by the name of Jim Thorsell.''

''I'm Thorsell!'' he exclaimed. ''You must be Morrow!''

Everyone in the car sat stunned for a second and then burst into laughter.

Baiba Auders' summit smile is more in response to the camera than our situation. We spent 15 minutes on our backs in the lee of the mountaintop preparing ourselves for the descent, risking snow blindness every time we peered over our goggles for a clearer look at the path.

Thor and his friend Julia Crossley had just returned the day before from a month-long holiday in Banff and, on a whim that day, had come out to the airport to see if a part for his Toyota Land Cruiser had arrived. Laughing, he promised to bring me up to date on the latest Banff gossip.

## THAWING OUT

The 20-mile drive across the Sanya Juu plains from the airport to Moshi took us past herds of Masai cattle and a family of grazing ostriches. My nerve endings began to tingle as the roadside smells of clay and straw, mixed with the diesel fumes of passing trucks, penetrated my nostrils. The sky was choked with heavy clouds. ''Unusual for August; the rains normally come in April and November,'' said Thor, as he jockeyed the Land Cruiser over the greasy road surface. From Moshi, the town of 50,000 at the core of Tanzania's coffee industry, the dirt road wound its way through run-down coffee plantations to the college.

Thor's tidy three-bedroom bungalow was enclosed in a stockade for college instructors. It was a welcome sight for our travel-weary bodies; the unmistakable shape of Kilimanjaro loomed in the distance.

As we lounged on the patio guiltily sipping Thor's domestically brewed Safari beer (beer and all other luxury items are at a premium in commodity-poor Tanzania), he motioned toward the exotic spectacle of several hornbills flitting among the branches of heavily scented trees. ''Having weathered as many Canadian winters as I have, I'm quite happy to look back at them with only a slight twinge of nostalgia,'' he smiled. With my toes still numb from Elbrus and clear vision slowly seeping back into my storm-battered left eye, I could appreciate his affinity for this place. At an elevation of 7,000 feet (2,134 m), just 200 miles south of the equator, the residents of Mweka enjoy a year-round temperature of 70 degrees F (21°C).

Debilitated by a rather pernicious flu bug at Thor and Julia's, I took the opportunity to get a better feel for East Africa. Since Julia had lived in Kenya from birth, and Thor had spent the past several years in both Kenya and Tanzania, they quickly put us at ease with a few precautionary notes.

Tanzania was in a sorry state by Western standards. Fuel shortages created transportation difficulties, but there was also a scarcity of certain merchandise, and we were warned to stock up on basic items whenever we could. This fact became painfully apparent when I blasted Thor's last squash ball irretrievably into a field of tall grass during a game at the college's open-air court. He remained amazingly calm for a dedicated squash enthusiast who would now have to wait a month until he could get replacements from Nairobi.

Money changing was tricky, and the government was cracking down on the black market, which favoured a rate of 60 shillings to the American dollar compared with the official bank rate of 10. We learned from other travellers that we should deal only with the East Indian merchants and remain wary of the black Tanzanians trading on the streets, as some of them were acting as government agents and received a commission for reporting offenders. As risky as it was, the black market seemed a necessity if we were to keep our stay from becoming prohibitively expensive.

As we sat on the veranda in the refreshing evening air, Thor fed us roasted impala that he had shot himself in a nearby hunting reserve, claiming the meat would make us bound up the mountain.

It was Thor's lifelong love and dedication to the preservation of the animal kingdom that had landed him this job a year before as the only white instructor at the game college, where students from all over Africa are trained to patrol their nation's parks. Their curriculum for the two-year programme includes park-management techniques, biology, ornithology and antipoaching practices. A $25,000 grant from the African Wildlife Leadership Foundation permitted the founding of the college in 1962, while the Tanzanian government financed the buildings. More aid came later from the U.S. Agency for International Development, the British and West German governments and private donations, until in 1965, the United Nations made the college a special project of the Food and Agriculture Organization.

One of the most direct routes to the summit of Kilimanjaro originated from the back door of the college and was created by the faculty and students in the days when the graduates' final test involved climbing the mountain and killing an elephant. While the elephant requirement remains—accomplished with the help of an SSG slug from a 10-gauge shotgun—the gruelling climb was discarded several years ago, and the trail has been all but reclaimed by the rainforest. Still, we made up our minds to climb the mountain by the normal route and descend directly back to Jim's patio by the more interesting Mweka route.

Situated 160 miles from the Indian Ocean, Mount Kilimanjaro is more easily reached overland from the Kenyan capital of Nairobi than from Tanzania's capital, Dar es Salaam. But at the time of our visit in August 1983, the border between the two countries was closed, so we had chosen the direct jet link from Europe to the Kilimanjaro International Airport, about 56 miles from the Marangu Park gates at the east end of the mountain. Our decision to avoid Dar es Salaam seemed wise, as we were to learn from other travellers that the city has serious accommodation shortages and finding transportation to the mountain was an effort requiring far more energy than one would expend in climbing.

## DIRE STRAITS

Tanzania, with a population of 18 million, was formerly called Tanganyika and gained its independence from Britain in 1961, the first country south of the Sahara to do so. Three years later, it joined the island republic of Zanzibar to form the United Republic of Tanzania, ''a one-party state created to provide a framework for uniting the energies and allegiances of people of 120 tribes, while allowing the citizens to freely choose by whom they shall be governed.'' This seemingly impossible mandate led the government, under President Julius Nyerere, to begin nationalization of its industry. The large coffee plantations were divided among the people into small homesteads that today provide them with a subsistence form of agriculture. The resultant loss of foreign exchange has seriously hurt the economy, and the

Our Chagga porter carries a ski bag across the oxygen-starved desert saddle that stretches between the volcanic peaks of Kibo and Mawenzi. The sight of skis brought incredulous stares from fellow hikers, but we were determined to ski Kilimanjaro's upper slopes. Reports of snow on the mountain in 1849 were greeted with indignant skepticism in British academic circles as armchair experts sneered at the observations of field observers reporting their findings back home.

Giant groundsels tower above the Norwegian prefab huts at the 12,000-foot Horombo campsite. Having only seen 12-inch-high groundsels in Scotland, I did a double take when I saw these plants, wondering if the altitude had affected my sense of proportion. As I was still recovering from a flu bug, we spent an extra day here to rest and fully acclimatize to the altitude. Many hikers climb the gentle trail too quickly and begin to pay the physical toll for recklessness around Horombo.

country has slipped back into a simpler, less productive era while its population continues to mushroom.

Tanzania closed its border with Kenya in February 1977, ostensibly to try to corner the tourism market of Kilimanjaro, Olduvai Gorge, Ngorongoro Crater, Serengeti and the other game parks. Unfortunately, the flood of foreign currency never materialized, and the country continued to sink into dire economic straits, further aggravated by the use of Tanzanian troops to oust Idi Amin from Uganda in 1979—a war that drained the national treasury overnight. The country has still not recovered, and the shortages and delays are now a part of life.

## IMAGINATIVE VISION

Kilimanjaro, rising out of the clouds of myth and romance, was first considered in European geographical circles when a Swiss missionary, Johann Rebmann, brought back reports of snow on the equator. It was 1848, and the malarial plains of East Africa spread out in strong resistance to the ambitions of both the centuries-old Arab slave trade and the men of the cloth, who had only recently entered this wilderness on soul-gathering safaris. But Rebmann, undaunted and determined, penetrated the natural barriers and subsequently came to publish the news of his find in the *Church Missionary Intelligencer* of April 1849, triggering a storm of controversy in Europe—particularly at the British Royal Geographical Society. Most vociferous in the debate was William Desborough Cooley, an eminent and outspoken geographer who had made Africa his specialty without ever leaving London.

The snows of Kilimanjaro, wrote Cooley, were "a most delightful mental recognition only, not supported by the evidence of [Rebmann's] senses." After all, he reasoned, the fellow was a missionary, not a trained geographer like himself. It was irrelevant that Rebmann, a Swiss and so familiar with mountains, had actually been there. "I deny altogether the existence of snow on Mount Kilimanjaro," Cooley continued. "It rests entirely on the testimony of Mr. Rebmann . . . and he ascertained it not with his eyes but by inference and in the visions of his imagination."

We were to get the same incredulous response early in our ascent of the mountain from a French tour guide who had just come back from Gilman's Point, at the rim of Kilimanjaro's crater—still a mile from the main summit—the point at which most tourists turn back because of mild altitude sickness.

"You have a hang glider?" he queried, spying our ski bag.

"No," we said, "these are skis."

"You want to ski?" He shook his head in disbelief. "Impossible. There is no snow up there." We could see the snow-lacquered tongue of the Decken Glacier glistening in the sun over his left shoulder but decided it wasn't worth arguing. We were content with the knowledge that Jeremy, on his previous visit to Kilimanjaro in February 1977, had had to wade through calf-deep snow at Kibo Hut.

Kilimanjaro, king of the African continent at an altitude of 19,340 feet (5,895 m) and one of the highest volcanoes in the world, rises out of an otherwise flat landscape. The mountain is actually composed of three major cones. At its west end stands Shira, the oldest and most eroded cone. Kibo, the youngest, is the tallest, with its main summit, Uhuru (a Swahili word meaning freedom), extending a mile west of what is called Gilman's Point. Mawenzi, the second cone, is a jagged volcanic plug joined to the Kilimanjaro massif by a high saddle and is recognized as the third highest point in Africa, after Kibo and Mount Kenya. While Mawenzi's sharp-edged, crumbly buttresses have received only a handful of ascents, thousands of sunburned pilgrims annually ply the trail that contours its lower slopes on their way to its taller neighbour.

Measuring 31 by 50 miles at its base, Kilimanjaro stands alone in the surrounding plains as an island ecosystem, containing samplings of virtually every environment on earth. Tropical jungle, savannah, alpine moorland, desert, snowfield and glacier are all found on the mountain, making ascent from base to summit analogous to travelling from the equator to the Arctic. The summit gets only an estimated five inches of precipitation per year, whereas the rainforest below receives more than six feet. The mountain can be climbed in almost any month, except during the long rains in

Jeremy Schmidt taste-tests some of our porters' food at Horombo Hut. Park regulations stipulate that a guide and porters be hired for the ascent, making an already gentle climb easier.

April and May, but the ideal months are January and February and from August to October.

A thick belt of montane forest, with giant trees such as the cone-bearing podocarpus, fig, cedar and camphor, encircles Kilimanjaro between 6,200 and 9,000 feet. On the south and east flanks, coffee and banana farms often penetrate as high as 6,000 feet. These are cultivated by the prosperous and industrious Chagga tribe, one of the most progressive in the country, numbering about half a million. Over the centuries, they have replaced lowland forest below the montane zone with agriculture and settlement to produce cash crops of coffee and their major sources of food—corn, yams and 17 varieties of banana.

## DO NOT OVERDO

After three days of the flu, I finally felt up to climbing. Thor gave us a lift down to Moshi, where we hoped to catch a bus to the Kilimanjaro Park gates at Marangu. In Moshi, we made a short detour to the marketplace in search of more rice to supplement the basic supplies we had brought along with us. Having hired a taxi driver who had connections, we managed to get a couple of pounds of that scarce staple. Jeremy remarked that the food selection was much better than six years before, when the store shelves had carried mainly canned pet foods.

At the park headquarters, we were confronted by a bewildering set of fees. Regulations stipulate that anyone going onto the mountain must hire a guide. The guide needs a porter to carry his belongings and food. And that porter needs a porter to carry extra water. One Nepalese porter could have handled the task alone, but it was an affordable enough make-work project that was especially welcome given the extra weight of our ski gear. We, in turn, had only one stipulation for the guide: that after our summit day, we would descend the little-used Mweka route. Our guide, a 27-year-old Chagga named Didas, had been over the Mweka route 10 years before and readily agreed.

Ten other tourists had assembled at the gates and were in the process of renting warm-weather gear and sleep-

Didas, our Chagga guide, took time off from working his small piece of land on the slopes below to lead us up the trail for his thirtieth ascent of Kilimanjaro. Like most guides, he seemed indifferent to the mountain and seldom broke his gloomy silence.

ing bags. Theirs was part of a package trip from the nearby Marangu Hotel, which included a catering service at each of the three mountain camps: Mandara, Horombo and Kibo. It occurred to me later that had we brought multiple layers of such second-hand clothing as sweaters, heavy pants, wool mitts and socks instead of expensive pile and down clothing, we could have given our winter clothing away to our porters at the end of the trip. It would have avoided the trouble of lugging huge packs for the remainder of our visit.

On August 10, our ponderous little expedition headed up the trail, past posters urging hikers: "Do not overdo!" Already, sweat was streaming from our foreheads in the close heat of the afternoon, sweat that would turn to ice higher on the mountain. We knew that if we were to reach Mandara Hut, at 9,022 feet (2,750 m), five miles away at the upper edge of the dense forest, before the equatorial darkness engulfed us at 7 p.m., we couldn't afford to linger. We caught glimpses of screeching colobus monkeys that scampered occasionally into view on the slender branches of the dense canopy overhead. The cacophony was intensified by the calls of the great-crested hornbill.

At dusk, we arrived at a smoke-filled clearing encircled by a cluster of eight huts that accommodated 60 people. They were only half full, and Didas found us a place after quick consultation with the hut custodian. A weathered sign hanging on the custodian's hut read "Karibu," Swahili for welcome. The comfortable A-frames (prefabricated in Norway and assembled here as a most effective and practical foreign-aid project) were named after Mandara, a Chagga chief who was infamous for taking advantage of early missionaries. Beginning with Rebmann, Mandara greeted explorers to his country for decades, graciously accepting their gifts and just as happily demanding everything else they possessed. Occasionally, his victims died on their way back to the coast, defenceless against the merciless heat.

In the congenial atmosphere of this international encampment, we were able to engage in a pleasantly strenuous evening of socializing. A pair of expatriate Australians who worked as geologists at

**Kilimanjaro**

1. To Marangu Park Gates
2. Horombo Hut (12,000 feet)
3. Kibo Hut (15,000 feet)
4. The Saddle
5. Gilman's Point (18,640 feet)
6. Uhuru (main) Summit (19,340 feet)
7. Breach Wall
8. Heim Glacier
9. Kersten Glacier
10. Decken Glacier
11. Mweka Route (descent)
12. Kibo
13. Mawenzi

High above the plains of Africa, Jeremy Schmidt cruises on his telemark skis along the rhinoceros-hide surface of one of the glaciers on Kilimanjaro. Having proved the skeptics wrong, Jeremy logically concluded that "snow is where you find it." Wendy Baylor and our guide, Didas, opted to finish the climb on foot. Mount Mawenzi and the saddle that stretches toward Kibo are in the distance.

a lead/zinc/silver mine in Zambia talked of wanting to leave that country after seven years. With the increasingly unpredictable political scene there, they were looking around for another country to which they might relocate. We also met a party of Germans who had been living in Moshi for several years and had decided to shake off the dust of the plains and "do" Kilimanjaro.

## SETTING A SNAIL'S PACE

The weather to this point had been depressingly sullen and overcast, but by morning, the sun had risen in a clear sky, and we set off for Horombo Hut only a five-hour walk away. My sense of well-being soared as I played Tarzan games through the giant heath forest, which was hung with curtains of wispy lichen that reminded me of a tattered t-shirt I had once used to put out a grass fire in the heart of the Grand Canyon. Our emergence from the forest was sudden, when, with just a few steps, we left the surreal canopy and came out onto the open moorlands on the southern slopes of Mawenzi.

We were greeted by descending porters, balancing the latest high-tech backpacks on their heads and calling out in Swahili, "*Jambo, habari*?" (Hello, how are you?). We had picked up enough of this voluble Bantu language, Tanzania's official tongue and the language of commerce spoken up and down Africa's east coast, to make ourselves understood and used it whenever we had a chance, even though English was common everywhere we went.

Although the trail rises gradually over its entire 24-mile (40 km) length, we shuffled along at a snail's pace, enjoying the changing perspective on the dun-coloured plains below. In fact, Jeremy and Wendy, who had used their mountain bikes on various exotic trips, thought that they could have ridden all the way to Kibo Hut. Mountain bikers, however, are now turned back from the park gates because of the disruption they would cause on the one-lane path. The gentle nature of the climb allows time to enjoy the tremendous variety that the mountain has to offer, and yet the considerable gain in elevation is enough to cause problems. We came across several victims of altitude sickness who had not taken the posted warnings seriously. Up the trail at Horombo, we saw a semiconscious, blue-lipped Japanese tourist suffering from pulmonary edema being carried down to medical help by his porters. And later, we heard that a group of fit-looking Spaniards who had sprinted ahead of us, their drumstick thighs sprouting from skin-tight gym shorts, had all ended up by the trailside, violently retching.

As the day progressed, we stumbled upon a scene from *Alice's Adventures in Wonderland*. As if we had nibbled some of Alice's magic mushrooms, it seemed we were reduced to miniature beings, dwarfed by giant 12-foot-tall groundsels, a plant I had seen in Scotland growing only to a height of 12 inches. They stood out as mutants, giraffelike necks inquisitively extended upward. Their long, thick trunks, bristling with a dense mass of dead leaves that insulated them from the freezing night temperatures, terminated in a crown of green leaves up to three feet wide. Their reassuring presence indicated a good water supply.

We opted to spend an extra day at Horombo, partly so that I could shake off the effects of the flu bug not yet completely exorcized from my body and partly to give us all a better chance to acclimatize to the altitude, now hitting the 12,000-foot (3,657 m) mark.

It was here that we met with the first incredulous response to our ski bag. The French and German tourists who had just come down from the summit could not understand why we would want to take skis along, further complicating an experience most of them had found to be already quite gruelling.

## ACROSS THE MOONSCAPE

Midway through our fourth day, on the way to Kibo Hut, at 15,000 feet (4,572 m), we paused to drink from a spring that provides the climb's last year-round water supply. Our porters filled all our containers and trudged onward across the high five-mile-wide (8 km) plateau between Mawenzi and Kibo known as the Saddle, which stretches out in a desolate moonscape scattered with random boulders. Since the other lower routes to Kilimanjaro are remote and overgrown, parties wishing to reach more demanding lines on the mountain branch off the standard route at this point and contour onto the southern slopes of Kibo or approach from West Kilimanjaro. A direct ascent can then be made via such imposing routes on the south face as the Breach Wall, a 4,000-foot (1,219 m) climb up vertical rock and ice steps, or through the jumbled ice blocks of the Heim Glacier.

Kibo Hut, a cheerless stone and concrete box with space for 60 people, was empty save for the custodian, a friendly lad of maybe 22 who was equipped with a shortwave radio to call in emergency help for stricken climbers. We spread out regally in the vastness of an empty 20-bunk room, although our meal of soup and bread was more suitable fare for peasants.

We promptly retreated to our bunks and dozed fitfully before an early-morning start that would allow us a solid footing on the frozen scree and give us a view of the sun rising behind Mawenzi from high up. It was probably just as well to climb in darkness, as the endless stretch of scree ahead can be discouraging and sleep at that altitude is almost impossible anyway.

We wakened Didas at midnight, thinking it odd that our guide was not waking us, and stumbled out into the dormant world. Although many hikers wear sneakers to the rim in good conditions, this was one time when we were glad of our sturdy, warm ski boots. In the stinging cold blackness, we could see a few flickering fires out on the plains of Kenya to the north and Tanzania to the east and south. Didas really came into his own this day, leading the way with his coal-oil lamp, which swung with the slow rhythm of his stride. Like a Mexican truck driver trying to extend the life of his headlights, he snuffed out the flame in a number of places where the light-coloured scree allowed him to navigate by starlight. He didn't miss a switchback on the trail up the interminable 4,000-foot-long (1,219 m) scree slope, testimony to the 30 or more previous ascents he had made on this mountain. With glazed eyes, we followed the pendulum of light as though we were hypnotized zombies being led to a pagan ritual.

A Swedish family with an 11-year-old

girl overtook us at about 2 a.m., but we caught up to them later when we stopped to warm up in a pockmarked feature called Meyer's Cave. Two of the older party members were collapsed on the ground, retching, which made me wonder whether some guides intentionally speed their way up the trail with the hope of debilitating their clients so that they can retreat to their quarters. In an effort to keep warm, we set off once again into the darkness.

We were too intent on the slippery scree slope and the exertion of placing one foot in front of the other to notice the full effect of the sun as it came up behind Mawenzi. It was only when the sunlight actually gilded the rock outcrops of Gilman's Point at 18,640 feet (5,681 m) that we turned around to admire the fantastic castle ruin of Mawenzi, whose serrated battlements were backlit by a blood-red sky. Since we had skipped breakfast before leaving, we decided to lie in the sun and have a bite to eat.

Wendy, who had never been this high before, found herself breaking the climb into increments of one step, determined to continue the 700 vertical feet (213 m) to the true summit of Uhuru.

The top of Kilimanjaro is an immense, rather flat snow-covered expanse with two distinct but shallow craters—one occupies the entire two-mile (3.2 km) span, while the other smaller one rises within it. The only active sign of volcanic energy is the pungent smell of sulphur from the steaming fumaroles on the floor of the inner crater. The entire Kilimanjaro complex contains as many as 250 cones and craters.

Leaving Didas and Wendy to make the ascent by the rocky rim, Jeremy and I cast off along the summit caldera on our lightweight telemark skis into the world of snow on the roof of Africa. It was perfect Nordic touring terrain—almost. In places, the direct overhead rays of the equatorial sun had drilled troughs every six inches on the flat stretches, creating a corrugated effect. Brittle arms of ice, some of which looked as though they had been sculpted by Tanzanian Makonde carvers, jutted out over the south-facing cinder slopes and clung to rocky outcrops. Suddenly, the lack of sensation in our leaden legs was replaced by a light, silky feeling that matched the

Standing on a towering serac, Jeremy Schmidt pauses to consider his options. The snow conditions were mixed, often rock-hard and corrugated, but occasional smooth patches tempted us closer to the brink of the glacier—a lure we avoided most of the time.

ethereal landscape perfectly. We glided effortlessly toward the summit across a surface resembling the coarse hide of a rhinoceros.

As we approached the drop-off toward the plains, the snow surface smoothed out, and we cranked a few telemark turns that drew us tantalizingly close to what could have become a screamer of a run into the clouds below. If there had been a layer of corn snow to give our edges purchase, we could have carved turns several hundred yards farther down to the end of the convex glaciers, but the sun's early rays glinted off an iron-hard skin of ice, warning us away from the edge.

We contoured along the brink, exploring the breathless world of skiing in an atmosphere containing less than half the oxygen than that at sea level. Knowing that Lutheran pastor Richard Reusch, a former officer in the Cossack Army of Imperial Russia, had found a frozen leopard carcass on the rim of Kibo at just under 19,000 feet (5,791 m) in 1926, Jeremy bent over and picked up a piece of bright blue sweater fluff, exclaiming in his best colonial accent, "Leopard fur! Send out the trackers, and have your weapons ready!" We were thrilled to be there, the plains of Africa spread out at our feet.

We basked on the warm rocks at the summit for an hour until Wendy and Didas, summit grins flashing all over their faces, joined us. In all aspects, this was by far the most enjoyable of my seven-continents climbs. Affordable and easily accessible by conventional transportation, there were no major political restrictions to battle and no need for months of planning and logistical foreplay.

We tramped back along the well-worn trail to Gilman's Point. Directly to the east, a great belching cloud of smoke rose to 20,000 feet in an ominous black mushroom over Mawenzi. We romantically envisaged a volcanic eruption, but in reality, careless hikers had set ablaze the whole hillside above the trail between the Marangu and Horombo huts, blocking the flow of climbers on Kilimanjaro for several days.

Having skied 1,000-foot sand dunes in 1981 during our Muztagh Ata expedition in western China, I was tempted to try my luck on the perfect 4,000-vertical-foot scree run from Gilman's Point. But whereas the fine silica flecks of sand in China had no more than dulled my edges, this coarser scree would have worn the bases right through to the soles of my boots, a rather abrasive experience. Instead, still wearing my leather ski boots, I bounded down the scree slope in tandem with the wind and my friends to arrive at the hut, totally refreshed, by midday.

## TANZANIAN SAFARI

Back at Kibo, I traded my favourite Karhu ski tuque to the custodian for 2½ quarts of precious water and wondered, as we drank, just how many such trades he had already made and imagined a whole hut full of Western paraphernalia somewhere on the plain. Since the next closest water source for us was 4,500 feet (1,371 m) below and several miles distant at Mweka Hut, we decided to spend the night here and get an early start the next day.

Just before dawn, we paid our porters for one more day and sent them down the trail to Marangu with our ski gear and instructions to leave it there to be picked up in a couple of days. We struck off directly down the fall line of the slope, hoping to find the stone cairns marking the Mweka route. Here, as everywhere above the timberline, an abandoned trail usually remains intact for dozens of years, but we knew that as soon as it entered the forest below, it would become lost in a wall of green, unless human or animal passage kept it open.

Our only route-finding difficulties on the descent arose when we came to a sheer 25-foot wall created by lava that had flowed down from the summit to the tussocks of the highland moors and solidified. We dropped our packs in order to search for an egress, and just as we began to joke about tying our bootlaces together to lower ourselves down, Didas gave a small triumphant shout. He had found a perfect descending cave, replete with handholds, that would deliver us to the slope below. This was one of the few times we had seen any sign of excitement on our new friend's otherwise gloomy countenance. The joy of discovery had transformed him from a guide leading groups of often anaemic,

disgruntled foreigners on an endless mountain treadmill to a member of a party that could savour each and every step. Up to this moment, Didas had seemed to treat his job with some disdain, as if wondering what he had done to deserve such a hard life. His attention was usually focused on his wife and six children and their *shamba*, with its grass-roofed hut, two or three cows and tiny courtyard; climbing Kilimanjaro simply helped to pay the bills.

We dropped through the skeletal remains of an otherworldly, burned-out heather forest alongside the steep Msoo Valley to a pair of expropriated metal grain sheds that Mweka Hut comprised. Here, we stopped early to avoid being caught without adequate flashlights out in the jungle that skirts the base of the mountain.

While heating some water from the nearby spring on our tiny kerosene stove, we marvelled at the scope of adventure open to the early climbers on this mountain. Given the endless trudge they had to make across unbroken tussock land and through thick forests, the approach was probably more eventful than the actual ascent. In those days, they would have had to contend with the odd elephant and Cape buffalo in the lower elevations and even would have stood a chance of sighting leopards or a serval cat in the upper regions.

On our last day, we spent five hours fighting our way down the heavily overgrown trail through alternating patches of flesh-tearing bramble and giant ferns. A machete would have come in handy, but instead, Didas was able to use resources at hand and beat back the foliage with one of my state-of-the-art ski poles. In the end, I gave him the pair, undoubtedly in use now as status symbols guaranteed to impress his clients.

The fog that smothered the dripping heather forest gradually began to dissipate as we came across the first signs of selective logging and the upper edges of the *shamba* clearings. The sounds and smells of civilization permeated the air, and as we burst into a clearing, we surprised a swarm of schoolchildren on their way home. Our smiles were greeted with puzzled looks, for it was not every day that a troop of hikers emerged from the forest into their backyards.

Upon our arrival at the college, we gave Didas bus fare to return to the park gates and bade him farewell with the passive handshake that seemed customary with his people. Back at the bungalow, we relaxed on the veranda, having washed off the dust of travel in the luxury of Thor and Julia's shower and began to plan a safari into the region's game parks.

Tanzania's 11 national parks, including Kilimanjaro, cover 20,920 square miles, approximately 3.6 percent of the nation's land area. When combined with the 10 federal game reserves that allow controlled hunting, that figure jumps to 14 percent. Canada, by comparison, has set aside only 1.3 percent of its land area for this purpose. The world's largest game reserve, Selous, is spread over 31,068 square miles in the remote southern part of Tanzania, and we had been tempted to visit it, attracted by its population of 50,000 elephants and some of the largest herds of buffalo anywhere. But with our limited time, we opted for the closer parks: Ngorongoro Crater, Lake Manyara and Tarangire.

Julia advised us to economize on our week-long photo safari in Arusha by rounding up a few other people to share the cost of renting a van or Land Rover with a driver, available through a private tour operator or directly through the Tanzania Tourist Corporation, which offers competitive rates.

After we stored our cold-weather gear, which was of absolutely no use to us here in the African veldt, Jim dropped us off once again in Moshi. We elbowed our way onto a bus crowded with women laden with produce who were bound for the market 67 miles away in Arusha, the administrative centre for the northern region. The open-air markets there were well stocked, and we filled a couple of big wicker baskets with fresh fruit and vegetables, cheese, dried catfish and several bottles of Dodoma red wine (at $1 a bottle).

While making our safari arrangements, we found the perfect complement to our group in a young German university student who shared our photographic aspirations. He had already made contact with a small company, Executive Tours Ltd., and he introduced us to a worldly Chagga driver by the name of Joseph Thaka. Joseph, in his late 40s, had been in the business for 15 years and was known for his dexterity in adjusting to and juggling the demands of whimsical tourists on game-watching trips.

## HIPPO CLUSTER

Heading west from town, we entered the distinct blue haze of the dry season. Kilimanjaro popped in and out of view over our shoulders to the east, reminding us that just a few days ago, we had been up there gazing out toward the plains. Occasionally, we found ourselves thinking wistfully of its snowfields as the searing sun burned down on us. In the wake of our moving vehicle, we left a cloud of dust that enveloped the thatch-roofed huts and scrawny cattle being tended by young Masai shepherds wrapped in their traditional blankets.

In a couple of hours, we arrived at Lake Manyara, just in time to bask in the rich afternoon light, perfect for photography. The sun-baked rock and talus wall of the Great Rift Valley rose up as an imposing backdrop more than 1,000 feet high. This fracture in the earth's crust is slowly tearing the continent along a 3,000-mile front from Syria to Mozambique, but with only one wall, it looked to me like a half-finished Grand Canyon.

To stretch our legs after the drive, we strolled along the white alkali flats of the lake, scattering a neurotic flock of off-pink flamingos that had been grazing in the shallow, fishy-smelling soda water. This desolate beach seemed safe from four-footed marauders such as buffalos or big cats, but Joseph cautioned us against walking away from our vehicle unaccompanied by an armed guide anywhere else. We drove up to a herd of hippopotamuses clustered together in a mud wallow in apparent bliss, most of them asleep or close to it. In an awesome display of nature, one of the larger creatures casually stood up and, with its ladle-like tail, started to spray feces all over its neighbour. We debated whether they were courting or lifemates but reached no conclusion.

Although small in landmass, the park has more than 350 recorded species of birds, including exotic lilac-breasted rollers, hornbills, marabou storks, starlings and secretary birds. My favourites

On the plains of Lake Manyara Park, we spent an evening watching a small herd of elephants tearing branches off trees a short distance from our camp. Ironically, it is a practice that can lead to their demise, for it often kills the trees, destroying a vital part of their habitat.

During one of the stops in our van, two young Masai boys came over for a better look. While the driver made some repairs, they stood off to one side, maintaining a silent vigil until Wendy Baylor beckoned them closer. Spotting a colourful coffee mug among our gear, one of them traded some of his jewellery for it before drifting back to his herd of cattle and out of sight. It was our only encounter with the Masai, a tribe whose nomadic life style transgresses the government's policy of land use.

were the cattle egrets that, when congregated in a tree, adorned the branches with their tufted, thistle-down heads like the blossoms of so many giant bell-flowers.

## PRIMORDIAL MOMENT

In an effort to reach our campground before the equatorial curtain came crashing down at 7 p.m., we rushed from the field. Aided by the feeble illumination of our flashlights, we gathered firewood from beneath the dense thicket of the nearby acacia forest. A park employee, toting an ancient Lee Enfield .303-calibre rifle with the blueing faded off the barrel, dropped by our campfire to assure us that he would maintain a dusk-till-dawn vigil to ward off any real or imagined human or animal thieves. We spent a fitful night in our tent nonetheless, listening with trepidation to a small herd of feeding elephants tearing branches off the trees just outside the range of the firelight.

The next day, our van toiled its way up from the dry and barren flatlands where we were bombarded by colour. The fertile hills were painted a startling vermilion by volcanic deposits, which complemented the jade belt of forest garnishing the 7,000-foot crater rim. We were on our way to a campsite overlooking the world's largest intact caldera, the 160-square-mile Ngorongoro Crater. Scientists have speculated that, judging from the circumference of the crater, the volcano which originally stood there could have been much taller than Kilimanjaro—before it blew its top, that is. Joseph would stay in the park lodge along with the other drivers and guests, while we spread out our lightweight sleeping bags on the ground beside two young Germans and five Italians who were fellow travellers.

We awoke to a cold fog rolling up from the 2,000-foot-deep crater, and as morning unfolded, a weak, low-angled sun penetrated from the east, crosslighting the solitary bushy-topped euphorbia tree that we had all camped beneath. For a moment, it seemed a primordial moment in history: cold human forms huddled under the protective canopy of a tree, nurturing a small cooking fire that gave them sustenance. But such visions

were interrupted by the Italians, who had brought with them a demitasse espresso-maker. It quickly became the focus of attention as it bubbled happily in the foreground, wafting its lush, vaporous essence toward us. The mist rolled back to reveal the pure estate of nature as the thick black coffee blasted the cobwebs out of our brains.

Joseph arrived just as the sun reached our stiff limbs, and he informed us that if we wanted to travel to the centre of the crater, we were obliged by park regulations to hire a Land Rover—at 1,760 shillings ($175 U.S.) per day. Knowing we would have a chance to see all of the "big five" (elephant, rhinoceros, lion, leopard and Cape buffalo) in one day here, we did not balk at the extra expense. In the parking lot outside the lodge, we offered extra wages to Elvis, the driver, and John, the naturalist guide, for staying in the bowels of the crater until the end of day when the light for photography would be best.

Elvis was the first driver we encountered in Tanzania who understood that a vehicle has a finite life span on those atrocious roads, and he eased his Land Rover skilfully over the ruts.

## HYPOXIC SHUFFLE

The descent into the crater took nearly an hour on a spectacularly rough and narrow dirt track. The driver and guide speed-read the landscape without binoculars and led us to all the game we could have asked for. Near the centre, we were delivered to the tender scene of the tank-like shape of a female rhinoceros nursing her young, itself the size of an armour-plated golf cart. We knew there were only half a dozen of this endangered species in the park, if not the country, and were grateful to our guides for their effective sleuthing.

Just as the light was peaking for our photographic purposes, Elvis called it quits for the day and began to steer the vehicle back toward the rim, despite our protests. We trimmed his tip accordingly, but he badgered Joseph until he added another hundred shillings. We wondered if he were a direct descendant of the notorious Chagga chief Mandara, who had ''accepted gifts'' in this manner from early missionaries.

Our last stop was Tarangire Park, only five miles off the Cape-to-Cairo highway, 79 miles from Arusha and touted as having a wildlife population density comparable to that of the Serengeti.

The only wildlife spectacle that I could relate to from my past which even came close to the size and abundance of the animals on these plains was on the bare Arctic tundra of the northern Yukon where, on two occasions, I had seen concentrations of the 120,000-strong Porcupine caribou herd in a land otherwise devoid of obvious life. Yet here, an empty horizon seemed to be the exception, and as an added bonus, the parks were so large that we rarely saw other tourists. There was standing room only for the wall-to-wall herds of zebras, wildebeest, gazelles and elephants. Smaller numbers of species such as impalas and giraffes wove through the slalom course of grazing and moving animals. The diminutive duiker, standing 18 inches tall at the shoulder, provided a delicate contrast as it grazed among the forest of legs of the much larger antelopes.

We came close to a herd of 30 elephants watering in a small river, some of them doing the "hypoxic shuffle" (as we had done in the thin air of Kilimanjaro) up the hill in the stupefying heat of the day. Our sudden presence spooked a couple of them, and they flung their trunks in the air toward us, trumpeting their warning. Couched as we were in our little Volkswagen tin box, we suddenly got a taste of the fear that had been, so far, gratuitously absent on the trip. Fortunately, fate had other plans for us, and the herd stampeded in the other direction in a furious cloud of dust.

During our last night in the game parks, in a moonlit camp overlooking a broad river bottom, ghostly beast forms of all sizes drifted by in a nightlong procession 100 yards away. Even in our state of heightened alertness, the only sound we heard coming from the apparitions was the rustling of a thousand legs brushing against the long grass until a cough spilling from the throat of a hunting lion broke the silence. Giddy with our taste of African wildlife, we called it a night and climbed into our tents. I had more mountains to climb and, the next day, had to start for home and my biggest logistical and financial safari ever.

A herd of wildebeests drifts across
the plains of Tarangire Park, a
reserve with a wildlife population density
approaching that of the world-renowned
Serengeti. Empty horizons were a rarity,
for the park was crowded with herds of
wildebeests, zebras, gazelles and
elephants. At night, we often lay sleepless in our tent, listening to the sounds of
feeding elephants and hunting lions, a
marked change from our nights on the
barren upper slopes of Kilimanjaro.

# Vinson

## Journey across the Antarctic desert

During a stopover on the Antarctic Peninsula, we joined a flock of Adélie penguins for a walk to their nesting site. While the birds still outnumber humans, retired Chilean General Don Javier Lopetegui, *inset*, shown with pilot Giles Kershaw, has plans to start a tourism industry on the polar continent.

A sledgehammer wind, gusting up to 120 miles per hour, assaulted the small fibreglass house. With banshee wails, it pummelled the building again and again, tearing at the web of steel cables that secured it to the underlying rock. Inside, our small group of would-be mountaineers lay sleepless at 2 a.m., each silently contemplating the tensile strength of steel, trying to imagine what he might do if the shelter were suddenly to become airborne. Outside, on a long, gently sloping glacier, our plane had broken its tether and was being driven before the wind, dragging two large snowcats to which it had been supplementally anchored. Tangled together, the three machines lurched down the ice toward a 500-foot cliff and the Southern Ocean below.

I had reached Antarctica only late that afternoon, touching down at the Argentine base of Esperanza on my way to Antarctica's Vinson Massif. After 18 months of planning, the storm that greeted us was a cruel, if not entirely unexpected, welcome. I had gathered together a party of 10, several of them paying clients, and while we were prepared for the worst, we had hoped we might not have to face it on the first day. But face it we did, and while we did not know it at the time, the storm was the beginning of the end. By the time it was over, our $250,000 (U.S.) expedition would lie in shambles. For the others, the 30-hour tempest represented a failed adventure. For me, it meant another year and finding $400,000 to regain ground lost in my seven-summits bid.

Our destination was Antarctica's highest peak, Vinson Massif, 16,067 feet (4,897 m), lying deep in the continent's interior in the Ellsworth Mountains. The Esperanza stop was a social debt to Colonel Gatica, the Argentine officer who had offered us fuel, a rare Antarctic commodity usually not available at any price.

Due to its remoteness and the hostility of its climate, the interior of Antarctica is effectively closed to all but highly organized, massively funded private expeditions and to tightly controlled government-sponsored scientific operations. My first tentative efforts to launch my own expedition began in September 1983, shortly after returning from Tanza-

nia and the Kilimanjaro ascent. After spending two weeks in Buenos Aires in December trying vainly to coax the Argentine military to let me and my partner Martyn Williams hitch a ride on one of their Antarctic supply runs, I became painfully aware that the crux of the expedition would not lie on the mountain itself—which offered a technically easy climb of maybe a week's duration—but in a horrific swamp of finances, logistics and politics. Not the least of my problems was the attitude of the scientific organizations that dominate the continent's settlement and thus control movement over it. The U.S. Siple station is a mere 150 miles from Vinson, but no power other than a presidential writ could grant us permission to embark on skis from there. Faced with a short four-month working season, high overhead (the U.S. National Science Foundation spends nearly $1 million a day on its Antarctic research) and often menacing operating conditions, they are loath to mount rescue missions for private parties and therefore do all that they can to discourage individuals from even coming to Antarctica.

## WEALTHY ADVENTURERS

In the fall of 1983, I had eagerly entered into what was to become two years of correspondence with the bureaucracies of five governments, the old-boy networks of an equal number of scientific organizations and the boardrooms of airlines, potential financial backers, cinematographers, equipment manufacturers and curious individuals. There would be a glimmer of hope, and I would rush off to New York or Toronto and even, on one occasion, to Buenos Aires to meet potential backers. But nothing seemed to click, and the web of red tape quickly began to smother me. The endless calls and letters were totally foreign to my style of doing things on the spur of the moment, either alone or with a few friends. As I called on well-heeled businessmen, instead of climbing friends, nostalgic thoughts of the 1977 Mount McKinley expedition would come to mind, and I sometimes wondered if I was out of my league.

In the fall of 1983, Baiba had left her job in Ottawa to join me in the West. We

wanted to become a full-time adventuring team, but the high costs involved in this leg of the project meant that while she would be working on it full time, she had no prospects of joining me. Baiba proved to be a persistent manager and kept me on track, and although progress was snail-like, by the summer of 1984, I realized that an expedition was, in fact, taking shape. Moreover, the international group of participants was eclectic and interesting. Peter Bruchausen, a 46-year-old expatriate Argentine oceanographer with more than 30 scientific expeditions to Antarctica, entered the game in its early phases after a chance meeting at the Explorer's Club in New York City. He used his contacts to persuade the Argentine army to allow us to buy fuel at cost from that country's Antarctic bases, support we desperately needed, given the 2,000 miles from the tip of South America to the mountain.

Because there was no suitable aircraft available in South America, Peter recommended a one-of-a-kind long-range, ski-equipped Tri Turbo DC3, owned and operated by a defence contractor from California. Our pilot was 37-year-old British ace Giles Kershaw, who had well over 5,000 hours of Antarctic flying—far more than any living pilot. Accompanying him were copilot Ric Airey, a Scot, and Alaskan flight engineer Rick Mason.

My chief backer was Steve Drogin, a San Diego real estate magnate and avid Antarcticaphile, who had agreed to finance the trip and assume overall leadership, while 35-year-old Mike Dunn, a Nevadan who customizes exotic tours for wealthy adventurers, eased Steve's financial commitment by finding three paying clients at up to $35,000 a head. They included Bob Peebles, Jean Neshiem and Steve Fossett, a Chicago stockbroker with a penchant for endurance sports. Martyn Williams, a 36-year-old Yukon mountain and river guide and an old friend, would share climbing leadership with me once we reached Vinson.

On November 17, 1984, the Tri Turbo raised its nose from the runway at Punta Arenas, Chile, and headed south into the wind. Its eight passengers sat in cramped quarters, surrounded by mounds of gear, each lost in his own mental space, staring out the window toward the world's least explored horizon.

Three thousand feet above the frigid waters of Hope Bay, Mike Dunn, Steve Fossett and Martyn Williams (left to right) languish in the Antarctic sun atop Mount Florida. Taking advantage of a break in the weather, we climbed the peak just outside the Esperanza Base to pass the time while we awaited the return of British pilot Giles Kershaw and our Tri-Turbo DC-3 from Argentina. What we assumed would be a few days' routine flight for repairs turned into a delay of more than a week when, upon landing at Rio Gallegos, Giles and his crew were placed under house arrest because they did not have visas. The bitterness over the Falklands war seemed destined to scuttle our expedition.

As he flew, Giles began passing back notes, "Beagle Channel below . . . Tierra del Fuego . . . this is it, folks, the Drake Passage." The horizon was sullied by heavy cumulus clouds, and despite our precarious position over the vast body of water, I breathed a sigh of relief, for it seemed that nothing could stop us now. The mountains were finally within reach, and I would soon be in my element.

Five hours later, the plane eased down on a glacier above Esperanza for what was supposed to be a quick stop to pick up Argentine army observer Colonel Gatica. However, although he knew that a weather front was moving in and that we should fly immediately on to the next base where the plane could be properly tied down against high winds, Gatica had planned an evening full of Argentine hospitality and rhetoric. Giles' alternate pleadings and threats, reinforced by his quickly rising blood pressure, did no good, and so it was that we crawled from our dwelling late the next day to find the plane tangled with the snowcats at the lip of the ice cliff. Miraculously, one of the snowcats had jammed itself between the plane's fuselage and the ice, halting the ocean-bound parade. Still, the fuselage had been damaged, and Giles, jettisoning our gear, headed north to Argentina for repairs, accompanied by his crew—a risky proposition for two British subjects without visas in the wake of the Falklands crisis. But the Colonel told them that if they landed in the city of Ushuaia, at the tip of Tierra del Fuego, the name of Gatica would open all the necessary doors.

The rest of us settled in to learn what we could of the continent and of those who live there. We were versed, of course, in the history of Antarctica, epitomized by the 1911 race to the pole between the highly touted government-backed expedition led by the British naval officer Robert Scott and the shoestring private venture of the consummate Norwegian explorer Roald Amundsen. Amundsen, using dogsled and skis, reached the pole days before Scott, who, encumbered by both ignorance of travel over snow and a Victorian rigidity of thought, lost his entire polar party. Scott's men started the 1,600-mile round-trip glacial journey with ponies but spent

their final desperate days hauling heavy sledges with their skis tied to the top of the loads. Although better prepared, Amundsen found the continent no more hospitable than did Scott. As a journalist once aptly put it, Antarctica is a place "colder than Siberia, drier than the Gobi Desert, windier than the summit of New Hampshire's Mount Washington, and emptier than the empty quarter of Arabia." It still is.

## ESPERANZA-BY-THE-SEA

Although there is a variety of historic claims, Antarctica is today the only continent without national boundaries, and what little civilization exists there does so by virtue of scientific research rather than settlement. Theoretically, it is a symbol of cooperation among nations, and by international treaty, it is open to anyone, regardless of citizenship or national origin. In December 1959, 12 countries signed the Antarctic Treaty, a 30-year moratorium on all sovereignty issues that would ensure the continent would "continue forever to be used exclusively for peaceful purposes." In effect, a continent half the size of Africa was reserved for free and nonpolitical scientific investigation, a sanctum where the dangerous proliferation of missiles and other nuclear gadgets was banned. Some 2,000 people live in Antarctica during the brief summer months from late November to March in some 40 bases on the continent and its surrounding islands. In winter, the human population drops to about 800.

The Antarctic Treaty expires in 1991, and despite its idealistic sentiment, both the signatories and a number of non-signatories are actively working to heighten their profiles on the continent amid growing evidence of mineral wealth and vast oil and coal deposits. It is the feeling of many that the control of Antarctica and its resources should be handed over to the United Nations in a global gesture that would benefit all nations.

Esperanza, our unscheduled stopover, is a cluster of comfortable fibreglass and wood buildings that sits near the now vacant British base of Hope Bay, and it exists primarily to provide an Argentine presence on the Antarctic

Kids are kids the world over, and these three have found the Antarctic equivalent of a mud puddle. To strengthen their claim on a slice of Antarctica, the Argentine government maintains 50 people — including 21 children — at their Esperanza Base.

Gale-force winds up to 200 miles per hour sweep down the Antarctic Peninsula quite regularly, tossing aside anything that blocks their path. On our first night at the Esperanza Base, one of the storms pushed our DC-3 down the sloping glacier upon which it was tethered and almost into the ocean. Luckily, one of the snowcats we had tied it to got tangled in its undercarriage, thereby saving it from a watery demise. The incident delayed and finally ended our first bid for Vinson.

Peninsula. Serious about its claim on the continent's future, Argentina maintains nine permanent bases, more than any other country.

Martyn and I were billeted with Pablo and Lilliana Dankiewicz and their two boys in a prefabricated house every bit as comfortable and modern as those used in the Canadian north. Pablo, a neurosurgeon, was the base physician. His office was equipped with a direct radio link to Buenos Aires in case the delicate manoeuvres on the operating table got out of hand. Lilliana was a physiotherapist who, with the base commander's wife, ran the southernmost AM radio station in the world.

The glacier-capped mountains rising 3,000 feet straight out of the ocean were as stunning as anything I could remember from my world travels. The Antarctic Peninsula is a natural masterpiece composed of a thousand of Alaska's Glacier Bays laid out in a row. And unlike the Arctic, there are no mosquitoes or polar bears with which to contend. Tabular icebergs as large as some countries ply the channels between the mainland and hundreds of islands. If we had to be stranded for a week or more, we decided, there could be no finer place.

A rookery of about 250,000 Adélie penguins shares the exposed rocks near Esperanza and, being the perfect little characters they are, won us over immediately. During the windstorm, Martyn and I had staggered out, arm in arm, to see how they were faring. Slipping and sliding on heaps of excrement, we stumbled into the midst of the birds, finding them prostrate over their nests, beaks pointed into the wind. They did not dare lift their heads to look at us, lest the wind turn them end over end, black-and-white tumbleweeds in the vast barrens. There are 21 species of penguins scattered throughout the latitudes of the southern hemisphere, from the coast of Antarctica to the equator, but most species are found between 45 and 55 degrees south. Of all the warm-blooded animals on the Antarctic continent— penguins, other seabirds, seals and whales—the only one that remains during the bitterly cold winter is the emperor penguin.

As we stumbled back to the comforts

While our 250-gallon auxiliary fuel tank rode in the first-class section, the rest of us flew economy class. Our second 2,000-mile flight to Vinson Massif was less than comfortable, especially since pilot Giles Kershaw had to take us high enough in the unpressurized Twin Otter to clear a series of mountain ranges. However, on the positive side, it meant a bit of acclimatization en route.

of our warm prefab home, we marvelled at the endurance of the early explorers who struggled into these same gale-force winds, sometimes for weeks on end in ice-encrusted clothing. The epic 1911 trip described by Apsley Cherry-Garrard in his book *The Worst Journey in the World; Antarctic, 1910-1913* is probably the most astounding description ever of the Antarctic. The team of three (Wilson, Bowers and Cherry-Garrard) set out for the Ross Ice Shelf at 11 a.m. on June 27, the height of the dark winter. Their mission was to visit Cape Crozier 65 miles away and retrieve an egg of an emperor penguin in the hope that the primitive embryo would establish a conclusive link between reptilian scales and feathers. For 36 days, they endured the harshest conditions possible. Cherry-Garrard wrote: "Such extremity of suffering cannot be measured. Madness or death may give relief. But this I know: we on this journey were already beginning to think of death as a friend." Yet they survived. At journey's end, their frozen clothes had to be cut from their bodies, and Cherry-Garrard's sleeping bag had turned into a mass of ice weighing 45 pounds, up from its original weight of 18 pounds.

The wonders of Esperanza and Hope Bay began to pale on our fifth day as we worried about the crew and the plane. High winds over Ushuaia had forced them to fly on to Rio Gallegos, where the Colonel's name had little influence. They were embraced not with open arms but with a fierce Argentine nationalism and three days' house arrest in a hotel. We found out later that Gatica had failed to inform either the air force or the navy that the army was assisting us, and neither of the two rival military branches took the news well. Working by radiotelephone in Esperanza, Peter used all of his considerable powers of negotiation to patch up the misunderstandings our group had engendered. Even then, the results were far from satisfying. Our flight crew was freed and the plane repaired, but we were denied any further Argentine assistance. When the pilots returned to Esperanza after seven days, it was only to pick us up and head back to Punta Arenas, Chile, leaving a nervous Colonel Gatica behind to face the consequences of his British fraternizing.

It was a tense week in Punta Arenas as we desperately looked for a fresh start. Finally, General Don Javier Lopetegui, a retired air force general working as an advisor on Antarctic matters to the Chilean department of tourism, came forth with help. General Lopetegui, like many who believe that the Antarctic's climate and its isolation preclude cost-effective resource extraction, is convinced the future of the continent lies in its preservation and in tourism. He saw in our plans a chance to develop some of his own and offered to sell us Chilean fuel from a cache near the British base of Rothera on Adelaide Island for our second attempt to reach Vinson. His only stipulation was that we comply with the conditions of the Antarctic Treaty by taking along a Chilean observer, and thus we added 25-year-old Alejo Contreras, one of the finest climbers in Chile, to our team.

At this point, Peter graciously bowed out to make room for Alejo. Having already forfeited his job at New York's Columbia University by joining us (he had been taking too much time off work), he now gave up his chance to climb the mountain he had been striving to reach since the mid-1960s.

But not even Lopetegui's goodwill could save us. Seven hours after leaving Punta Arenas for the second time, we landed near Rothera, the base for the British Antarctic Survey, where a routine inspection of the plane revealed that 8 out of 32 rotor blades inside one of the engines had been flattened. Giles lost little time in informing the team that their beloved and beleaguered expedition was lost. The engine obviously worked well at lower elevations, he told us, but he was unwilling to trust it on takeoff at the altitudes of more than 7,500 feet we would encounter in the interior. "There are 51 known plane skeletons in Antarctica, and some of them are DC3s," he said simply. "I don't want to add another one to the list." Sick at heart, we turned back again. The expedition had collapsed, and it would take another year to put it back on its feet.

The realities of the 1984 expedition were to haunt my efforts at every turn. Steve Drogin took its failure personally and, treating it as an unsuccessful business venture, withdrew his support.

As the crew refuelled on Chilean aviation gas stored near the British Antarctic Survey's Rothera Base on Adelaide Island, Martyn Williams and I took time out for a quick ski down the slopes of Marguerite Bay.

Just 600 miles from the South Pole, we landed the Twin Otter and set up our Base Camp on a dramatically desolate site not far from Mount Tyree (left) and Mount Epperly (right). Martyn Williams and I cast longing eyes toward Tyree as it is one of the world's most challenging mountains, and its 6,000-foot west face has yet to be climbed. Aware of the area's winds, we immediately built thick snow walls around the camp as a defence for our tents and then began to ferry supplies to the base of Vinson three hours away. At 3 a.m. the next day, the Chilean Air Force parachuted fuel to us so that Giles Kershaw could begin his flights back and forth to Chile to pick up two more teams intent on following in our footsteps.

Having lost my financial patron, I had to get back into high gear and return to potential corporate sponsors—failure looming darkly in the background.

## CIRCUITOUS ROUTES

Worst of all, four months after my return to Canada, I learned that Texas millionaire businessman Dick Bass, after joining four Mount Everest expeditions in two years, had finally summited—claiming, at age 55, to be not only the oldest person to stand atop Everest but the first person to stand atop all the continents. My chances for sponsorship were now considerably lessened, as my project no longer had the same media impact.

What the media had dubbed "the seven-summits race" was over, even though, in my mind, the game still lacked satisfactory definition. Bass had chosen to include Australia's 7,310-foot (2,228 m) Kosciusko in his bid, a mountain I had climbed in 1983 during a 54-hour stopover in Sydney. From a climber's point of view, Kosciusko is the weak link in the series. In the first place, that modest peak is not the highest mountain in Australia. That distinction goes to Big Ben, a spectacular snow-capped volcano rising 9,003 feet (2,745 m) from sea level in the remote territory of Heard Island.

From the outset, I had decided that the highest peak on the continental shelf of Australasia, which encompasses Australia, New Zealand and New Guinea —16,023-foot (4,884 m) Carstensz Pyramid, an isolated jungle-bound summit—seemed more worthy of highest peak status. Early that spring, I had met with *The Vancouver Sun*'s managing editor, who had offered to put on a public fund-raising drive through his newspaper, but upon hearing that Dick Bass had completed his quest, he immediately withdrew his support.

Perversely, the setbacks only fuelled my determination to continue. With Martyn and Mike, I began to follow a path even more circuitous than that of the year before. Before year's end, I joined Sir Edmund Hillary and astronaut Neil Armstrong at the North Pole as part of a promotional package, helped to found an adventure-tour company and became part-owner of an airline.

The flight to the pole was an idea of Mike Dunn's, who had already organized six previous excursions. He reasoned that publicity of any kind might attract a Vinson sponsor, and so he included Martyn and me on his big-bill Hillary/Armstrong trip—offering profits from his paying clients toward the Antarctic attempt.

On our return from the pole, we stopped off for four days to make a ski ascent of the 5,000-foot (1,524 m) Ad Astram peak on western Ellesmere Island, encountering conditions even more severe than those expected in Antarctica. With temperatures hovering at minus 56 degrees F (-49°C) and lower for our entire climb, we had ample opportunity to test our equipment and ourselves. While the others were turned back on foot by snow conditions, Martyn and I finished the climb on skis and learned some valuable lessons. We found that the tent fabric shrank 25 percent, making it difficult to erect correctly, and foods with high water content, such as cheese and salami, became immutable chunks of steel.

Bart Lewis, a Calgary-based promoter, had been flogging the seven-summits project all over the continent, looking for sponsors, showering me with an endless stream of phone calls. He considered every trick in his fund-raising bag—from motivational slide lectures, product endorsements and limited-edition prints to t-shirts, adventure films and magazine features—but nothing ever seemed to work out.

Hearing of my plight, family friends Russ and Bette Davis called up to offer an interest-free loan of $24,000 (U.S.) to be used as a down payment in securing a plane and fuel, but it was the continued enthusiasm of General Lopetegui in Chile and a surprise call from South Korea in August that ultimately took us back to Antarctica. General Lopetegui told us he could deliver supplies and fuel to the mountain once we had a plane. The airdrop of 36 drums of fuel from a Chilean Hercules would cost a hefty $40 (U.S.) per gallon, but it was a fair price, given the circumstances. More important, the Chileans promised rescue assistance, if necessary. This was the most generous offer ever made by any Antarctic Treaty nation to a private expedi-

tion, and we were determined to live up to the safety measures stipulated by Chile.

Soon after the general's offer, a long-distance call for help came from South Korea via one of Mike's worldwide connections. South Korea, it seemed, wanted to enter the Antarctic sweepstakes by putting seven climbers on top of the continent and sending nine marine biologists on a circumnavigation of King George Island, at the tip of the peninsula. By hiring our expediting services, they would help pay for our expenses. I had already been in touch with a group of eight Americans led by Dan Emmett of Santa Monica that included renowned climbers Yvon Chouinard and Doug Thompkins, who were interested in the Antarctic climb, so the Korean interest cemented our plans. With three planeloads of paying climbers, we would just barely be able to cover the costs of our own expedition—providing nothing went wrong. At an overall price tag of $400,000 (U.S.) for the trip, we would be offering not only one of the world's most expensive seat sales but one of the riskiest.

## KOREAN CONNECTION

By midsummer of 1985, Adventure Network International, Inc. was established, an idea born of the aspirations of a group that included Martyn and his partner Maureen Garrity (who together operate the Yukon branch of Ecosummer Canada Expeditions), Mike Dunn, pilot Giles Kershaw, Bart Lewis, Baiba and me. Our intention was to pool the talents not only of expediters the world over but also of resource people from other fields to assist individuals and groups in gaining access to the world's most isolated regions. After the completion of the Vinson expedition, we agreed to keep the infrastructure intact for future projects. We also created a subsidiary company, Antarctic Airways, with a fleet of one leased aircraft to handle our transportation needs. "This must be the first time an airline has been founded in order to climb a mountain," scoffed Martyn.

In mid-August, Mike met for five days in Seoul with the Sea Explorers of Korea, laying down the terms of the contract for

Adventure Network's involvement. The trip, it seemed, was definitely on. Again. On August 29, only two months prior to our scheduled departure, the fabric began to unravel when the owners of the the Tri Turbo we had chartered in 1984 informed us it was no longer available to us. Scrambling to find a Twin Otter capable of the journey, I was told that even if I found a plane, due to the past year's global rash of aviation accidents and hijackings, insurance was unavailable to us at any cost.

Martyn, a boisterous, red-haired Viking of Welsh extraction, known for his high performance in the mountain world, took on the task of preparing an official itinerary and expedition plan, also arranging for the charter of a Twin Otter from Calgary's Kenn Borek Air, conditional on the acquisition of insurance.

Circumstances had changed incredibly since our original budget, which had been based on the use of the Tri Turbo. We were now looking at $70,000 (U.S.) for the fuel drop at the mountain. (As General Lopetegui had told us, "You cannot expect to go to the remote regions of Antarctica on a shoestring budget. Once you leave South America, costs add up quickly.")

Our latest paying teammate was Bill Hackett, a sporting-goods distributor. The 64-year-old veteran climber had climbed Aconcagua, Elbrus, Kilimanjaro and McKinley 20 years before but had shelved a very active climbing career for a more lucrative profession. Only recently, he had climbed Mount Hood, outside his hometown of Portland, Oregon, for the 88th time. We had planned three teams for Vinson: a Korean team, the Emmett team, and our own, of which Bill would be a member. Once I had met him, the project began to take on a human element.

At the 11th hour, we procured liability coverage through Gordon Luna at Westar Insurance, but at $60,000 (U.S.) for two months, it cost twice as much as that for the Otter used in the Trans Globe expedition of 1979-81. Giles called and said we would need additional fuel at Rothera if we were to accommodate the Koreans' rigid timetable. The Korean and Emmett teams were on conflicting schedules that did not allow the most efficient use of the plane, meaning that

it had to be flown empty on two occasions, elevating costs once again. It almost meant that our group would be forced to go early in the season when temperatures are colder than at midseason. Once at the mountain, we would also have the pressure of knowing that two more groups were waiting on our heels, wanting to get to the mountain regardless of what our situation was.

---

## SPRING IN PATAGONIA

In Kimberley, Baiba and I relied on the telephone for a continuous stream of calls to England, Chile, Alaska, Vancouver and Calgary to prop up our shaky dispositions.

With fewer than 10 days to departure, Mike returned from leading a safari in Africa just in time to rush to Los Angeles for a final hectic week to try to pacify the Koreans, who were incensed that their plane tickets to the centre of Antarctica were so expensive.

On October 28, I bade an emotional goodbye to Baiba who, by all rights, deserved a seat on the plane for all her work. Instead, she headed to Montreal to visit her parents, while I flew off for round three in the Antarctic. With the accumulated stress from the past three months clogging my system and the lack of time for any appreciable physical exercise, I was probably in the worst condition that I had been in many years. Once on the jet, though, I slumped into my seat and managed to have a completely relaxing sleep.

The Patagonian spring was miserable, and a heavy wind drove falling snow sideways across the runway when we landed in Punta Arenas. It took a few days for the members of our team to appear. Giles and Rick Mason were flying the Twin Otter south from Calgary in a seven-day trip, with piloting help from Giles' friend John Patterson. Steve Fossett arrived, his voice still hoarse from a successful September swim across the English Channel, a fourth attempt that had left him in the water for 22 hours. Our team doctor, Roger Mitchell, a friend from the Yukon, prescribed quantum doses of "pisco sour," a delicious but tangy Chilean alcoholic drink. The other members of the 1985 expedition included Maureen Garrity, who would act

as liaison in Punta Arenas with the Chilean authorities and the other two climbing teams; Pat Caffrey, a Montana forester with several altitude climbs to his credit; Bill Hackett; and Alejo Contreras, our Chilean climber-cum-observer, who belongs to the mountain rescue organization Cuerpo Soccoro Andino, and has been on more than 130 missions into the Andes. Alejo had arrived with his vintage Sony Walkman, bound together with wire and tape, and his only cassette, Steppenwolf's "Born to be Wild." Whenever he played it, his eyes looked into some dreamy world that belied the music's raucous nature. We signed on the Hugh Macleay family of Punta Arenas as honorary team members, since they had opened their house for use as a staging area, as well as airport manager Juan Radic, who relayed messages to Maureen from Antarctica and who would ensure that our airdrop was sent out on schedule.

Punta Arenas has received the full benefit of European taste and investment capital, and large stately stone houses are interspersed among the more modest but colourfully painted wooden clapboard structures. It is an attractive town with architectural lines from 19th-century Europe, kept clean by an incessant wind that picks up any loose refuse and carries it off across the dusty pampas. The friendly residents, a mixture of mestizos and northern European descendants, wear windbreakers out of habit, even on warm, sunny days.

On November 9, Giles arrived at the Punta Arenas airport and telephoned to say he had obtained flight clearances as far as the Chilean Teniente Marsh Base on King George Island.

The next day, I found myself once again above the Drake Passage, winging south, praying for an uneventful trip. As we throbbed our way out of sight of Punta Arenas, I felt even smaller and more insignificant than one does when in the mountains. With only enough fuel for 900 miles, we had to make it to Teniente Marsh. Turning back was not an option. There were eight of us crammed into the tiny airplane alongside a 250-gallon auxiliary gas tank and 950 pounds of gear, and we were forced to sit bolt upright, with no legroom. Yet as the oxygen content dropped in the unpressur-

The peculiar pyramid-shaped summit of "Flamingo Point," clearly visible from our vantage point at the top of Vinson's first icefall, rises 500 feet from the 8,000-foot-thick ice of the Polar Plateau. Exhausted physically and mentally from months of logistical problems and affected by the altitude, I felt somewhat like an inebriated penguin stumbling about the slopes. To make matters worse, the sun shone 24 hours a day, and my internal clock was having trouble keeping track of what time it was. Finally, I stashed my watch until the climb was over.

Above Camp Two, we caught a glimpse of Vinson's summit, just over the left shoulder of a black ridge. Camp Two is far below on the broad glacier to the left.

ized cabin, we all nodded off—a rare chance to rest before the climb.

The cloud cover was heavy, but after refuelling at Teniente Marsh, Giles got word by radio of an unexpected window in the weather. We took to the air once more, flying into brilliant sunshine that lasted for the entire three-hour 450-mile flight to Adelaide Island. A rosy blanket of cloud coated most of the peninsula below us, and in the distance, the icy flanks of the Forbidden Plateau (Graham Land) shone in the evening sun. Passing close by Brabant Island, a spectacular peak with heavily crenulated ridges caught our attention. Clear of open water, I was breathing easier, and any lingering sense of foreboding was washed away by the cleansing rays of the sun. In our ski-equipped air taxi, we had the wonderful capability of setting down almost anywhere we wanted on the Antarctic "runway" of ice.

Our final refuelling, and a night's stopover, was at a Chilean fuel cache near the British Rothera Base. Base commander Andy Perry and several of his men travelled out by snowmobile to greet us and exchange news. Our good fortune with the weather thus far was reinforced by the fact that it had just cleared for the first time in 34 days.

The next day, we began the final leg of our flight to Vinson Massif, our departure marred only by the arrival of a telex from England saying the Rothera Base was not in any way to assist or approve our expedition or others like it. Giles, who had suggested the location for the base 10 years before while in the employ of the British Antarctic Survey, shook his head in disbelief.

Four hours later, the Otter broke through a blanket of cloud, and for the first time, we saw the Ellsworth Mountains, 190 miles away. The range was broadside to us, presenting a jagged coxcomb profile, and our little plane was suddenly alive with excited chatter. I crawled up into the cockpit with Rick and Giles to get a better look. To avoid possible turbulence, Giles ascended to 17,000 feet as we crossed the range from north to south, leaving us gasping for breath, heads pounding. We soared over a high snow-wreathed shoulder, while further below, the mountains met the flow of the Nimitz Glacier on the edge of the Polar Plateau, a vast interior ice sheet.

Our amazement at the abruptness of the range was probably no less intense than that of the first aviators to sight it. In 1935, American millionaire Lincoln Ellsworth and Canadian pilot Herbert Hollick-Kenyon made the first aerial crossing of west Antarctica, and when they returned, they named the 210-by-54-mile mountain system the Sentinel Range. (Vinson Massif was named after U.S. Congressman Carl Vinson, who had been a strong proponent of Antarctic research and exploration from 1935 until he retired in 1961.) During the next 51 years, Vinson Massif, in the Ellsworth Mountains of the Sentinel Range, was climbed only three times: twice by American teams (the first a National Science Foundation-backed team in 1966 and one sponsored by Dick Bass in 1983) and once by a team of German and Russian geologists.

## SNOWY DEFENCES

As we circled our landing site, four or five miles from the foot of an icefall where we would establish Camp One, we were relieved to note that it had been some time since the wind last scoured the glacier. Giles' landing was as smooth as the surface of the snow, and he taxied for half a mile in a straight line to leave a target for the Hercules that was to drop food and fuel for us. As the engines died, we became acutely aware of our dependence on our flight crew. The closest base, should we have to ski for it, was the U.S. Siple station, 150 miles to the north, and the next closest was 600 miles away at the South Pole. Aware that we were unwelcome at either base (despite a banner at the latter that reads "The United States welcomes you to the South Pole"), we strengthened our resolve to remain autonomous.

Hopping out of the plane into the crisp minus-31-degree-F (-35°C) air, we stretched our cramped limbs and slapped each other on the back. More than half of the battle had been won.

Our celebration was short, though, for we were in an extremely exposed position and our first instinct was to dig in. Nothing but a barren expanse of ice separated us from the steep ridge of

Although much of the climbing above Camp Two was easy, we had to exercise caution going through the second icefall and belayed one another through a series of crevasses.

Mount Shinn, over which we would have to climb to reach Vinson Massif. To the other side of the glacier rose the rock wall of the Tyree/Gardner massif, soaring vertically out of the ice for nearly 8,000 feet (2,438 m) to its summit of just under 16,000 feet (4,876 m). Stiff summit winds whipped a two-mile spindrift contrail out to the north, over the Ronne Ice Shelf. Remembering the storm at Esperanza, we quickly began to prepare our defences. The infamous Antarctic winds, known to meteorologists as katabatic winds, are generated as gravity pulls the dense cold air down from the icecap toward the ocean at speeds of up to 200 miles per hour. We knew all too well their potential for destruction.

The winds pack the Antarctic spindrift into a dense crystalline material more reminiscent of iron plate than of snow, and we had to use carpenter saws with ripsaw blades to cut it. The walls we built at each of the four camps would each take half a day but were intended for use by all three climbing parties. Martyn's extensive experience travelling and living in the harsh environment of Canada's north, especially the St. Elias ice cap in the Yukon, stood us in good stead.

With thick four-foot-high walls at our back, we snacked on chocolate and then began a three-hour trip ferrying supplies to the foot of the mountain. Giles had been the pilot for the Bass expedition in 1983, and he started out ahead to show us the way. We had to scramble to keep up with him. He was fitter than most of us, and the week or more of flying at altitude in an unpressurized cabin had given him a head start on acclimatization. We were ready to sign him on as a climber on the spot. Unfortunately, he and Rick were scheduled to return to Punta Arenas to pick up the Korean climbers as soon as the Chilean Herc made its airdrop.

The 36 drums of aviation fuel descended from the sky at three the following morning just 500 yards from camp. Nine parachutes carried four drums per plywood pallet each, and a ton of food and supplies occupied a 10th and an 11th parachute. The expert packaging by the Chilean Air Force ensured that not one bag of food had been ruptured on impact. The 11 giant parachutes each

Always mindful of the danger of high winds and our isolation if there were an accident, we built snow walls around each of our camps, cutting snow blocks with a carpenter's ripsaw. Camp Three (above) was especially vulnerable, located on an exposed saddle within view of Mount Shinn (background). Three weeks later, Yvon Chouinard and Doug Thompkins climbed Shinn, the continent's third highest peak, and upon returning to Camp One, they were trapped in their tent for 30 hours by the infamous Antarctic gale-force winds.

weighed almost as much as a person and had to be bundled up and returned in the empty Otter.

Although the airdrop shattered any chance of meaningful rest that first night, we all felt we would rather climb than sleep. We didn't know how long the still, clear weather would last, and we didn't feel comfortable about letting any time slip away that might move us farther up the mountain.

## TELEMARK SPECTACLE

As we arrived at the site of Camp One, the sun slid behind a ridge of Mount Shinn, plunging us into deep shade and minus-22-degree-F (-30°C) temperatures. Exhausted, we staggered about like inebriated penguins as we erected our two tents, dived inside and fired up the stoves. Slowly, a little warmth began to seep back into our bodies. The months of high stress and nonstop effort necessary just to reach the mountain had taken their toll, and now, on top of that, we found the 24 hours of sunlight in the Antarctic summer playing brand-new games with our minds and bodies. Charged with energy from the continual sunlight, our minds told us to keep moving while our bodies said, "Whoa, slow down!"

A four-inch coating of powder on the 1,500-foot (457 m) icefall made for easy climbing. So easy, in fact, that we considered not even fixing a hand line up its upper 600 feet (183 m), where it steepened to 40 degrees. Where Dick Bass's group had had to use utmost caution on the slippery wind-packed slope two years before, Martyn was able to ski down, carving 108 symmetrical telemark turns in a row from the top. I regretted having cached the video camera at Camp One that day, thereby missing the chance to record this graceful spectacle.

When we broke out onto a tight notch on the Shinn ridge, catching our best view of Vinson Massif, its true summit was still hidden from us. The site of Camp Two was clearly visible, however, on the edge of a cirque, or glacially carved bowl, where maximum sun exposure would ensure we were gently awakened every morning. Camp Three lay on a broad saddle between Shinn and Vinson. Between the two camps, we would have to climb 2,000 vertical feet (610 m) up the cirque, the upper section of which was dominated by a moderately crevassed icefall.

At Camp Two, we stacked a double row of marshmallow snow blocks against each other, hoping that the bonding effect of disturbed snow would help solidify them. A large, half-open crevasse 300 feet away would be our only escape if a big storm destroyed our tents.

On ski and on foot, we established a route through the crevasses on the upper glacier, cut a platform in the saddle, where we cached four days' worth of food, and returned to a much-needed 11-hour sleep at Camp Two. The wind rattled us out of our dreams the next day, and without even looking outside, we knew we were in for a rest day. On the pass, the wind was busy burying our platform cache in three feet of compacted spindrift.

It was during that day that Bill Hackett, who had torn a cartilage in his neck earlier, decided to abandon the climb, and the next morning, he headed down the mountain. Martyn, worried about Bill working back through crevasse country by himself, dashed up to Camp Three, deposited his load, skied back to Camp Two, roped up to Bill and continued down to Base Camp with him. Here he greeted the Koreans who had arrived at Base Camp the day before, then skied and climbed back up with another load of food to join us at Camp Three. He had descended a total of 4,000 vertical feet (1,219 m) and ascended 6,000 (1,829 m) in one long, long day, earning Bill's praise: "In all my years of climbing, Martyn is the strongest person I have ever had the good fortune to climb with."

Meanwhile, we had been in contact with Giles by VHF radio, telling him that Bill was on his way down, and he asked if he could join us on the summit push. "No problem," we answered, and with that, he tucked his sleeping bag, a thermos of tea and our Base Camp pink flamingo mascot into his pack and started off for Camp Three. Both he and Martyn pulled into camp at 4 a.m., eyeballs frozen open. The rest of the team was groggy from their own minor climb of 2,000 feet (610 m) but managed to brew a pot of tea for the hardworking arrivals.

After an astonishing one-day trip to Base Camp and back, Martyn Williams, tired and caked with frozen water vapour from his push up 6,000 vertical feet, rejoined us at Camp Three with Giles Kershaw.

The next day was clear and cool, the air mentholated. Despite the promising conditions, though, we declared another rest day, ostensibly for the benefit of Martyn and Giles but really for all of us. Plumes of wind-driven snow were coming off the lovely summit of the continent's third highest mountain, Shinn, directly above us. And although we were becalmed for the moment, the snow and ice around us told the story of far less gentle times. Vertical crevices between ice towers had been carved into gaping holes, and even on the smooth surface of the glacier, the wind's steely fingers had gouged two-foot-deep troughs, stripping snow down to cobalt-blue ice.

## TOP OF THE BOTTOM

Day eight dawned clear, and we were out on the slopes by the time the sun hit. We had some 4,000 vertical feet (1,219 m) ahead of us and needed an early start. Roger, Steve, Martyn and I were on Nordic skis, while the others, roped together, followed Alejo at a slow but steady pace on foot. The climbing consisted of straightforward, tedious plodding up the side of a massive snow basin, and it seemed like centuries before we reached the foot of the final 700-foot (213 m) summit wedge. Roger and Steve cached their skis here, while Martyn and I strapped ours to our packs. We all donned crampons and began kicking our way to the top.

Less than an hour later, Martyn pulled himself onto the summit cornice, and the rest of us followed, hugging each other, shouting out to the empty continent and dancing at the top of the bottom of the world. Blubbering through my ice-encrusted moustache, I grabbed Martyn and gave him my heartfelt thanks. "You don't have to tell me that," he said, and began to laugh. "I can tell it by the way you're crushing me." At the point of tears, I looked out on the mountains and fell silent. I had finally reached what had seemed an impossible goal. My friends had helped me on every leg of the journey, sorting out solutions to extreme logistical and financial problems, and now I found it impossible to convey to them my feelings of appreciation. While Everest had been physically the most demanding peak, Vinson, isolated and

A t the summit, we chose to display the United Nations flag on the only continent that knows no sovereignty. Standing (left to right) are Steve Fossett, Alejo Contreras, Martyn Williams; kneeling, me, Pat Caffrey, Giles Kershaw, Mike Dunn and Roger Mitchell.

wrapped in red tape, had seemed the most impossible, and here I was finally on top of it, surrounded by friends.

Amazingly, there wasn't a breath of wind, and we had to hold open our United Nations flag for the inevitable summit photographs. Because the Antarctic continent enjoys no sovereignty, we had magnanimously claimed the continent for the world. We also left a plastic garden-variety flamingo as a symbol of the Flamingo Party we had formed to rule this newly founded nation. The Canadian flag also came out, along with the flags of the United States, Britain and Chile. Beyond us, the Tyree/Gardner massif dominated the horizon, with dozens of other pristine unclimbed peaks lined up behind and to the side of it. To the north, the Ronne Ice Shelf dissolved in the distance into a wall of incoming cumulus clouds. Our noisy celebration became a silent appreciation of a magnificent, unfettered and untrammelled land. The great polar plateau rolled off to the south, the horizon bending toward the South Pole, a scant 600 miles away. Unconsciously, we found ourselves tracing possible ski routes and descents for traverses of the range itself.

For almost two hours after the others had begun their descent, Martyn and I lingered on top in the windless, minus-22-degree-F (-30°C) air. Somewhere out there this season, scientific teams of two would be dropped off to spend up to three months in the field. Even though the more adventurous would run their eyes wantonly over the sensuous skyline of rocky peaks, they would have to suppress their desire to climb. Edicts issued from home offices half a world away would prohibit them from even thinking about scaling a peak for nonscientific purposes.

Finally, we reluctantly stepped onto our skis and pushed off gently from the summit, traversing the edge of a cornice that stretched half a mile down one of the summit ridges. We yelped and whooped our way across the dragon-hide snow which was so rough that we heard the terrible scraping sounds of Roger's and Steve's ski edges trying to find a grip, less than a mile away.

As we came to the edge of the cornice, Martyn tried to sideslip down the 70-degree slope to easier ground. But suddenly, he was gaining momentum all too quickly. A rooster tail of snow shot 10 feet in the air as his ice axe scraped the impenetrable surface, his skis flailing impotently below him, rocks looming too close. After an eternity of three seconds, his iron-hard grip on the head of his axe finally drove it into the hilt, nearly pulling his arms out of their sockets. With his body suspended limply a few feet above an assortment of multicoloured meat-grinder rocks, he breathed a huge sigh of relief, which I echoed from my perch above. "Are you okay?" I squeaked. "Yeah, but this isn't my idea of the perfect ski run," he replied. Wanting desperately to avoid such dramatics, I chose a different route to descend the cornice. As I came to a point directly above him along a border of red-coloured sedimentary rocks, I could feel my edges starting to wash out. My fist instinctively pushed me back upright, but I was quickly losing control in an accelerating slide. Twice more I hit the snow, but the last time, I couldn't regain my stance and went screaming into the rocks, skis and legs outstretched to absorb the shock.

Shaken and slightly dizzy from hyperventilating in the cold, thin air, we both exchanged skis for crampons and descended the next 400 feet (121 m) to less intimidating ground. At the top of the basin, we launched out again on snow that varied in its hardness and consistency from turn to turn. Periodically, we were thrown into involuntary daffy jumps over the two-foot-deep trenches in between the wind-carved ridges. It was one of the most technically demanding telemark descents of our lives, and it took every trick we had learned in our combined 30 years of skiing to negotiate the 3,000-vertical-foot (914 m) run back to the high camp. Each turn had to be precise and every recovery spectacular. With a delicate video camera tucked into my pack, I couldn't afford to take any more bone-crushing falls.

But finally, we came upon more forgiving terrain on the lower third of the basin, which spilled onto the Shinn Col. Glass-smooth ice dunes, coated with a quarter-inch of hoar crystals took an edge as easily as frozen butter. A hushed calm came over our soaring spirits as we

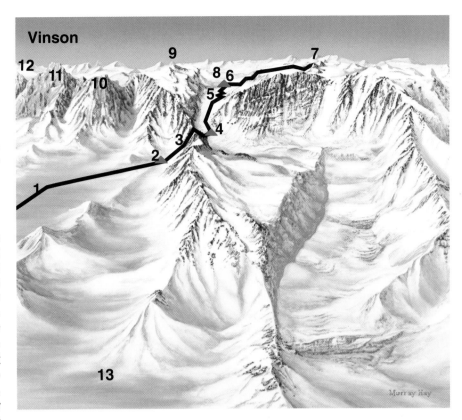

1. To Base Camp
2. Camp One (8,500 feet)
3. First Icefall
4. Camp Two (10,000 feet)
5. Second Icefall
6. Camp Three (12,000 feet)
7. Vinson Summit (16,067 feet)
8. Shinn-Vinson Col
9. Mount Shinn (15,356 feet)
10. Mount Epperly (15,238 feet)
11. Mount Tyree (15,903 feet)
12. Mount Gardner (14,983)
13. Nimitz Glacier

glided into the shadow of one of Vinson's ridges. Suddenly, it made a lot of sense to be here. We no longer felt like interlopers from another world.

All too soon, we reached the door of our tent. With Vinson under our belts, Martyn and I now gazed longingly toward Mount Tyree, the range's second-highest peak, which offered a more challenging ascent. If we climbed alpine style and the weather was cooperative, we could be back within several days. Our interest was piqued because of some claims that Tyree might be higher than Vinson. Prior to our departure from Canada, there had been some controversy as to which of the two mountains was actually the highest on the continent, and while new measurements had recently been taken of the whole range, only half of them had been published. We had seen the new official altitude of Tyree (15,903 feet [4,847 m]), but Vinson's was still a secret. Giles was quite confident of Vinson's stature, but still, the thought of having climbed the lower one was devastating.

We looked at our time schedule vis-à-vis the imminence of the next group's arrival date and the fickleness of Antarctic weather and decided that time was not our own. The others on the team were anxious to leave, a feeling that Martyn and I did not share, having both worked for more than two years to reach one of the world's most inaccessible mountains.

We dismantled the camp and descended into the heavy fog that had developed in the valley below. Miraculously, the mist lifted just as we reached the brink of the most dramatic part of the icefall. The mountain's most impressive features unfolded at a time when we could appreciate them the most. On our way up, we had been labouring under monstrous packs and paying homage to the snow in front of our noses.

Far below, the others appeared as microdots on a constantly changing spreadsheet. We were now on the lower slopes of the upper icefall, and the snow's consistency turned into one of the skiing world's least desirable surfaces—breakable crud. With teetering packs forcing us to concentrate completely, we wallowed our way across the endless slopes. Tired of walking, Mike tried skiing these lower slopes, but as he broke through the crust, he fell face first, and his pack plunged forward, driving his head into the ground. During the fall, he twisted his leg, partially tearing bits of binding tissue from the inside of his knee, and we found him near the top of the fixed rope, limping painfully along, under a pack festooned with skis. With another person, it would have been a worst-case scenario and meant a difficult evacuation, but Mike is a man with exemplary willpower, and he assured us he would be all right.

We made our way down the fixed rope, then reverted to a more primitive form of propulsion as we glissaded down on our backsides until we hit powder. It was perfect powder atop a stainless-steel-smooth base, living up to the promise of a "Ski Antarctica" bumper sticker at home that boasts: "half-inch powder on a 10,000-foot base." We were sufficiently inspired to genuflect under our loads and left the best and only set of telemark tracks that the Ellsworth Mountains have ever seen.

Exuberant, we glided into the Koreans' advance Base Camp. They were characteristically cheerful and immediately poured us some ginseng tea, laced with whisky. "How is the route above Camp One?" we were asked. "We will carry the generator to recharge our Beta video camera batteries as far as Camp Three." Good luck, buddies, I thought. Their ambition was to use their fine international-calibre climbers, one re-

porter and one cameraman to move an entire outdoor movie studio to the top of Antarctica.

We departed, wishing them all the luck that we had had. In fact, just after we left, a nine-day storm blew in. In these fierce conditions, only three members of the Korean team were able to make it to the summit, and they were not able to get the camera above Camp Two. Things did not improve for the next group either. When Giles brought the Americans in, poor flying conditions forced them to land and wait twice for better weather while en route to the fuel stops. Then, at the mountain, two of them were pinned in Camp One by a wind they estimated to be more than 100 miles per hour. Battling continuous storms, six of their eight climbers attempted Vinson, and only two made it. One of the two, Gerry Roach, had been engaged in his own seven-summits quest and completed it with this climb.

## WINGING NORTH

It had been nine days since we had left Base Camp, but in this land of the midnight sun, it seemed like one exceedingly long day. Without further delay, we threw our gear into the plane and gave Alejo a round of hearty farewell hugs. He had to remain there until the final climbing group had left, thereby satisfying the conditions of the Antarctic Treaty and providing a radio link with the outside world in case he had to bring in the Chilean Air Force to handle an emergency.

As we winged north, perfect atmospheric conditions gave us infinite visibility, and Giles excitedly pointed out old familiar features in the icy landscape. Just after midnight, we put down at the Chilean base of Carvajal on the west side of Adelaide Island, where Hector Peligro, the base commander, bunked

On his way down from the summit, Martyn Williams skis delicately across the lip of a crevasse on the upper icefall. The rugged terrain and snow conditions that varied from perfect powder to dragon-hide crust made the descent a suitably challenging end to a long and hard-fought expedition.

us with the rest of his men. Early the next morning, we flew around the south end of the island to the fuelling station at Rothera. The flight was absolutely breathtaking, and now we could see why General Lopetegui was so much in favour of developing tourism on and around Adelaide.

We headed on to King George Island. More spectacular low-level flying took us through Le Maire Channel, where great cusps of unclimbed snow-studded peaks soared straight up from the water's edge. The rest of the peninsula was cloaked in the typical cloud shroud that hangs over the turbulent waters of the Drake Passage.

Our landing in horizontal sleet at Teniente Marsh Base brought about our re-introduction to the world we had left behind aeons ago. We spent several hours indoors while the wind howled outside, reminding us of the windstorm at Esperanza Base the year before. We were not the only visitors, though, and were swept into a buzzing social scene. General Lopetegui, the kingpin of our own expedition, and his associate Monica Krassa were there attending to a group of 20 American tourists. Coincidentally, one of them happened to have some slide duplicates of the first ascent of Vinson, so I was invited to give a short presentation. To the group of about 50 in the hotel, I expressed our team's appreciation for the General's efforts in helping to stimulate adventure travel in Antarctica and, in particular, for his boldness in helping us with our own rather ambitious project.

We left the next day, tired but pleased with our success. I had only one mountain left in my seven-summits bid, and despite its jungle location in the Indonesian territory of Irian Jaya, I was convinced that overcoming Vinson's odds was a sure sign of success in reaching the slopes of Carstensz Pyramid.

# Carstensz

## Stone Age encounters in Australasia

It was 4:30 a.m., and darkness still clung to the Indonesian capital of Jakarta. The heavy silence was broken by the first of five daily calls to prayer sent over powerful loudspeakers, directed at the city's predominantly Muslim population. Mercifully, the sound was filtered by the double-paned glass of our hotel room 17 floors above the ground, but nonetheless, we were wide awake, victims of jet lag from a 30-hour flight that had taken us from Toronto to the opposite side of the world.

At least this time, we were familiar with Muslim customs. Two years before, in August 1984, Baiba and I had been awakened here at the same hour, but we were on the ground floor of another less soundproof hotel, shaken from a deep sleep by the mullah's piercing falsetto. Confused by the haunting wail, we had groped our way to consciousness, taking several minutes to reassure ourselves that it was not a fire alarm or some bizarre air-raid warning.

We had come to Indonesia on both occasions to climb the highest mountain between the Andes and the Himalayas, Carstensz Pyramid, a grey rocky peak that rises 16,023 feet (4,884 m) out of the steamy jungles of remote Irian Jaya. This easternmost province of Indonesia lies on the western half of New Guinea, the second largest island (next to Greenland) in the world, stretching 1,500 miles from tip to tail. Located between Australia and the equator, at the crossroads of Southeast Asia and the South Pacific, the island consists of two distinct regions—the swamps and jungles of the coastal lowlands and the temperate mountain highlands of the interior.

Exotic equatorial glaciers, jagged limestone ridges and a firm waterworn north face make Carstensz Pyramid (also called Jayakesuma) a coveted but seldom-climbed mountaineering prize. In addition to its pleasing aesthetics and challenging routes, it is the highest summit on the continental shelf of Australasia, and I had been drawn to it not only by its seven-summits stature but also by its mystique. Like Vinson Massif, it is all but inaccessible. Today, its seclusion is guaranteed by a defensive wall of rainforest and a government that discourages visitors to the area because of occasional guerrilla activity.

Even the mountain's early visitors were affected by the province's political obstacles. When Carstensz was first climbed by Austrian Heinrich Harrer and New Zealander Phil Temple in 1962, the undeveloped territory of Netherlands New Guinea was in the process of being acceded to Indonesia and was, consequently, unstable. Finally, in 1966, when the American-owned company Freeport Indonesia, Inc., was granted the contract to mine the world's largest known aboveground copper deposit at Carstensz's eastern base, the area relinquished its primordial silence to the roar of bulldozers. Concerned with the business of mining in a region subject to periodic uprisings among the indigenous highland people, both Freeport and the Indonesian government go to great lengths to prevent casual visits to Carstensz. Security is the major local priority, and until recently, tourism has been considered an inconvenience.

## BACK TO THE STONE AGE

On our first foray into the highlands of Irian Jaya in 1984, we had secured what we thought was the correct travel permit from the police in Jakarta only to find, after jet-hopping 3,000 miles across Indonesia's vast archipelago of 13,677 islands, that the heavily stamped document had no influence on the military powers of Irian Jaya. It took almost three weeks on the bureaucratic merry-go-round, both in Jakarta and Jayapura, the capital of Irian Jaya, to realize that the only inland place to which we could travel would be the mile-high Baliem Valley, a tantalizing 125 miles east of our mountain.

Having heard fascinating stories of the valley's Dani people from friends who had spent a month roaming through the villages, we saw this opportunity as a way to salvage our trip.

Within several hours of making our decision to visit the Baliem Valley, we had obtained valid travel permits, booked a flight and stored our climbing and cold-weather gear in Jayapura. As we boarded a Twin Otter for the journey to the interior, we subconsciously turned back our watches to the Stone Age.

Not until 1938, during an expedition sponsored by the American Museum of Natural History, did the Baliem Valley come to the attention of modern society. Under the leadership of Richard Archbold, the party flew to Lake Habbema in the Snow Mountains of the interior to explore the region and collect specimens from the flanks of 15,580-foot (4,749 m) Mount Wilhelmina (now known as Trikora). Its major discovery, however, had nothing to do with alpine flora and fauna. During a reconnaissance flight from the lake, Archbold and his colleagues were thrilled to spot the unmapped 10-by-40-mile valley of the Baliem River. Subsequent meetings with the people convinced them that they were the first white men ever to penetrate their isolated domain.

Archbold's contact with the Dani, however, was brief, and it was not until 1954 that Western missionaries arrived by floatplane to start a permanent settlement in the valley. Two years later, the Dutch, who had claimed the western half of New Guinea in 1828 (and were to lose it in 1963 to the Indonesians, who had been seeking independence for all of the Netherlands Indies since 1945), established a government post and an airstrip at Wamena, near the lower end of the valley beside the Baliem River.

Today, air travel remains the only realistic means of reaching the Baliem Valley, and Wamena—now a settlement of 10,000 merchants, missionaries, Indonesian administrators and elementary-school-educated Dani civil servants—is the staging area for journeys into the heart of the valley.

Our flight, a one-hour hop from Jayapura, was marred by a heavy mist that obscured the highland scenery. Perhaps it was just as well, for our pulses quickened alarmingly whenever the clouds parted; even at 12,000 feet, the Otter was threading its way through mountain passes, the wings skimming past heavily wooded slopes.

We interpreted our safe landing in Wamena as an auspicious beginning to our adventure. This feeling was confirmed minutes later when we bumped into one of the few Dani in the valley who spoke a smattering of English and regularly guided foreigners who wanted to know more about Dani culture than could be learned within the walls of Wamena's two hotels. He was Justinus

A Dani tribesman, *previous page*, decorated with bird-of-paradise feathers and cowrie shells plays his people's only traditional musical instrument, a bamboo mouth harp. Refused permission to climb Carstensz Pyramid by Indonesian security forces, Baiba and I ventured into Irian Jaya's Baliem Valley, 120 miles from the mountain. It was a trip back to the Stone Age, and we felt like intruders from the future. The precarious trip across the Baliem River, *above*, started on a vine-bound raft of logs.

Daby, a short, athletically built airport security guard. Tinus indicated that he would be happy to take us through the Baliem Valley.

## NEUTRAL GROUND

Tinus glowed with excitement as we prepared for the trip. We had come at an opportune time, he explained. Once every four to five years, at the decree of a great *kain* (chief, or big man), a series of weddings is held throughout the valley. It is an institution that some anthropologists believe will not survive another five years because of the inevitable impact of the 20th century. We had walked into the middle of what might be the last of the traditional Dani wedding cycles.

When we had bought a month's supply of canned goods, rice, kerosene, cooking oil and gift items, such as salt and axe heads, Tinus mustered three friends as porters, and we departed Wamena for his home village of Jiwika, following a muddy track that was built under the earlier Dutch administration. Until the mid-1970s, intertribal warfare was a major component of the Dani culture, and in an attempt to curb the constant fighting, the Dutch had set the various tribes to work constructing two broad trails that ran up either side of the valley for its entire length. A former district officer claimed that the roads ''become neutral ground between tribes that used to kill one another on sight. Once they have roads, the Baliem natives can safely walk to and from Wamena. They stay in the exact centre on the theory that it's the safest place.''

As we moved up the valley, strolling through fields green with the Dani's staple crop, *hiperi* (sweet potato), we were struck by the lush beauty of the circumvallate Snow Mountains, which spring straight up from the broad, flat valley floor with the abruptness of the Canadian Rockies. At a base altitude of over 5,000 feet, the Baliem Valley enjoys a much more comfortable climate than the coastal regions less than a hundred miles to the south.

We had left Wamena in the late afternoon, and darkness overtook us only a few miles out, near the settlement of Akima. We decided to spend the night there with some of Tinus's relatives. Akima was typical of the many Dani compounds we were to visit, embodying a layout of dollhouse compactness. We approached two gates, one for pigs, the other for humans, and passed through a rough six-foot stave fence into the barnyard smells of the rectangular enclosure. The circular straw-roofed men's *honai*, always the largest sleeping hut, occupied the far end of the compound. Abutting the *honai* and running down the right side of the village were the pigsties and the shelters for women and children, while to the left was a long communal kitchen. Perhaps a dozen villages in the valley also accommodate tin-roofed administration buildings.

Although we had brought a small tent in order to be self-contained, we enthusiastically welcomed the offer to spend the night in a Dani guest hut. Crawling through a raised doorway in the split-level structure, we found ourselves crouched on a straw-covered floor in a low-ceilinged room that effectively trapped all the smoke from the earthen-floor fire pit. The rough-edged smell of the Dani's omnipresent *hanim* (cigarettes made from home-grown tobacco and rolled in leaves from the forest) permeated the room, and *noken* (net bags), containing dark mysteries, hung from the soot-blackened rafters.

As the fire died, we squeezed ourselves up into the windowless sleeping platform through a trapdoor in the ceiling. When the floor hatch was closed, mosquitoes and ghosts were shut out along with, we quickly discovered, any hint of fresh air. The novelty wore off immediately, and we spent the rest of the night alternately gasping and cursing in the hot, dead air of that claustrophobic little sauna. It was our single attempt at sleeping native.

The next morning, yawning, scratching fleabites and blinking our way into a new day, we got a better look at one of our hosts, Tinus's Uncle Saba. Blessed with an infectious grin, the powerfully built man was clad in the traditional Dani clothing: a long, slender *horim* (penis gourd). The *horim* reached almost to his chest, and when he dropped on his haunches to rest, he took care to hold the tip aside lest he impale the underside of his chin or poke out an eye. His hair

and shoulders had been cosmetically greased with pig fat, and his curly locks were trimmed straight across his forehead. His wife, Waga, wore the traditional married woman's *yokel*, a nonfunctional brace of brightly woven strands that hangs below the buttocks in loops. A couple of hand-knotted *noken* —made from a hand-rolled string of dried, shredded bark and dyed with natural vegetable colouring—swung from the apex of her head, cradling a baby and a bundle of freshly picked *hiperi*.

## RITUAL WARFARE

Our next stop was Jiwika, where we stayed with Wempi, Tinus's brother, in a tin-roofed thatch hut provided by the government. We arrived on August 17, Indonesia's Independence Day, and a small contingent of soldiers and uniformed officials, addressing a soccer field full of clothed and naked Dani, read from the *Pancasila* (the five principles of Indonesian-style democracy) and fired rifles into the air. There was no end to the rhetoric, and we abandoned it for a walk on the outskirts of the village, where we met the aged *kain* Kurelu. The diminutive man, whose name translates to "wise egret," carried himself proudly, a serene but tired smile on his face. He wore a smart red t-shirt and shorts with a tiny pair of tennis racquets silk-screened above the words "Nice Smash." During the early 1960s, Kurelu had presided over nearly a third of the valley's population. In 1966, however, he lost his power to younger men when he opposed a major war within his tribal alliance, and he now spends his days making wraithlike rounds of Jiwika.

In 1961, writer Peter Matthieson visited the valley with the anthropologists, botanists and filmmakers of the Harvard Peabody expedition. Their objective was to observe a living Neolithic community that practised "ritual warfare"—a regularly repeated conflict indispensable to the culture. They found the Dani of the Baliem Valley to be organized into some 12 alliances that were involved in almost continual fighting among themselves, either in open battle or by raiding party. In 5½ months of observing the southern frontier of one alliance's territory, the study group witnessed an

**S**howing signs of both past and current mourning, a Dani woman pauses for a smoke during a funeral ceremony. She has covered herself in mud to grieve the recent loss of a relative; the amputated distal joints on her fingers indicate earlier losses when she was a young girl.

The women of Upatem village wail as the flames of a pyre consume the remains of a 35-year-old woman named Koalaro on the second day of her funeral. On the periphery, a score of old men sit pouting and whimpering, tears on their cheeks, creating a cacophony that could be heard for miles. Funerals are a time for complex ceremonies that climax with the eating of *wam*, crudely butchered pigs baked in pits.

Anxious that tradition be well served, Wenekolik (centre), a popular *kain*, or chief, in the region, consults with his sons on the serious matter of which pig should be killed first for an upcoming wedding. Pigs are an important sign of wealth, and their slaughter is only acceptable during weddings and funerals. Weddings are held throughout the valley every four to five years, at the discretion of a *kain*, who personally oversees the ceremonies.

average of one battle or raid per week. In a year, the death toll resulting from wounds received in warfare between two villages numbered between 10 and 20 on both sides. At the end of the study, anthropologist Robert Gardner concluded that "the Dani engage in 'war' to promote the success and well-being of their social order. In large measure, their health, welfare and happiness depend on the pursuit of aggression against their traditional enemies . . . without it, the culture would be entirely different; indeed, perhaps it could not find sufficient meaning to survive."

Armed Dutch patrols started to pacify the valley residents in the early 1960s, a task the Indonesians continued when they came to power, and by the end of the decade, the valley was essentially war-free. The Dani seemed to take the end of violence with aplomb, and Karl Heider, one of the Peabody anthropologists, revised his opinion on the necessity of war: "Warfare touched many parts of the Dani life but was not essential. . . . Warfare was in many respects not consistent . . . with the basic pattern of Dani culture and therefore relatively easily ended."

It may have been the Dani's long allegiance to aggression that kept them locked in the Stone Age for so many centuries. It could be why the Dani never developed any major art or music forms, ceramic cooking vessels or a written language, and why they never cultivated any stimulants or depressants other than tobacco. Father Hochenbaum of the Catholic mission in Wamena believes that there have been so many factions created through the millennia by the feuding tribes that a collective intelligence, a pooling of ideas and new developments, has never been possible.

"Now that the senseless raiding and warfare have come to an end, we [the church and government] must help to guide the people into the modern age," he told us. "Change is inevitable, but it is the extent of change that is critical. The Dani don't need or want all of the values the rest of the world will try to force on them." We recalled Hochenbaum's words frequently as we travelled up the valley.

In Jiwiki, we met Tinus's father, Ibika.

Her head covered by a net bag, as tradition dictates, a bride stands patiently while she is fitted with her nuptial skirt. The process takes two or three hours as her single-status grass skirt is replaced with one made of orchid and fern fibres tied tightly together with bark string. The skirt impedes her walking ability, but she will wear a lighter-weight version once the wedding ceremony is over. At her feet on a palm frond lie the choicest cuts of a pork rump.

A dandy at the remote village of Watlangku adorns himself with a headdress of rare birds' feathers. As part of the wedding ceremony, 30 similarly dressed men and women danced in an endless circle while hundreds of guests filed into the village with gifts of pork.

The two men did not speak much, having had words in the past about Tinus's abandoning his expected role as farmer and slipping away to Wamena and another century. The father showed us how to light a fire with a split stick, a strand of fire-hardened bamboo and some tinder. As he fumbled with the apparatus, his blue-jeaned son dropped down to help him. Speaking in Dani, the only language Ibika would ever understand, Tinus, with matches in his pocket, gathered up the scattered tinder, unconsciously bridging a generation gap of 4,000 years.

## LIFE AND DEATH

Tinus led us on a tour of the extensive community gardens. In a valley with such a high population density, labour-intensive agriculture has developed along with a sophisticated system of irrigation and drainage ditches. Adhering to tradition, the men occasionally break new ground with a simple spade and prepare it for drainage, while the women are tied to the ceaseless tedium of the planting, maintenance and harvesting of *hiperi*. The men have thus managed to preempt most of the drama and excitement in Dani society, devoting their working hours primarily to decorative rather than functional ends.

After several days in Jiwika, we decided to press on. The trip was made memorable by a crossing of the Baliem River, not far out of Jiwika. As we approached the bank of the broad, muddy current, Tinus shouted out in Dani, and a boatman soon appeared astride four half-submerged vine-bound logs. "Hop on," urged Tinus. "This is the only way we can get to Upatem unless we walk many hours and cross on the new steel footbridge." We approached hesitantly, thinking that the long way around might not be such a bad idea. Pride, though, is a difficult master, and we were soon on the first of what would be four aquaphobic crossings of the Baliem.

Even before we reached Upatem, we could hear dissonant wailing coming from a hut, where a funeral vigil for a 35-year-old woman named Koalaro was well into its second day. A score of old men sat on the ground outside, pouting and whimpering, with tears on their cheeks. Some women emerged from the hut caked from head to heel in a light-coloured mud, a measure of their sorrow.

Until recently, a funeral in the Dani culture was a time of physical pain as well as sorrow, since tradition called for the severing of two distal joints of a young girl's fingers to appease the ghost of the deceased. The girl's lower arm was effectively anaesthetized by a sharp rap on the elbow, and a stone adze was used to chop through the bone. One is not likely to shake hands with as many amputees in one's life as in the Baliem Valley.

Like most other Dani ceremonies, a funeral is an occasion for eating *wam*. Two pigs had been baked, and the meat was distributed on banana leaves among the mourners. A few drops of rain splattered in the already muddy courtyard, and Koalaro's uncle ducked into the hut and returned, carrying her corpse to a funeral pyre. The wailing reached a crescendo as the body was laid down and a pallet of coals scattered on the wooden logs. In seconds, long flames leapt skyward, and a furnace heat drove the mourners back.

Within half an hour, the pyre still ablaze, most of the people, save for a handful of the deceased's closest relatives, had drifted away. Life resumed as usual, smiles returning to the people's faces in their quiet conversations.

We found it difficult to turn down an invitation to a pig feast—signalling an upcoming wedding—at another nearby settlement, Wo'ogi. The marriage cycle was beginning, and within days, the entire valley was infected with the excitement of dozens of weddings. The invitation to Wo'ogi was extended by Wenekolik, one of the better-loved *kain*s in the region. A warrior from the old days, Wenekolik proudly wore a double ring of cowry shells on his upper arm, denoting that he had killed a rival *kain*.

On our arrival at Wo'ogi, we heard the men chanting inside their hut, the traditional means of greeting Dani visitors. They soon emerged, and Wenekolik, who had come to preside over the feast, was with them. Three pigs brought in from the range were casually snuffling around inside the compound. The smallest pig was grabbed by the snout and

At a village near Akima, tribesmen brought out a mummified *kain* that was purported to be 250 years old. For a small fee, we were allowed to photograph it.

held broadside to its young executioner. His arrows, with a bamboo-blade tip but no fletching, had to be aimed from a distance of four feet or less to ensure accuracy, and the crude split-bamboo string of his bow gave minimum weight to the draw. The larger boars were simply goaded into a corner and held at bay with a pole while the not-so-wily hunter sneaked outside the fence and let loose his arrows through an opening in the boards.

Heavy logs that had been hauled into the compound by the men were set afire and the pigs were then tossed whole into the flames, where they swelled up like balloons. The hair was singed and quickly scraped off with sticks. The butchering techniques were basic: a blade of bamboo slit through the pig's hide; hands disgorged the viscera; and a heavy stone axe split the brisket, splaying open the carcass.

At the far end of the compound, the women had lined a two-foot-deep cooking pit with grass, ferns and reeds. Once the pigs were butchered, the women and men began layering the pit with hot rocks from the fire, lush green *hiperi* tops, *hiperi* tubers, cabbages and the splayed pigs. Small stones were tucked into the pigs' "armpits" to ensure complete cooking. When they were finished, they had a three-foot stack of vegetation, hot rocks and pig swathed in a grass cocoon and bound together by a coil of squashed bamboo stalks.

Darkness was flooding into the compound when we finally sat down to eat, tearing flesh off bone, sucking fat and munching on *hiperi*. Grease from the hands was rubbed casually into the scalp and onto the shoulders. Mosquitoes viciously attacked our unprotected backs, but we shrugged them off in the excitement of the moment. The open fire exuded a magical warmth, and we were soon struggling to articulate, in our sorely abbreviated vocabularies, how we felt about each other. The young men wanted us to stay on in their village to give them a chance to learn about Canada in the unlikely event that they would someday travel there. They nodded knowingly to everything we said, but we knew that the world we described lay beyond their understanding.

The party lasted longer than we did.

Feeling no need to burden himself with clothing or ropes, this young Dani rock climber demonstrates his prowess at bouldering.

As fatigue overcame us, we slipped off to the warmth of our sleeping bags, where the repetitive syllables of the Dani's songs made their way into our dreams. Responding to the life pulse of a distant past that yet lives on, the soles of the singers' feet traced ancestral dance patterns in the earth from which legend says they were born.

The pig feast is merely a warm-up for a wedding, which is an equally complicated affair. When a suitor requests the hand of a bride, Tinus explained, he must deal with her brother. The formalities centre on the value of the woman, who usually commands a trade of three to seven pigs. Later in marriage, if the couple are not getting along and the wife wishes to leave with another man, the husband can generally be mollified with a payment of the same number of pigs. The Dani abstain from sexual intercourse from the sixth month of pregnancy until the child is weaned, which in some cases does not take place until the child is more than four years old. That, combined with the practice of limiting childbirth to two offspring per woman, has helped foster polygamy.

Preparing the nuptial skirt consumes much time and energy. Traditionally, the woman's close male relatives spend weeks weaving strands of brightly coloured orchid and fern fibres onto bark strings. The skirt is then custom-fitted to the young bride by removing her grass skirt, which denotes an unmarried woman, and then wrapping and tying the prepared strands around her hips in an operation that lasts over two hours. The bride stands upright for the duration, receiving emotional and physical support from her friends. For most of the time, her head is covered with a net bag. The wedding skirt is much more cumbersome than the *yokel* the woman will eventually wear. It acts as a kind of hobble, making it difficult for her to walk any distance.

A Dani marriage is not consummated until one or two days after the celebration. The bride remains in the cooking hut surrounded by her gifts of net bags and a cured pig carcass. Women from the groom's village, who wear men's headdresses for the occasion, eventually come singing and dancing to collect the bride and carry her off to her new village. During the trip, a scouting party of several women charges ahead of the main group wielding small, sharp planting spears in defiance of any ghosts that may be in the way of the procession. At the new compound, the men and women of the village install the bride in the communal kitchen by chanting and pacing back and forth outside. The bride remains there until nightfall, when her husband appears from his hiding place in the darkness and shares the cured pig meat with her in silence. One of the bride's last acts before leaving the home she has lived in since birth is to start a banana plant in the enclave at the end of the courtyard. If it grows straight and true, it will bring good luck to her and her offspring.

During our stay at Wo'ogi, we slipped into a comfortable centuries-old village rhythm, winning partial acceptance by helping with everyday chores and by joining in during the wild guttural singsongs. Today dissolved into a mirror image of yesterday, and tomorrow became today.

It was, then, with mixed emotions that we organized our packs and said goodbye to Wenekolik. It was hard to leave Wo'ogi, but at the same time, we were excited by the prospects of the final leg of our journey, a trip from the valley into the mountains. Crossing the Baliem River for the last time, we turned east up one of its tributaries, the Wosiela.

As we worked our way toward the mountain ramparts, the *hiperi* fields began to shrink before the forest. Eventually, we reached the margin of primary growth and revelled in the magnificence of the untouched rainforest of mixed hardwoods and araucaria pines. It was a magical place, and we were pleased to learn that the Dani held it in high esteem. Approaching an overlook above a deep amphitheatre, we came upon a rectangular structure couched in the lee of a prominent boulder. Tinus said that it was a spot where people came from as far away as Jiwika to leave the drinking gourds and planting sticks of deceased relatives so that their spirits would live on in the mountain wind.

Of that final hike, Watlangku was our favourite mountain village. Its inhabitants were free-spirited and warmly accommodating, and we romantically attrib-

The porous limestone of the highlands is riddled with karst formations such as the Kontilola cave near Usilimo, features that will no doubt lure more and more cavers and climbers to the area. The Dani, used to dealing with the peculiar ways of interlopers, viewed our interest in the recreational possibilities of the valley with amusement. Sadly, having already established contact with successive Dutch and Indonesian administrations and a string of missionaries, the Dani people will likely not be able to resist modern Western influences much longer.

A small, traditional walled Dani village is perched 2,000 feet above the sweet potato fields to which the women descend daily for the village's food.

uted it to the spectacular setting. The tri-cluster of compounds floated on an island in the sky surrounded by a moat of clear, invigorating air. The tree-clad mountains, at last shedding their mantles of cloud, soared above us on all sides. We hiked up to explore their slopes one morning, guided by a group of small boys, and as we wound our way along the slippery trail, through taller and taller trees, a raucous bird call knifed through the green canopy. Tinus pointed out the dens where giant tree rats are hunted at night. With the string of boys toiling uphill, Tinus playfully shouted, "Expedition to Puncak Jaya!"—alluding to our recent unsuccessful attempt to reach Irian Jaya's highest peak.

At a trail junction that day, we met the *kain* of a nearby village, and he, in the manner we had grown to know so well, invited us to visit his home before we left the mountains. And we, as we had done so often before, accepted the offer of hospitality.

When we reached the village a day later, we found one of the few clear streams in the region draining one side of the property and a breathtaking backdrop of blue-green broad-leaved giants climbing several thousand feet into the swirling mists above. Transfixed, we stood speechless, gazing at the pristine beauty. Shangri-la, we thought, at last. It was a short-lived moment, for when the grinning chief popped out of his hut, he was proudly clutching a ghetto blaster in his hand. In a single second, the magnificence of that remote, idyllic setting was lost to a loud, tinny noise in a plastic box, and we saw our shadow falling onto an old man and his people with the weight of a toppling araucaria.

The next morning, with our chins dug into our chests, we started our long trudge back toward the shank end of the 20th century. It would be fully 20 months before we returned for round two, bolstered with enough paperwork to overcome, we hoped, any hitch in reaching the mountain.

## COOPERATIVE VENTURES

Baiba and I had welcomed the offer of one of my Antarctica climbing partners, Steve Fossett, to join our expedition, and together we had launched into a 17-

month correspondence with official-dom. Once again, I found myself cast as a diplomatic acrobat, jumping through an endless series of bureaucratic hoops while trying to convince myself that I was still a free spirit.

Our first step was to meet with the president of the Freeport mining company in New York, an adventurous sort who was sympathetic to our cause but reluctant to commit his company to accommodating a flood of tourists around the mine site. Steve, a Chicago stockbroker with an office in New York City, kept in constant contact with him, and we were subsequently told that we could secure permission to pass through the mine site only if Indonesian authority was forthcoming. In turn, the Indonesians wanted proof that we had the appropriate clearances from the mine—a Catch-22 of the first order. Nevertheless, we doggedly pushed our enquiries with the foreign affairs departments of the respective governments in Ottawa and Jakarta and, most important, with the Commissioner General of the Indonesian pavilion at Expo 86 in Vancouver, British Columbia.

My proposal to the Expo representatives was for a joint Indonesian-Canadian expedition to Carstensz that could be documented and presented as an audiovisual show at the Indonesian pavilion. In addition, we would pay the transportation and food costs for two of their team members. We pointed out that a logical follow-up to this would be to host these same Indonesians on a climbing trip to Canada's Rocky Mountains a few months later to bring the project full circle. The Indonesians liked the idea and saw it as a tangible return for their cooperation with us. The persistent lobbying efforts of Dahlia Soemolang, director of social and cultural relations in the Foreign Affairs Department in Jakarta, to convince the military that our intentions were harmless and that adventure tourism has a place in their beautiful country finally won out.

At the end of April 1986, the pieces all fell together, just five days prior to our scheduled departure for Indonesia. But even upon arrival in Jakarta, some of the details were still shaky, and telexes had yet to be sent to the military post in Timika and to Freeport Indonesia, Inc., for reconfirmation. We were a noteworthy exception to government policy, but I could not help still harbouring doubts that our expedition would actually be given the go-ahead. After all, no foreign climbing parties had received permission to climb Carstensz since 1975.

## MOUNTAIN PARADISE

Our team of Baiba, Steve and me was complemented by three Indonesian students from the University of Indonesia's Mapala Club, an organization whose members are venturing out beyond Indonesia's overcrowded urban world into such leisure-time sports as climbing, caving and white-water rafting. They were Adi Seno, 27 years old, Titus Pramono, at 25 the leader of the club, and Yura Katoppo, 20. Adi and Titus were in the final stages of their schooling, in geography and economics, respectively, and had taken time out from working on their undergraduate theses to join us. We had met Adi in 1984 in the company of another Mapala Club member, Norman Edwin, who had been instrumental in helping us on our previous attempt to reach Carstensz. Since then, both of them had spent many hours working on our case, through repeated contact with government officials, but unfortunately, Norman had other commitments and could not join us on the second attempt. Yura was a young biology student covering his own expenses for the trip. He had only recently become active in climbing, whereas the other two were, by Indonesian standards, more seasoned mountaineers. Both Adi and Titus had been to Carstensz before (making the seven-day approach from Ilaga in the north) and were more than willing to provide us with interesting information on the area.

Sticky heat smothered us as we wobbled down the stairs onto the tarmac at Timika, on the southern coast of Irian Jaya, 10 hours after leaving our air-conditioned hotel in Jakarta, and our nostrils almost quivered at the promise of cool mountain air. Our stay in Jakarta had seemed like purgatory, a constant assault of sweltering automobile-exhaust fumes aggravated by blaring, beeping car horns. Yet our mountain paradise was not far away, and we were about to

**B**ridging a 4,000-year generation gap, a Dani youngster walks hand-in-hand with his father at Jiwika.

begin exploring this fascinating corner of a vast country that harbours over 300 different ethnic groups, speaking more than 250 languages and dialects.

## WALL OF CLOUDS

From the air above Timika, we had tried to catch a glimpse of the Snow Mountains, also known by the Indonesian name, the Jayawijaya Range. But unfortunately, they were shrouded in a secretive layer of high cumulus that predictably accumulates by noon every day because of the warm, humid air rising from the mangrove swamps of the lowlands.

Rudi Tobing, the government relations representative for Freeport, which is Irian Jaya's largest private employer, met us at the airport. Over the screaming engines of a transport C-130 that had just landed, he yelled that there had been some insurgent activity the previous day and that we would have to stay overnight in Timika. On the flat jungle plain, midway between the ocean and the dripping ramparts of the mountains, the straggling mine service town of 5,000 swayed before us in the heat of a sweating mirage. Transmigration settlements, a politician's alternative to birth control, had been hacked out of the jungle on the outskirts of town in an attempt by the government to relieve the strain of serious overpopulation in Java, where there are nearly 1,500 people per square mile. Indonesia has an estimated population of 160 million, and more than 65 percent of its people are concentrated on 8 percent of its land on the islands of Java and Madura. Boatloads of hopeful Javanese who have taken the opportunity to start a fresh life arrive every month in Timika and ports on the other less densely populated islands.

We were graciously guided to a simple three-bedroom concrete bungalow, but we began to worry when we saw that it had air vents but no mosquito netting. We feared mosquitoes more than the heat, for this coast is known to be one of the world's worst areas for a strain of malaria that is resistant to chloroquine, the anti-malarial drug we were taking. Also, as in all of the dwellings, there was no air-conditioning to neutralize the 100 percent humidity and 88-degree-F

Having received official permission to proceed to Carstensz on our second visit to Irian Jaya, we trekked the rugged terrain above the tree line, sighting peaks such as the distant Idenburg Top and the Zebra Wall (centre).

(31°C) heat. We lay in the stifling room with the sound of raindrops the size of ping-pong balls bouncing off the corrugated tin roof all night long until dawn released us. By the time Rudi drove up in the company vehicle in the morning, I was never so relieved to see a ride, and we were soon happily on our way toward the cool air of Tembagapura, an exemplary, attractively planned mining town with modern facilities for nearly 400 families (most of whom are Indonesian), at 6,500 feet (1,980 m).

Our attention was quickly diverted from the heat by the demands of travel. The road, a technological miracle, cut through the chaotic vegetation for a total of 64 miles, from the barge landing near the coast, past Timika and up to the mining town. Rudi put the mud-splattered vehicle in four-wheel drive at the foot of the first hill, and it snarled its way up the steep road. We followed a sinuous crest toward a wall of clouds and soon were floating in and out of mist, past dripping hillsides coated in a mat of moss and vine-covered forest. In places, the ribbon of gravel balanced on the spur of a ridge that was only as wide as the road itself, and our glimpses into the depths made us gasp. It seemed impossible that a road existed there. We spent the night at the town site, and with the dawning of the next day, we set out again.

As we jostled for position alongside the miners on the world's longest single-span aerial tramway (it was close to a mile in length and stretched over a vertical rise of 2,700 feet [822 m]), the dense fog dissipated to reveal the dramatic landscape. The 10 Irian porters we had hired to carry our loads to Base Camp charged off across the boggy Carstensz Meadow beyond the noise and activity of the mine, apparently familiar with the terrain. Most of them came from northern highland villages and had somehow avoided the guardpost at the edge of the clearing to make their homes in a small shantytown near Tembagapura. The radical change in altitude made me almost giddy. We had come up to 11,000 feet (3,352 m) from sea level in 24 hours and, before the day was out, would be making camp at 13,200 feet (4,023 m). Because we were on a tight time schedule, circumstances didn't allow for

The firm, waterworn limestone on the central section of Carstensz's north face was a climber's delight, and without the constant problems posed by cold-temperature peaks, Adi (left) and I scrambled quickly upward with a series of trouble-free belays.

slower progress, and I was worried that at least one of us would develop serious altitude illness.

The heartening view of limestone peaks shining in the early-morning brightness burned away my apprehension. At the end of the 1,300-foot-long meadow, the trail veered east up a fault line choked with intermontane forest. The other direction led to Bilorai, a day and a half away for a surefooted native. We were entering the high Kemabu Plateau world of such tribes as the Dani, Moni, Damal and Ekagi, who, clad only in penis sheaths or grass skirts, occasionally travel these high routes on trading and hunting missions. Their bodies are sometimes found huddled against rocks where they have died from exposure.

We planned to end the day at a campsite at the foot of the Meren Glacier, just over 300 yards from where the trail branches northward over the steep New Zealand Pass toward Ilaga. The route continues from Ilaga eastward to Wamena in the Baliem Valley, where we had been in 1984. It would have taken us a month to trek from Wamena to the mountain. The one-week walk to Carstensz from the airstrip at Ilaga is much preferred to the approach we were taking, not only because it offers a unique opportunity to observe the native people in their own setting but also because it allows for a more gradual and natural process of acclimatization.

## GLACIAL IDYLL

By midday, after we had been hiking for five hours, we arrived near the top end of the Meren Valley, and a drizzle turned into an outright downpour. We quickly dispensed the agreed-upon 3,000 rupiahs ($3) to each shivering porter, who smiled with relief at the thought of being able to return home. They were only wearing shorts, t-shirts and mine-issued rain jackets in various stages of disintegration, with the exception of one, who had only a grimy t-shirt. Baiba, exhibiting both practicality and kindness, tore holes in a plastic garbage bag and stuffed it over his head.

During our previous visit to Jayapura, we had contacted Ron Petosz, a parks manager working on a master plan for

Irian Jaya on assignment for the World Wildlife Fund and the Indonesian government. He had been into the Carstensz area twice to study park parameters and to determine the need for enforced protection of the over 4-million-acre Lorentz Reserve. At the campsite below the Meren Glacier, he had found the accumulated mess left by an Australian university group during their glacial studies in 1971 and 1973 and the bits and pieces left by subsequent visitors from the mine site. He had beseeched the mining company, as a good corporate citizen, to help clean up the campsite and to encourage its employees who go to the glacier for Sunday picnics to retrieve their garbage. Not only did Freeport respond favourably by hauling out four oil drums full of residual debris, but we were told that they also asked their employees to post a 10,000-rupiah bond before going to the area, which would be forfeited if it was found they had breached their agreement.

Our campsite was beside one of several alpine lakes, the gravel shore barren except for isolated clumps of grass and a purple-flowered *Epilobium*. The effects of intense ice action were everywhere: the overhanging north wall of Mount Wollaston was polished by centuries of glacier advance and retreat, and moraine fields rolled gently away from the tongue of the Meren Glacier, just a 20-minute walk from our tents. This glacier has retreated one mile in the past 40 years and is but a remnant of the great ice sheet that once spilled over onto Kemabu Plateau. Friends had chided me for not bringing skis on this trip. There were 3 square miles (7 sq km) of skiable terrain left in the Carstensz, Meren and Dugundugu icefields, all lying above 13,000 feet (3,962 m). If we had used telemark equipment, the summits of East Carstensz Top and Dugundugu would have been within a day's ski. However, the mushy surface of the glacier's snow, which gets rained on daily, would have made the runs down horrendous.

Baiba, Steve and I were up early the next morning but postponed any ambitious activity when we saw that the weather was a continuation of the previous day's grey rain. Anxious to find out how the rest of our team was faring at this

altitude, I shouted over to the other tent, "Hey, how are you feeling?" Adi responded with "*Taik*! Do you know what that means in Indonesian? Like shit! But I feel better now after throwing up." Both Adi and Yura remained tent-bound all day, while the rest of us made a one-hour carry over a steep pass to the foot of Carstensz in the Yellow Valley.

Our camp there was idyllic. In the foreground, a saucer-shaped lake nestled in a bed of slate, its glacial silt turning the water an intense turquoise colour. To the west, the valley tapered off into a lush alpine meadow before plunging toward the jungle below. We were only a five-minute walk from the broad face of Carstensz, which soared up in a shield of waterworn grey dolomite, sustaining a 40-to-60-degree angle for nearly 2,000 vertical feet (609 m). Moss-filled serrated cracks carved by water runoff from the daily deluge patterned the face in continuous lines to the summit.

## SOLID ROCK

While several routes have been established on Carstensz's cracks (with North American climbing standards' ratings of 5.7 and higher on a scale that runs as high as 5.13), the climbing possibilities of the area seemed endless. The region forms the apex of the Merauke Range, which runs for 1,242 miles along the centre of the island of New Guinea. Blind valleys, sinkholes and isolated towers of limestone are common throughout, making it a potential mecca for both cavers and climbers. One of the two buttresses on the steep north wall of Dugundugu, on the flip side of the snow slope that we could see from our camp, was climbed by British mountaineers Peter Boardman and Hilary Collins in 1979. Farther east, inviting 3,000-foot (914 m) north walls plunge from the three summits of Ngga Pulu.

We scrambled around on the lower face of Carstensz, amazed at how well the soles of our lightweight Scarpa hiking boots stuck to the holds. I had almost forgotten how fine it felt to be on good solid rock. The familiar fluidity and coordination of movement required for this kind of climbing triggered an excitement in me that had been dormant since the previous summer's climbing on crags

Baiba Morrow

By 2 o'clock each afternoon, mists rolled in from the coastal jungle plain, obliterating our fantastic view of the highlands with sheets of rain and cloud. The rain was an element I had not encountered on my other seven-summits climbs, and we had to protect ourselves from the threat of hypothermia, despite our tropical location.

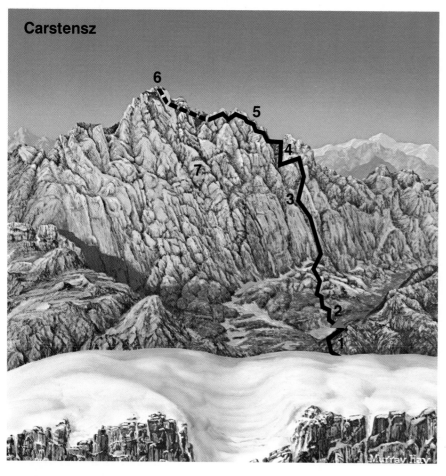

**Carstensz**

1. To Meren Valley
2. Base Camp (13,200 feet)
3. Slab and Gully Climbing
4. Traverse
5. Summit Ridge
6. Summit (16,023 feet)
7. North Face
8. East Ridge
9. Yellow Valley
10. Dugundugu Icefield and Mountain

Route Hidden From View ▬ ▬ ▬

near home. Because Carstensz was the only rock climb of all the seven summits, I savoured the experience even more.

The weather in the Irian highlands deals a predictable hand each day. Around noon, the first clouds come brimming up from the jungles behind the glaciers, sweep down the valley in a fine mist, and then within an hour, a heavy downpour forces trekkers to search for shelter. There is no greater comfort than to lie in a tent, listening to the rain pounding on the waterproof walls, while a purring gas stove warms up dinner. At night, as we read by candlelight, electrical storms filled the sky with flashes that penetrated even closed eyelids. Outside, the terrible roar of water cascading down the weathered rock faces warned us of the dangers of being caught outside during a storm.

For me, because I came from a cooler climate, it was the ideal therapy to calm my soul and reinforce my outlook on life. It was a different sort of revelation for our Indonesian comrades though—an abrupt change from a smog-filled, hot and humid city at sea level to this high, barren mountainscape, where the cold rain drove their bodies into hypothermic chills. Despite these interim discomforts, their spirits remained high.

On May 7, our fifth day since leaving sea level, we set off at 5 a.m., headlamps illuminating the scree and boulder field, to the base of our route. The skies had cleared after a nocturnal downpour, and the stars were already beginning to relinquish their brightness to the rising sun. The previous day, Adi and I had climbed up and fixed a rope on the first pitch to save time on summit day. It would also act as an escape rappel upon our descent, in case we needed it.

Now, in the predawn light, Steve, Baiba and I jumared up the rope, anchored by two pitons. When a muddy foothold broke off, Steve didn't have a good grip with his hands and went for a short joyride until Baiba caught him on the rope from her belay point above. Steve, a tireless, self-proclaimed snow-dome slogger, admitted that he was doing more rock climbing on this one peak than he had in his entire life. Knowing that I was pushing my own flaccid muscles close to their limits, having been away from mainstream climbing for several months, I was concerned for Steve's safety and, for that matter, the safety of the group. We would be moving slowly, exposing ourselves to the elements for longer than we had planned.

My fears were put at ease as his eyes brightened and he rose to the challenge. Even though we gave him a tight rope in a few places, he showed a fine, instinctive style, his hallmark of dogged determination winning in the end.

Our planned ascent followed the route Harrer had taken to first climb Carstensz. Two direct pitches of enjoyable slab-climbing gave way to easy scrambling up a 900-foot (274 m) diagonal trough to a broad ledge that ran far out onto the face. From there, a 500-foot (152 m) scree slope led to the long, undulating summit ridge. The central part of the route offered deceptively easy rock climbing. Everywhere we reached, there was a hold that our hands or boots stuck to like glue, even in the rain.

On the early part of the climb, where our superior acclimatization paid off, we pulled ahead of Adi and Titus. Yura had prudently decided to remain behind because of a persistent headache. However, as we slowly picked our way along the complicated ridge, the plucky Indonesian climbers caught up to us, and we stayed together for the duration. It had taken us four hours to reach the ridge, and just as we broke through into a panorama of leafy carpet rolling out toward the Arafura Sea, the ensuing vista was swallowed by fluffy cumulus clouds. The summit was blocked by jagged rock towers balancing on the ridge in an intricate and challenging sequence that demanded complete concentration.

As we made four separate rappels with lots of adrenaline-pumping exposure along the knife-edged ridge, we quickly came to appreciate the mist that helped to lessen the psychological impact of the sheer drop-offs below us. The razor-sharp rock crackled under our soles, lacerating our hands if we were a bit clumsy in steadying ourselves. All along, Baiba had shown a careful and controlled independence, which set my mind at ease. She and I worked well as a team, watching Steve in the middle of the rope whenever he needed a quick belay. At one point, she beamed up at me and said, "This is wonderful, I could

The seventh summit was a fitting place for a series of heartfelt hugs, and Titus Pramono fell into Steve Fossett's arms as he made it up to the top. Adi Seno (left) and Baiba Morrow wait their turn. It was Adi's second time on the summit, and Baiba was the fourth woman ever to make the climb.

After a scramble down from the summit through driving rain, we were greeted by the comforting sight of Yura Katoppo's candles glowing through our tents at the Yellow Valley Base Camp.

do it all day!'' ''Don't worry,'' I replied, ''you will be.'' Midway on the ridge, the route traversed out onto the south face and gave a delightful pitch of airy climbing with a few well-protected 5.8 moves.

The climbing was throwing me into a Zen-type frame of mind. A warm wave of pure awareness flushed out my thoughts; it was a cleansing, spiritual acclimatization period, and I knew the energy would lodge itself in my system for weeks after, like a medicinal time-release capsule.

## COMING HOME

Near the summit, I stamped knee-deep holes in steep, 150-foot-wide (45 m) patches of rotten snow, careful not to cut across diagonally, lest they slough off. Directly below, lay a glacier plateau and, paradoxically, beyond that, the jungle. The thin mist acted as a solar trap, and despite a light breeze, it felt muggy.

Only a few paces below the top, Steve, Baiba and I swarmed up the last bit of scree together. This was the second summit in this project that I had shared with them—Steve on Vinson and Baiba on Elbrus—and we made a pact right there to treat this as the beginning of a climbing triangle. Joined soon after by Adi and Titus, we brandished various flags for snapshots in true summit spirit (this was Adi's second time on the summit, and Baiba was the fourth woman to make the climb). The summit itself, littered with bottles and canisters marking the previous dozen or so ascents, held no magic for us, other than the knowledge that we had succeeded in our unique climbing experience. The view we had anticipated was left to our imaginations—fog enveloped our world. Only half the climb was over, and it was now time to get down safely. A commemorative plaque near the summit reminded us of the death in 1981 of a member of the Mapala Club who had perished during the descent after falling from a rappel. It was a reminder that one could not let one's guard down on this mountain until safely back at Base Camp.

The fine drizzle that had set in turned into a healthy downpour by the time darkness caught us out on the north face, just below the summit ridge. Ankle-deep water had channelled into the trough in the middle of our route, and with headlamps on, we felt like spelunkers, splashing through a gloomy subterranean river. By the end of the night, Adi was soaked through and in some pain: ''I am tired, cold, hungry and having to speak English. But still I am enjoying this!''

Paying close attention to our clumsy, drained bodies, we completed the last of the three rappels to the bottom by 9 p.m. Now, as we staggered toward the welcome illumination of a candle in Yura's tent, we could joke about the fact that we had probably set a record for having made the mountain's slowest ascent. Peeling off our soaked clothing, we collapsed into our warm sleeping bags. We were home.

# Chronology & Logistics

## NORTH AMERICA: MOUNT McKINLEY

Elevation: 20,320 feet/6,194 m

Date of summit: June 9, 1977

Route taken: New route, Southwest Rib; finish by Messner Couloir on west face

Time taken for climb (from Base Camp, return): 23 days

Team members: Bernhard Ehmann, Roger Marshall, Bugs McKeith, Ekhardt Grassman, Allan Derbyshire, Jon Jones, Dave Read, Patrick Morrow

Access to mountain: Fly to Anchorage, Alaska, and onward by train to Talkeetna, or drive Alaska Highway directly to Talkeetna. If you are climbing the west side of the mountain, fly by ski plane to Kahiltna Glacier from Talkeetna. If you are climbing from the east side, drive to the Denali Park gates, and take a bus to Wonder Lake at road's end.

Level of difficulty: Moderate to severe; allow two to three weeks for ascent

Climbing season: May to July

## SOUTH AMERICA: MOUNT ACONCAGUA

Elevation: 22,831 feet/6,959 m

Date of summit: February 9, 1981

Route taken: Polish Glacier

Time taken for climb: 14 days

Team members: Dave Read, Roger Marshall, Gordon "Speedy" Smith, Patrick Morrow

Access to mountain: Fly to Mendoza, Argentina, via Buenos Aires or Santiago, Chile. Hire a truck, take regularly scheduled bus or hitchhike to trailhead at Punta de Vacas or Punta del Inca, 60 miles west on the highway from Mendoza. Hire mules or carry your own loads for the 30-mile walk to Base Camp on the east or west side of mountain, depending on the route taken.

Level of difficulty: Moderate to severe; allow up to two weeks (or more) for acclimatization on ascent

Climbing season: December to March

## ASIA: MOUNT EVEREST

Elevation: 29,028 feet/8,848 m

Date of summit: October 7, 1982

Route taken: Southeast ridge

Time taken for climb: 55 days

Team members: Bill March, Laurie Skreslet, Peter Spear, Rusty Baillie, Jim Elzinga, Dave Jones, Dwayne Congdon, John Amatt, Al Burgess, Bruce Patterson, Tim Auger, James Blench, David McNab, Lloyd Gallagher, Dave Read, Blair Griffiths, Donald Serl, Gordon "Speedy" Smith, Roger Marshall, Stephen Bezruchka, Kurt Fuhrich, Patrick Morrow. Summit Sherpas: Lhakpa Tshering, Pema Dorje, Sungdare Sherpa, Lhakpa Dorje

Access to mountain: International flights to Kathmandu or bus from New Delhi; then, once in Nepal, fly to Lukla from Kathmandu or trek (10 to 14 days) from road's end at Jiri. Acclimatization gained from trekking in from Lamosangu or Jiri is invaluable. To reach Tibet, fly from either Hong Kong or Beijing to Chengdu, then on to Lhasa. Drive to Base Camp near the Rongbuk Glacier by bus or truck.

**Level of difficulty:** Moderate to severe

**Climbing season, Nepal side:** Pre- and post-monsoon periods of March to June and September to December

# EUROPE: MOUNT ELBRUS

**Elevation:** 18,481 feet/5,633 m

**Date of summit:** July 25, 1983

**Route taken:** Southwest face

**Time taken for climb:** 10 hours from Priut Hut at 13,780 feet (4,200 m)

**Team members:** Jeremy Schmidt, Baiba Morrow, Patrick Morrow

**Access to mountain:** Aeroflot flight from Moscow to Mineral'nyje Vody; four-hour bus to head of Baksan Valley

**Level of difficulty:** Snow slog of moderate difficulty; it is important to allow a few extra days for acclimatization

**Climbing season:** June to September

# AFRICA: MOUNT KILIMANJARO

**Elevation:** 19,340 feet/5,894 m

**Date of summit:** August 17, 1983

**Route taken:** Normal "tourist" route

**Time taken for climb:** 5 days

**Team members:** Jeremy Schmidt, Wendy Baylor, Patrick Morrow

**Access to mountain:** Fly directly to Kilimanjaro International Airport or to Nairobi, Kenya, and go overland, if border is open.

**Level of difficulty:** Easy, by the tourist route; allow 4 to 5 days for proper acclimatization for ascent and 2 days for descent

**Climbing season:** Optimum times are December to March and June to August, although it can be done anytime during the year

# ANTARCTICA: VINSON MASSIF

**Elevation:** 16,067 feet/4,897 m

**Date of summit:** November 9, 1985

**Route taken:** Via Shinn Icefall, Shinn-Vinson Col

**Time taken for climb:** 9 days

**Team members:** Martyn Williams, Mike Dunn, Giles Kershaw, Roger Mitchell, Stephen Fossett, Pat Caffrey, Bill Hackett, Alejo Contreras, Patrick Morrow

**Access to mountain:** The logistics involved in climbing this peak are by far the most difficult to arrange. Special aircraft and crew to reach the interior are required. Climbing and skiing side trips are attractive options on the Antarctic Peninsula. The only company offering trips into the interior of Antarctica is Adventure Network International, Inc., 44 West 4th Avenue, Vancouver, British Columbia, Canada V5Y 1G3, or Box 4118, Carson City, Nevada, U.S.A. 89702. Flights to Antarctica begin in Punta Arenas, Chile.

**Level of difficulty:** Moderate to severe

**Climbing season:** November to February, during austral summer

# AUSTRALASIA: CARSTENSZ PYRAMID

**Elevation:** 16,023 feet/4,884 m

**Date of summit:** May 7, 1986

**Route taken:** Normal route up north face

**Time taken for climb:** 16 hours

**Team members:** Stephen Fossett, Baiba Morrow, Adi Seno, Titus Pramono, Yura Katoppo, Patrick Morrow

**Access to mountain:** Located in the remote highlands of Indonesia's easternmost province, Irian Jaya. Approach by air from Jakarta or Australia to Biak and then Nabire, on the northern coast of Irian Jaya. From there, a Fokker F27 to Ilaga, the starting point for the 5-to-7-day walk in from the north.

**Level of difficulty:** Moderate to difficult

**Climbing season:** Weather pattern is the same year-round with clear skies until midday, then a heavy downpour until dusk, although technically, there is a rainy season from May to October

# PERMITS

Climbers should consult the nearest embassy or consulate of the country to which they intend to travel in order to determine visa and permit requirements. Addresses can be obtained from External Affairs Canada, Ottawa, K1A 0G2.

# Index